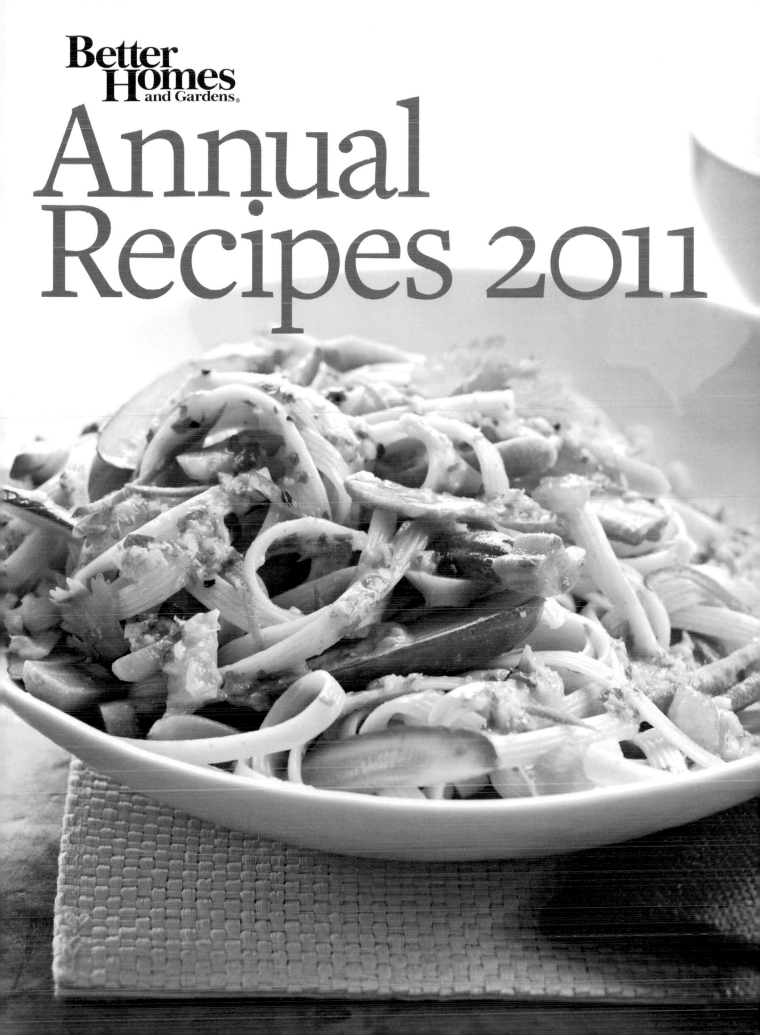

Better Homes and Gardens®

Annual Recipes 2011

MANGO CHICKEN
SALAD

At *Better Homes and Gardens®* magazine, our passion is coming up with simple ways to help you live better. Every issue is packed with ideas for making your home more beautiful and comfortable, for creating calming and peaceful gardens, and for making your family meals more delicious, more nutritious, and as simple as possible to prepare.

I feel so privileged to be a part of creating the magazine every month—and of course I love to see what's in store on the food pages. I am always inspired to get into the kitchen after reviewing the recipes and food stories. Everything always looks so delicious! As I page through this year's annual, I am struck by how vibrant, beautiful, and *fresh* everything looks.

In 2011, "fresh" was the operative word. We wanted to tap into our readers' growing interest in eating more locally grown fruits and vegetables—from gardens, farmers' markets, and local Community Supported Agriculture (CSA) farms.

In February, we feature comfort foods packed with colorful produce—such as a Sunday Beef Rib Roast with beautiful baby carrots and tender baby spinach. In April, chef Jamie Oliver brings his food revolution to our food pages with garden-inspired and kid-friendly recipes such as Cup-of-Garden Soup, Braised Peas with Scallions and Lettuce—and a yummy Easy Orange-Carrot Cake. In June, Watermelon Salad—a gelatin salad made with fresh ingredients—embodies our belief in food that is fresh and new, but tried and true.

One of the highlights of this year was in August when First Lady Michelle Obama graced the cover of our magazine. The garden she planted at the White House inspired us to create fun, delicious kid-friendly recipes packed with fruits and vegetables.

While the fresh foods trend is one we hope stays around indefinitely, we're also very fond of other trends in the world of food—such as the delicious and ubiquitous use of bacon in unexpected ways. In September, chocolatier Katrina Markhoff shares the recipe for her unbelievably luscious Bacon-Laced Chocolate Cake.

Responding to our readers' interests is our interest. We know that saving money on the grocery bill has become increasingly important to many families during this challenging economic time. A new feature, Delicious on a Dollar, focuses on recipes that deliver great taste for pennies.

We want to help you save money, save time, and eat well—and we know that the fresh ideas in this beautiful book will help you do just that. From our kitchen to yours—enjoy!

Gayle

Gayle Goodson Butler, Editor in Chief
Better Homes and Gardens® magazine

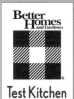

Our seal assures you that every recipe in *Better Homes and Gardens® Annual Recipes 2011* has been tested in the Better Homes and Gardens® Test Kitchen. This means that each recipe is practical and reliable, and meets our high standards of taste appeal. We guarantee your satisfaction with this book for as long as you own it.

All of us at Meredith Consumer Marketing are dedicated to providing you with information and ideas to enhance your home. We welcome your comments and suggestions. Write to us at: Meredith Consumer Marketing, 1716 Locust St., Des Moines, IA 50309-3023.

Pictured on front cover:
Glazed Buttery Rum Fruit Cake, page 220

Better Homes and Gardens®

Annual Recipes 2011

MEREDITH CONSUMER MARKETING
Vice President, Consumer Marketing: Janet Donnelly
Consumer Product Marketing Director: Steve Swanson
Consumer Product Marketing Manager: Wendy Merical
Business Director: Ron Clingman
Senior Production Manager: George Susral

WATERBURY PUBLICATIONS, INC.
Editorial Director: Lisa Kingsley
Associate Editor: Tricia Bergman
Creative Director: Ken Carlson
Associate Design Director: Doug Samuelson
Contributing Art Director: Bruce Yang
Contributing Copy Editors: Terri Fredrickson, Peg Smith
Contributing Indexer: Elizabeth T. Parson

BETTER HOMES AND GARDENS® MAGAZINE
Editor in Chief: Gayle Goodson Butler
Creative Director: Michael D. Belknap
Senior Deputy Editor: Nancy Wall Hopkins
Senior Editor: Richard Swearinger
Associate Editor: Erin Simpson
Editorial Assistant: Renee Irey

MEREDITH NATIONAL MEDIA GROUP
President: Tom Harty
Vice President, Production: Bruce Heston

MEREDITH CORPORATION
Chairman and Chief Executive Officer: Stephen M. Lacy

In Memoriam: E.T. Meredith III (1933–2003)

I need easy recipes for dinner sensations that use pantry staples! Would someone teach me how to dress up an ordinary chocolate or vanilla cake so it's extraordinary? What can I do with all of the tomatoes from my garden? Everyone loves a barbecue—I need tips on how to make it effortless! How do I know if an avocado is ripe enough—or overripe? And how do I make my own fresh pasta?

Whether you've been cooking for 20 years or 2 months you, probably have questions or need inspiration now and then. This book provides the recipes, ideas, tips, and solutions you're looking for.

LOOK FOR:

- **Our Monthly Feature** Foods are best when eaten in season. Each month we feature recipes that keep that very idea in mind. Whether it's chili to stave off winter's chill, cooking with locally grown produce in the summer, or holiday baking for family and friends, we have you covered.
- **Home Cooking** You can always learn something new in the kitchen—whether it's a cooking technique or a style. Special days require a special cake! Three-layer beauties with mix-and-match frostings and quick decorating ideas show you how. Build a triple-decker club—and try new spins on this classic sandwich. And enjoy summer's fresh produce with salads in all shapes—layered, tossed, chunked, and wiggly. Learn from a cocktail pro how to muddle, blend, and shake refreshing drinks. Not sure what to do with summer's tomato crop? We show you three cooking methods to keep the rave reviews coming. With Home Cooking you can take a cooking class at home!
- **Delicious on a Dollar** This feature keeps recipe food costs low without sacrificing flavor.
- **Good and Healthy** Keep your resolution to eat well all year with recipes that are fresh, flavorful, and good for you. Hearty and satisfying winter soups are on the table in January. With spring comes creamy and protein-packed hummus—ideal for healthful nibbling. In the heat of the summer we yearn for light and healthful foods, so in July we feature a nutrient-power-packed salad. Good food that's good for you.
- **Everyday Easy** Whip up fast and fresh weeknight dishes that are budget-friendly too.
- **American Classics** Chef Scott Peacock and his vision of southern cuisine emphasizes fresh, seasonal, and regionally grown ingredients. This award-winning chef shares delicious recipes and how-to techniques.
- **Prize Tested Recipes**® Look to page 256 for winners in our monthly recipe contest. Creative cooks share their best newly developed recipes. One winner is selected for each of two categories.
- **Recipe Icons** Many recipes are marked with icons that indicate whether they're Fast (less than 30 minutes), Kid-Friendly, or Low Fat (for nutrition guidelines, see page 335).

 **68**
 **82**
 **113**
 **137**

contents 2011

73

89

124

158

COZY UP Use a stack of mismatched bowls, grab a ladle, and welcome friends. Keep it casual. A simmering pot of soup makes the whole house feel warm.

21

23

25

CHEESE AND ALMOND GUACAMOLE

Winter Games

Need a nibble to go with the fun? Whether your party includes skiing or skating, Super Bowl or Super Mario, these appetizers are hearty enough for the hungriest guests.

CHIPOTLE KETTLE CORN

Cheese and Almond Guacamole

Serrano peppers are slightly smaller and hotter than jalapeños. If you like it spicy, add the peppers seeds and all, or remove them to reduce the heat.

START TO FINISH **20 min.**

4	avocados, halved, seeded, peeled, and coarsely chopped
½	cup chopped red onion
2	serrano peppers,* halved, seeded, and finely chopped
¾	cup crumbled feta or goat cheese (6 oz.)
1	lime, juiced
½	cup sliced almonds, toasted and chopped
⅓	cup chopped fresh cilantro
¾	tsp. salt
	Carrots, jicama strips, and/or pita chips
	Lime wedges and cilantro sprigs (optional)

1. In a large bowl combine the avocados, onion, and serrano peppers; mash slightly with a fork. Fold in the cheese, lime juice, almonds, cilantro, and salt. Spoon into serving bowl. Serve at once or cover surface directly with plastic wrap and refrigerate for up to 6 hours.
2. Serve with carrots, jicama, and/or pita chips, lime wedges, and cilantro sprigs. Makes about 10 (¼-cup) servings.

*Because hot chile peppers, such as serranos, contain oils that can burn your skin and eyes, avoid direct contact with them as much as possible. When working with chile peppers, wear plastic or rubber gloves. If bare hands do touch the chile pepper, wash your hands well with soap and water.

EACH SERVING *183 cal, 16 g fat, 13 mg chol, 268 mg sodium, 8 g carb, 5 g fiber, 6 g pro.*

Chipotle Kettle Corn

Find ground chipotle chile pepper in large supermarkets. Chili powder can be substituted in a pinch.

START TO FINISH **15 min.**

1	cup sugar
2	tsp. salt
2	tsp. ground cumin
1	tsp. ground chipotle chile pepper
⅓	cup canola oil
⅔	cup popcorn kernels

1. In a small bowl combine sugar, salt, cumin, and chipotle pepper. Heat the oil in an 8-quart pan over medium-high heat. Add the popcorn and cook, shaking occasionally, 2 minutes. Add ½ cup of the sugar mixture. Cover and cook, shaking often, until popcorn begins to pop. Once popcorn begins to pop, shake continuously until the popping slows. Immediately remove from heat and carefully pour into a large bowl (popcorn will be very hot).

2. Place remaining sugar mixture in shaker jar. Sprinkle some on the popped corn and pass the remaining. Makes 16 (1-cup) servings.
Microwave Version Prepare sugar mixture as above. One at a time, pop two 3.3-ounce bags microwave kettle corn. Immediately after popping pour into a very large bowl and toss with 2 tablespoons of the sugar mixture. Repeat with remaining bag of popcorn and 2 more tablespoons of sugar mixture. Pass remaining sugar mixture as above. Makes 20 (1-cup) servings.
EACH SERVING *78 cal, 3 g fat, 0 mg chol, 266 mg sodium, 15 g carb, 1 g fiber, 1 g pro.*

SPICY CHICKEN
WITH CUCUMBER
YOGURT SAUCE

Spicy Chicken

A meaty mix of wings and small drumsticks
will satisfy the heartiest of appetites.
Marinate and bake chicken ahead of time,
then reheat on the grill for a hint of smoky
flavor (or serve straight from the oven).
PREP 30 min. MARINATE 6 hr.
BAKE 25 min. GRILL 10 min. OVEN 400°F

1½ cups plain yogurt
2   Tbsp. grated fresh ginger
3   cloves garlic, minced
2   tsp. curry powder
1   tsp. salt
1   tsp. paprika
¾   tsp. ground cinnamon
½   tsp. cayenne pepper
4   lb. chicken wings and/or small
     chicken drumsticks
     Fresh mint (optional)
1   recipe Cucumber-Yogurt Sauce

1. For the marinade, in a medium bowl
combine yogurt, ginger, garlic, curry
powder, salt, paprika, cinnamon, and
cayenne; let stand 15 minutes, stirring
occasionally.
2. Meanwhile, if using chicken wings cut
each wing into two portions at the first
joint. Place wings and/or drumsticks in
a 2-gallon resealable plastic bag set in a
shallow dish; add yogurt marinade. Seal
and refrigerate 6 to 24 hours, turning bag
occasionally.
3. Preheat oven to 400°F. Drain chicken
from marinade; discard marinade. Line
two 15×10×1-inch baking pans with foil;
lightly coat with nonstick cooking spray.
Arrange chicken in prepared pans
(if using both drumsticks and wings,
place them on separate pans). Bake small
drumsticks 35 minutes; bake chicken
wings 25 minutes or until chicken is
cooked through (180°F).
4. Serve immediately, or cool chicken
slightly and transfer to storage containers.
Cover and refrigerate overnight and reheat
(see Grill Reheat, right).
5. Transfer chicken to platter and sprinkle
with mint. Serve with Cucumber-Yogurt
Sauce. Makes 8 to 12 servings.

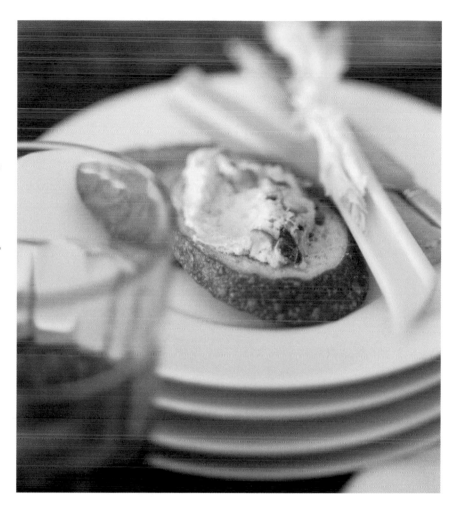

Grill Reheat For a charcoal or gas grill,
place chicken on a well-greased grill rack
directly over medium heat. Cover and grill
10 to 15 minutes or until heated through,
turning once after 5 minutes. (Do not turn
too soon or chicken may stick to grill. If
chicken does stick, loosen with a metal
spatula before turning.) For a grill pan,
reheat chicken in batches. Grill directly
on a greased grill pan for 10 to 15 minutes
until heated through, turning once.
EACH SERVING (WITH SAUCE) 747 cal,
*21 g fat, 100 mg chol, 589 mg sodium,
10 g carb, 1 g fiber, 28 g pro.*

Cucumber-Yogurt Sauce
PREP 20 min. CHILL 1 hr.

2   8-oz. cartons plain yogurt
1   large cucumber, shredded and well
     drained
2   cloves garlic, minced
½   tsp. salt
¼   tsp. ground cumin
2   Tbsp. chopped mint or basil
     (optional)

In a bowl combine yogurt, cucumber,
garlic, salt, cumin, and mint; mix well.
Refrigerate 1 to 4 hours before serving.
Serve with Spicy Chicken. Makes
8 to 12 servings.

Winning Strategy

Frozen bread dough makes it easy to create these three-bite grilled pizzas. They're topped with tomatoes cooked slowly in garlic and herbs. Or go with a basic meatball recipe that can swing in two crowd-pleasing directions—Mexican and Italian. For drinks, serve margaritas and pomegranate juice-spiked ginger ale.

LOW FAT **KID FRIENDLY**

Roasted Cherry Tomato Pizza Poppers

These tasty little pizzas have a crisp texture when grilled and are chewy-crisp when baked (see Oven Method, *below*). Look for frozen pizza dough among frozen breakfast pastries and baked goods.
PREP **1 hr.** GRILL **4 min.** STAND **10 min.**

1   recipe Roasted Cherry Tomatoes
2   1-lb. loaves frozen pizza dough, thawed
¼   cup extra virgin olive oil
1   tsp. dried oregano
1   tsp. dried basil
12   to 14 oz. deli-sliced mozzarella or provolone, cut into 2-inch pieces
      Small fresh basil leaves (optional)

1. Prepare Roasted Cherry Tomatoes.
2. Meanwhile, on a lightly floured surface, roll pizza dough, one loaf at a time, into a 15×12-inch rectangle (if dough becomes difficult to roll, cover and let rest occasionally). Loosely cover dough then let rest 10 minutes. Cut circles using a 2- to 2½-inch round cutter (depending on your grill grate, the larger size may be easier to work with). Discard trimmings. Place dough rounds on lightly greased baking sheets. In a bowl combine olive oil, oregano, and basil; brush over both sides of dough rounds. Prick rounds all over with a fork.
3. For a charcoal or gas grill, using tongs place about 12* dough rounds directly on a well-oiled grill rack directly over medium heat. Cover and grill for 2 minutes. Carefully flip the rounds and press down lightly to flatten. Top each with a piece of cheese. Close grill and cook until cheese melts and dough is cooked through, about 2 minutes more. Remove rounds, transfer to a baking sheet. Repeat with remaining dough rounds and cheese. Keep warm in a 250°F oven until ready to serve. Top each round with a spoonful of Roasted Cherry Tomatoes and basil leaves. Serve warm or at room temperature. Makes 10 to 12 (4-popper) servings.
Oven Method Preheat oven to 450°F. Brush dough rounds with olive oil-basil mixture and bake on greased baking sheets for 7 minutes; turn and top with cheese. Return to oven and bake 2 minutes more. Top with tomatoes and basil as above.
Make Ahead Grill or bake dough rounds but do not top with cheese. Store up to 3 days at room temperature. Just before

serving, top with cheese and return to grill (about 12 at a time) over medium-low heat for 2 minutes. Or bake in a 350°F oven for 2 minutes or until cheese melts. Top with Roasted Cherry Tomatoes and basil.
*So dough rounds do not overcook on the grill, it's best to grill about 12 or so at a time.
EACH POPPER *64 cal, 2 g fat, 3 mg chol, 104 mg sodium, 8 g carb, 0 g fiber, 2 g pro.*

Roasted Cherry Tomatoes

Just a few ingredients yield a flavorful topping. Top the pizza rounds, then serve any remaining tomatoes alongside so guests can help themselves to more as they please.

2   pints red and/or yellow cherry or grape tomatoes, halved
1   Tbsp. extra virgin olive oil
2   to 4 cloves garlic, minced
2   tsp. balsamic vinegar
½   tsp. dried or 1 tsp. chopped fresh oregano

1. In a 13×9×2-inch disposable foil pan combine tomatoes, oil, garlic, vinegar, and oregano.
2. For charcoal grill, place pan on grill directly over medium coals for 8 to 9 minutes or until tomatoes are wilted, stirring occasionally. Remove from grill. (For a gas grill, preheat grill. Reduce heat to medium. Place pan on grill rack. Cover and grill as above.) Use to top the Pizza Poppers.
Oven Method Preheat oven to 450°F. Roast the tomato mixture in the 13×9×2-inch pan for 10 to 12 minutes, stirring occasionally.

ROASTED
CHERRY TOMATO
PIZZA POPPERS

KID-FRIENDLY

Bacon-Cheddar Cheese Balls

For a cheese ball, freshly shredded cheese works better than packaged shredded cheese. So flavors have a chance to blend, mix the cheese mixture the night before. Shape and roll in the crumbled bacon or pistachio nuts a few hours before serving.

PREP 40 min. STAND 45 min. CHILL 2 hr.

1   lb. extra sharp cheddar cheese, finely shredded
2   8-oz pkg. reduced-fat cream cheese (Neufchâtel)
1   2-oz. jar sliced pimientos, rinsed, drained, patted dry, and chopped
¼   cup apricot preserves
2   Tbsp. milk
1   tsp. Worcestershire sauce
¼   tsp. bottled hot pepper sauce
8   to 10 slices bacon, crisp-cooked and crumbled
⅓   cup pistachio nuts, chopped
    Celery stalks, cucumber slices, apricot halves, and/or toasted baguette slices

1. In a very large mixing bowl combine cheddar and cream cheese; let stand to come to room temperature (about 45 minutes). Add pimientos, apricot preserves, milk, Worcestershire, hot pepper sauce, and about half the cooked bacon (cover and refrigerate remaining bacon). Beat with an electric mixer on medium speed until almost smooth.

2. Cover and refrigerate cheese mixture 2 hours or up to overnight. Divide into two portions. On waxed paper shape portions into balls. Up to 4 hours before serving roll one cheese ball in bacon pieces and one in pistachio nuts.

3. Serve with celery, cucumber, apricot, and/or toasted bread slices. Makes 18 (¼-cup) servings.

EACH SERVING *218 cal, 17 g fat, 49 mg chol, 361 mg sodium, 6 g carb, 1 g fiber, 11 g pro.*

BACON-CHEDDAR
CHEESE BALLS

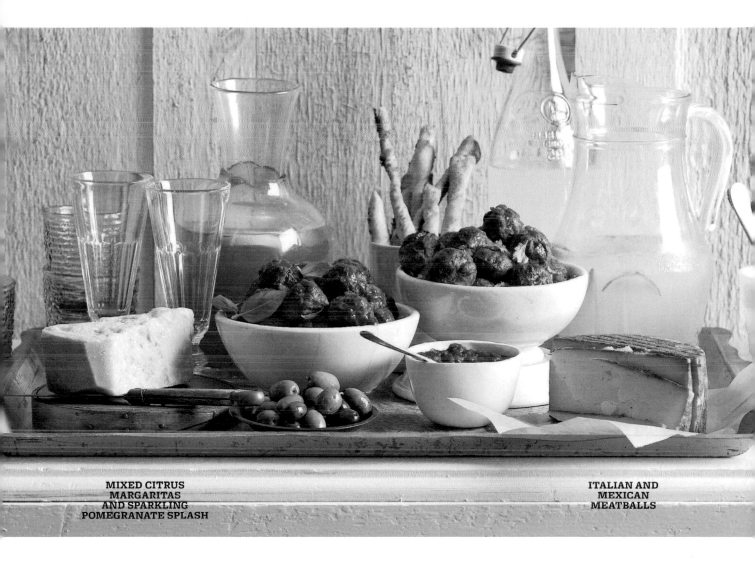

MIXED CITRUS
MARGARITAS
AND SPARKLING
POMEGRANATE SPLASH

ITALIAN AND
MEXICAN
MEATBALLS

Mexican Meatballs

PREP **35 min.** BAKE **22 min.**
OVEN **400°F**

Nonstick cooking spray
2 eggs, lightly beaten
⅔ cup fine dry bread crumbs
⅓ cup chopped fresh cilantro
4 cloves garlic, minced
2 tsp. dried or 2 Tbsp. fresh oregano
2 tsp. chili powder
1 tsp. salt
1 tsp. ground cumin
2 lb. lean ground turkey
8 oz. uncooked or cooked smoked chorizo sausage, finely chopped
2 Tbsp. olive oil
1 cup Smoky Tomato Sauce, *page 18*
Fresh cilantro leaves (optional)

1. Preheat oven to 400°F. Lightly coat 15×10×1-inch baking pan with nonstick cooking spray.
2. In a very large bowl mix together eggs, bread crumbs, chopped cilantro, garlic, oregano, 1½ teaspoons of the chili powder, the salt, and cumin. Add ground turkey and sausage; mix well. With damp hands or a small ice cream scoop form into twenty-four to thirty 1¾- to 2-inch meatballs (about 3 tablespoons).
3. Combine oil and remaining ½ teaspoon chili powder; brush on meatballs.
4. Bake meatballs 22 to 25 minutes or until cooked through (165°F on an instant-read thermometer). With slotted spoon, remove meatballs to a serving bowl; toss with Smoky Tomato Sauce. Top with cilantro leaves. Makes 12 to 15 (2-meatball) servings.
EACH SERVING *232 cal, 12 g fat, 89 mg chol, 572 mg sodium, 6 g carb, 1 g fiber, 24 g pro.*

Mixed Citrus Margaritas

START TO FINISH **10 min.**

2 cups tequila
1½ cups fresh-squeezed lime and/or orange juice
½ cup orange-flavor liqueur, such as triple sec
Powdered sugar
1 to 2 limes, cut in wedges

In a large pitcher or jug combine tequila, juice, liqueur, and sugar to taste. Serve over *ice* with lime wedges. Makes 8 to 10 servings.
EACH SERVING *190 cal, 0 g fat, 0 mg chol, 2 mg sodium, 12 g carb, 0 g fiber, 0 g pro.*

ITALIAN MEATBALLS

Smoky Tomato Sauce

Any leftover sauce is good served with sautéed chicken over pasta or as a dip for breadsticks. It can also be frozen for up to 6 months.

START TO FINISH **35 min.**

2   Tbsp. olive oil
1   large onion, finely chopped
8   cloves garlic, minced
2   tsp. dried or 2 Tbsp. chopped fresh basil
2   tsp. dried or 2 Tbsp. chopped fresh oregano
2   28-oz. cans crushed tomatoes
⅓   cup tomato paste
1½ tsp. smoked paprika or paprika
½   tsp. salt
½   tsp. ground black pepper
1   recipe Italian Meatballs and/or Mexican Meatballs

1. In a Dutch oven heat oil over medium-high heat. Add the onion, garlic, basil, and oregano; cook, stirring occasionally, until onion is tender, about 4 to 5 minutes. Add the tomatoes, tomato paste, smoked paprika, salt, and pepper. Bring to a boil; reduce heat to medium-low. Simmer, covered, stirring occasionally, for 20 minutes.
2. Gently toss about 1 cup of the warm sauce with each batch of the Italian and Mexican meatballs; pass remaining sauce. Makes 7 cups.

EACH ¼-CUP SERVING *34 cal, 1 g fat, 0 mg chol, 142 mg sodium, 6 g carb, 1 g fiber, 1 g pro.*

Sparkling Pomegranate Splash

START TO FINISH **10 min.**

2   1-liter bottles ginger ale or two 750 ml. bottles sparkling wine, chilled
2   16-oz. bottles pomegranate juice, chilled
1   to 2 lemons, sliced

In a large pitcher or jug combine the ginger ale, pomegranate juice, *ice,* and lemon slices. Makes about 10 servings.

EACH SERVING *158 cal, 0 g fat, 0 mg chol, 8 mg sodium, 17 g carb, 1 g fiber, 1 g pro.*

Italian Meatballs

PREP **35 min.**   BAKE **22 min.**
OVEN **400°F**

    Nonstick cooking spray
2   eggs, lightly beaten
½   cup seasoned Italian fine dry bread crumbs
⅓   cup grated Parmesan cheese
4   cloves garlic, minced
½   tsp. salt
½   tsp. black pepper
2   lb. lean ground turkey
8   oz. sweet Italian turkey sausage, removed from casings
2   Tbsp. olive oil
1   tsp. smoked paprika or paprika
1   cup Smoky Tomato Sauce, *right*
    Small fresh basil leaves (optional)

1. Preheat oven to 400°F. Lightly coat a 15×10×1-inch baking pan with nonstick cooking spray.
2. In very large bowl mix together eggs, bread crumbs, cheese, garlic, salt, and pepper. Add turkey and sausage; mix well. With damp hands or an ice cream scoop form twenty-four to thirty 1¾- to 2-inch meatballs (3 to 4 tablespoons each). Transfer to prepared baking sheet.
3. Combine oil and paprika; brush on meatballs. Bake meatballs 22 to 25 minutes or until cooked through (165°F on an instant-read thermometer). With a slotted spoon, transfer meatballs to a large serving bowl; gently toss with Smoky Tomato Sauce. Top with basil. Makes 12 to 15 (2-meatball) servings.

EACH SERVING *180 cal, 7 g fat, 89 mg chol, 416 mg sodium, 6 g carb, 1 g fiber, 24 g pro.*

Good and Healthy

Keep your resolution to eat well. Savor hearty winter vegetables in this light and satisfying soup.

LOW FAT

Chunky Vegetable-Lentil Soup

START TO FINISH 50 min.

1   Tbsp. olive oil
1   medium onion, cut into thin rings
1   clove garlic, minced
1   cup dry green (French) lentils, rinsed and drained
1   lb. whole small mushrooms (halve or quarter any large mushrooms)
4   medium carrots, thinly sliced (2 cups)
2   stalks celery, chopped
4   cups water
1   14-oz. can vegetable broth
¼   tsp. salt
¼   tsp. ground black pepper
¼   a head napa or red cabbage, sliced into strips (2 cups)

1. In a 4-quart saucepan or Dutch oven heat oil over medium heat. Add onion and garlic; cook for 4 to 5 minutes or until onion is tender, stirring occasionally. Stir in lentils; cook and stir 1 minute.
2. Add mushrooms, carrots, celery, the water, vegetable broth, salt, and pepper. Bring to boiling. Reduce heat and simmer, covered, about 25 minutes or until lentils are tender.
3. Divide among soup bowls; top with cabbage. Makes 6 (1½-cup) servings.
EACH SERVING 185 cal, 3 g fat, 0 mg chol, 408 mg sodium, 30 g carb, 13 g fiber, 12 g pro.

CHUNKY VEGETABLE-
LENTIL SOUP

Everyday Easy

Resolve to serve scrumptious
budget-friendly meals that take only minutes.

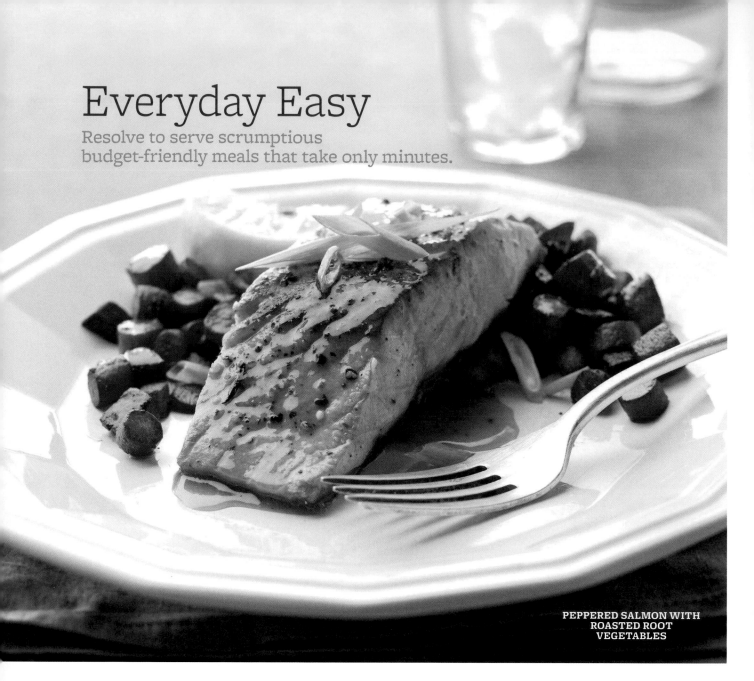

PEPPERED SALMON WITH
ROASTED ROOT
VEGETABLES

FAST

Peppered Salmon with Roasted Root Vegetables

START TO FINISH 30 min.

BUDGET $3.87 per serving

4 medium carrots, coarsely chopped
2 small beets, peeled and coarsely chopped
3 Tbsp. olive oil
1 tsp. sea salt or salt
4 4- to 5-oz. skinless salmon fillets
1 tsp. coarsely ground pepper blend or pepper
¼ cup frozen orange juice concentrate, thawed
   Chopped green onions (optional)

1. Preheat oven to 425°F. In a baking pan combine carrots, beets, half the oil, and half the salt. Roast, uncovered, for 20 minutes, stirring halfway through. Transfer to a platter; cover to keep warm.
2. Meanwhile, sprinkle salmon with remaining salt and the pepper. In a 12-inch skillet heat remaining oil over medium-high. Add salmon; cook 3 minutes. Turn; cook 3 minutes more or until fish flakes easily. Transfer to platter with vegetables. Add juice concentrate and 2 tablespoons *water* to skillet. Simmer, uncovered, about 1 minute or until thickened; spoon over salmon. Sprinkle green onions over all. Makes 4 servings.
EACH SERVING 392 cal, 26 g fat, 62 mg chol, 531 mg sodium, 16 g carb, 3 g fiber, 24 g pro.

FAST | **KID FRIENDLY**

New Year's Day Dumpling Soup

START TO FINISH 25 min.
BUDGET $3.25 per serving

1   32-oz. box mushroom or vegetable broth

1   cup water

2   tsp. grated fresh ginger

2   10-oz. pkg. frozen pork potstickers or dumplings with sauce

2   medium carrots, peeled and cut in thin 2-inch strips, or 1 cup shredded carrots

1   small bunch green onions, trimmed and diagonally sliced

1. In a Dutch oven combine broth, the water, ginger, and seasoning packet* from one package of potstickers. Bring to boiling over high heat.
2. Add potstickers, carrots, and most of the green onions. Return to simmering. Reduce heat and cook, covered, for 8 to 10 minutes or until potstickers are heated through.
3. Ladle soup into bowls. Sprinkle with remaining green onion slices. Makes 4 servings.
*If no seasoning packet is provided, add 2 teaspoons soy sauce and 1 teaspoon toasted sesame oil.
EACH SERVING *369 cal, 16 g fat, 18 mg chol, 1,207 mg sodium, 42 g carb, 4 g fiber, 14 g pro.*

NEW YEAR'S DAY DUMPLING SOUP

FRIZZLED EGGS OVER
GARLIC STEAK AND
MUSHROOM HASH

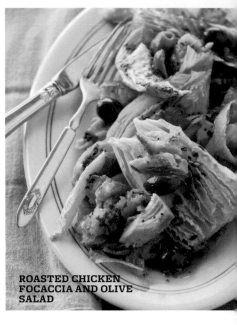

ROASTED CHICKEN
FOCACCIA AND OLIVE
SALAD

Roasted Chicken, Focaccia, and Olive Salad

FAST

START TO FINISH 30 min.
BUDGET $3.00 per serving

5   Tbsp. olive oil
¼   cup white wine or cider vinegar
2   tsp. Mediterranean seasoning blend
     or spaghetti seasoning
1   tsp. sugar
3   cups torn day-old garlic focaccia or
     Italian bread (6 oz.)
2   cups shredded deli-roasted chicken
     (12 oz.)
¾   cup pitted olives
3   romaine hearts, cored and coarsely
     chopped

1. For dressing, in a small bowl whisk together 4 tablespoons of the olive oil, the vinegar, seasoning blend, and sugar; set aside.
2. In a 12-inch skillet heat 1 tablespoon oil over medium-high. Add bread. Cook and stir 5 minutes until lightly toasted. Remove from skillet. Add dressing, chicken, and olives to skillet; cook and stir 2 to 3 minutes until chicken is heated through. Return bread to skillet; toss to coat.
3. Arrange romaine on 4 plates; top with chicken mixture. Serve immediately. Makes 4 servings.
EACH SERVING 478 cal, 34 g fat, 83 mg chol, 998 mg sodium, 22 g carb, 3 g fiber, 21 g pro.

Frizzled Eggs over Garlic Steak and Mushroom Hash

START TO FINISH 30 min.
BUDGET $2.25 per serving

2   Tbsp. vegetable oil
2   cups frozen diced hash brown
     potatoes with onions and peppers
1   8-oz. pkg. sliced fresh mushrooms
4   3- to 4-oz. thin breakfast steaks
4   to 6 cloves garlic, thinly sliced
4   eggs
     Fresh tarragon (optional)

1. In a 12-inch skillet heat 1 tablespoon oil. Cook potatoes and mushrooms, covered, over medium-high heat for 10 minutes. Stir occasionally. Remove from skillet; cover to keep warm.
2. Sprinkle steaks with *salt* and *pepper*. Heat remaining oil in skillet. Cook steaks and garlic for 3 to 4 minutes, turning once, until desired doneness. Remove from skillet; cover to keep warm.
3. Add each egg to the hot skillet; sprinkle *salt* and *pepper*. Cook to desired doneness. Place potatoes, steaks, and eggs on plates. Sprinkle fresh tarragon. Makes 4 servings.
EACH SERVING 324 cal, 15 g fat, 258 mg chol, 397 mg sodium, 17 g carb, 2 g fiber, 29 g pro.

FAST | **KID FRIENDLY**

Veggie Grilled Cheese

START TO FINISH **20 min.**
BUDGET **$2.32 per serving**

- 2   cups jarred pickled vegetable mix (giardiniera)
- 3   cups packed fresh baby spinach leaves
- 6   oz. fresh mozzarella cheese, chopped
- ½   cup oil-packed dried tomatoes, snipped
- 1   tsp. fresh chopped or dried minced garlic
- ½   tsp. ground pepper
- 12 slices whole grain bread, toasted

1. Rinse and drain the pickled vegetables well. For filling, in a large microwave-safe bowl combine all ingredients except the bread. Cook on high (100% power), uncovered, for about 2 minutes or just until the filling is warm, the spinach is wilted, and the cheese is beginning to melt.

2. To assemble sandwiches, divide half the filling among four slices of bread. Add a slice of bread and top with the remaining filling and another slice of bread. Slice diagonally. Makes 4 servings.

EACH SERVING *359 cal, 14 g fat, 30 mg chol, 782 mg sodium, 42 g carb, 7 g fiber, 17 g pro.*

VEGGIE GRILLED
CHEESE

Gatherings

Served it with flair, a first course can be the main attraction of the party.

ROASTED PEAR-SPANACH
SALAD

Roasted Pear Spinach Salad

PREP 20 min. BAKE 25 min.
OVEN 450°F/400°F

- 1 tsp. butter
- 2 firm-ripe pears
- 1½ tsp. sugar
- ½ cup sliced almonds
- 1 cup dried cranberries
- 8 slices ciabatta bread
- 3 oz. blue cheese
- ⅓ cup cider vinegar
- 2 Tbsp. pomegranate molasses or honey
- 1 Tbsp. Dijon mustard
- ⅓ cup extra virgin olive oil
- 6 oz. baby spinach

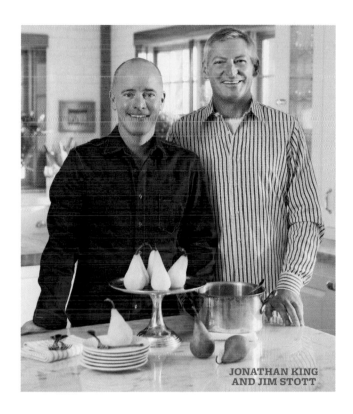

JONATHAN KING AND JIM STOTT

1. Preheat oven to 450°F. Grease baking sheet with butter. Core pears and cut each into 8 wedges; toss with sugar and place on baking sheet, cut sides down. Bake 15 minutes until soft and browned on undersides. Transfer to waxed paper to cool.
2. Place almonds on an ungreased baking sheet and toast 3 to 5 minutes. Transfer to a bowl. Stir in half the cranberries; set aside.
3. Reduce oven to 400°F. Cut each slice of bread in half. Brush both sides with a little *olive oil* and toast on baking sheet 3 minutes per side. Remove from oven; crumble cheese and divide among toasts. Return to oven and bake 4 to 5 minutes more.

4. Meanwhile, in blender combine remaining cranberries, the vinegar, molasses, and mustard. Blend until smooth. Season with *salt* and *pepper*. With blender running, add ⅓ cup oil in a slow, steady stream.
5. In bowl toss together the spinach, half the almond mixture, and vinaigrette to taste. Divide salad among tumblers; top with pears, toasts, and additional almond mixture. Serve immediately. Makes 8 to 10 appetizer servings.

Celebrate the distinctive flavors of winter

Stay simple
Tumblers are a fun way to serve the pear and blue cheese salad. "Food looks really appealing in clear glass," King says.

Create a look
"We like to use lots of small votive candles on the table," King says. "Then we intersperse a few very small flower arrangements."

Make it a main
To turn the salad into an entrée, Jonathan adds grilled chicken or salmon and serves it either on a buffet or on individual plates.

> "These little salads bring a smile wherever they go. They're a great way to get a party off on the right foot."

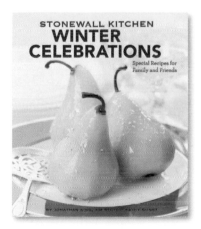

STONEWALL KITCHEN WINTER CELEBRATIONS
Special Recipes for Family and Friends

For more, read *Stonewall Kitchen Winter Celebrations* by Jonathan King, Jim Stott, and Kathy Gunst (Chronicle, $19.95).

food life

IDEAS AND INSPIRATION FOR SHARING TIME AROUND THE TABLE

Generous Gems

These ladies who lunch do so for a cause. This gathering featured jewelry for sale to benefit underprivileged communities, but the goods for sale—and the good the proceeds do—can be of your own choosing.

Women. Jewelry. The combination of the two is always a hit. Add an elegant salad, a sinful dessert, and a philanthropic cause to the mix, and a delightful autumn luncheon moves from "have-fun" to "do-good."

A new collection of jewelry designed by Noelle Leshan Hicks triggered a call by friend Lynn Williams Croft to party planners and Door Couture founders Catherine Bailly Dunne and Tanis McGregor. She wanted to organize a luncheon at her home where style is defined not only by an array of gorgeous jewelry but by her aim—and that of her invited guests—to

purchase for a purpose.

To set the tone, Catherine and Tanis crafted invitations adorned with metallic chenille stems that mimic links of a gold bracelet. They also fashioned an exaggerated version of the bracelet for Lynn's front door to greet guests with a friendly reminder of the luncheon's theme.

From the decorated door to the beautiful table, the subject of the event was always at the forefront of the gathering. In the dining room, the Indian-inspired dinnerware, rendered in vibrant hues of gold, aqua, and cranberry, was manufactured by Jacqueline Cambata

Above: The Indian-inspired dinnerware is designed to increase awareness of underprivileged communities. Proceeds from the dinnerware sales aid such impoverished areas. Guest Lynn Bird sparkles in her new multistrand pearl necklace. Each guest took home a pair of gold earrings in an initialed bag as a party favor. *Opposite:* Hostess Lynn Williams Croft serves roasted chicken salad to Catherine Bailly Dunne (left) and jewelry designer Noelle Leshan Hicks.

"Whatever your skill is—be it making jewelry or cooking dinners that can be frozen and sold to raise money—there is great value to working together to make a difference."

—Catherine Bailly Dunne

 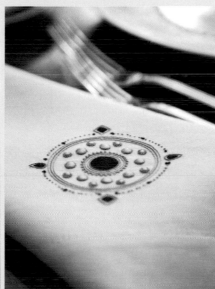 

with the specific goal of increasing awareness of underprivileged communities everywhere. Proceeds from dinnerware sales aid such impoverished areas.

"There are talented people who use their artistry to raise consciousness to those in need," says Tanis. "Making purchases of charitable merchandise benefits the buyer beyond the physical piece they receive."

Petite aqua vases filled with unassuming flowers and clear crystal glassware bow to a centerpiece that steals the show. Catherine and Tanis painted inexpensive vases and tree branches gold, then draped Noelle's creations on them, piquing anticipation of the full line of jewelry to be shown in the living room when coffee, tea, and a decadent pumpkin pie were served. To hold the heavier necklaces, each centerpiece vase was anchored by finish-friendly putty applied to its base.

"Whether it's a large-scale event or small, anyone can bring the community together to help," says Catherine. "Whatever your skill is— be it making jewelry or cooking dinners that can be frozen and sold to raise money—there is great value to working together to make a difference."

Opposite: Tree branches that have been painted gold and draped with pieces from jewelry designer Noelle Leshan Hicks' collection serve as a stunning centerpiece. *Above:* An oversize rendering of the signature charm bracelet made from crinkled gold paper welcomes guests at the front door. The embroidery on the linen napkins was inspired by Indian jewelry. Hostess Lynn Williams Croft enjoys her guests.

february

COLOR IT COZY There's still a chill in the air, but warmth at the table, thanks to satisfying comfort foods crafted with colorful produce.

33

42

46

Love Me Tender

Cooking meat on the bone leads to great flavor. Master butcher Kari Underly shares seven recipes to bring you the best bone-in cuts.

FRENCH ONION-BEEF
SHORT RIBS

French Onion-Beef Short Ribs

This is no-watch cooking. The short ribs are browned on the stove top then slow-cooked in the oven until tender. Each serving gets a short rib, so there's no carving needed. If the short ribs are in long sections, ask the butcher to cut them into smaller (about 3-inch) sections.

PREP 45 min. BAKE 2 hrs.
COOK 30 min. OVEN 325°F

3 lb. beef short ribs, cut in 3×2×2-inch sections (6 pieces)
4 cloves garlic, minced
1½ tsp. freshly ground black pepper
1 Tbsp. olive oil
¼ cup brandy or reduced-sodium beef broth
2 to 3 cups reduced-sodium beef broth
1 bay leaf
1 Tbsp. fresh thyme leaves
1½ lb. yellow onions
2 Tbsp. unsalted butter
   Salt and ground black pepper
4 ¾- to 1-inch diagonal slices baguette-style or other French bread
2 oz. Gruyère cheese, shredded
   Fresh Italian (flat-leaf) parsley sprigs
   Fresh thyme sprigs

1. Preheat oven to 325°F. Sprinkle short ribs with garlic and 1½ teaspoons black pepper. In a 6- to 8-quart Dutch oven brown short ribs, half at a time if necessary, in hot oil over medium heat, turning frequently to avoid burning garlic. Remove Dutch oven from heat; remove short ribs. Carefully add brandy to Dutch oven and return to heat. Cook and stir, scraping up any brown bits. Add 2 cups of the beef broth, the bay leaf, and 1 tablespoon fresh thyme. Return short ribs to Dutch oven. Bring to boiling. Cover and bake in the preheated oven for 2 to 2½ hours or until tender.
2. Meanwhile, slice onions crosswise. In a 12-inch skillet cook sliced onions in hot butter over medium heat for 5 minutes. Reduce heat; cook onions over medium-low heat for 25 to 35 minutes or until light brown and tender, stirring occasionally. Season to taste with salt.
3. Remove short ribs from Dutch oven. Strain the cooking liquid and discard solids. Skim fat from cooking liquid. In the same Dutch oven combine cooking liquid and cooked onion mixture over low heat until heated through. If desired, add additional beef broth until it reaches desired consistency. Season to taste with salt and pepper.

4. Meanwhile, on a baking sheet place bread slices. Broil 4 to 5 inches from heat for 1 to 2 minutes or until toasted. Turn bread slices and evenly divide cheese among bread slices. Broil 1 to 2 minutes more or until cheese is melted and bread is toasted on the under side.
5. To serve, place bread slices in four shallow bowls. Divide short ribs among bowls. Spoon broth mixture over beef. Sprinkle with parsley and thyme. Makes 6 servings.
EACH SERVING (*without toast*) *633 cal, 49 g fat, 101 mg chol, 333 mg sodium, 15 g carb, 2 g fiber, 27 g pro.*

Sunday Beef Rib Roast

This roast is ideal for celebrations and Sunday dinners because it requires little care and few spices. Vegetables are cooked alongside the roast for a flavorful one-pan meal.

PREP 30 min. ROAST 1 hr. 45 min.
STAND 15 min. OVEN 350°F

1 recipe Herb-Bacon Topper
1 4- to 5-lb. beef rib roast (chin bone removed)
1 tsp. cracked black peppercorns
½ tsp. salt
1 lb. baby carrots with tops, trimmed
1 lb. small red potatoes (halve large potatoes)
3 to 4 cups baby spinach
1 15-oz. can butter beans, rinsed and drained

1. Prepare Herb-Bacon Topper. Preheat oven to 350°F. Sprinkle beef roast with cracked pepper, salt, and half the Herb-Bacon Topper (refrigerate remaining topper and reserved bacon pieces). Place meat, bone side down, in a shallow roasting pan. Insert an oven-safe meat thermometer into center of roast.
2. Roast, uncovered, for 45 minutes. Arrange carrots and potatoes around roast; toss to gently coat. Roast 1 to 1¼ hours more or until meat thermometer registers 135°F for medium-rare. Sprinkle meat with remaining Herb-Bacon Topper; cover and let stand for 15 minutes. Temperature of meat after standing should be 145°F. Push meat, potatoes, and carrots to one side of pan. Stir spinach and beans into drippings in opposite side of pan; sprinkle with reserved bacon pieces. Makes 10 servings.
Herb-Bacon Topper Cook 4 slices of bacon until crisp; drain on paper towels. Chop half the bacon; stir in 1 tablespoon chopped fresh thyme and 1½ teaspoons chopped fresh rosemary. Break remaining bacon into pieces to sprinkle into the spinach and beans before serving.
EACH SERVING *492 cal, 32 g fat, 91 mg chol, 468 mg sodium, 19 g carb, 4 g fiber, 32 g pro.*

SUNDAY BEEF RIB ROAST

CHILI-RUBBED BONE-IN STRIP STEAKS

HONEY-GLAZED
PORK ROAST

Chili-Rubbed Bone-In Strip Steaks

Each of these thick-cut steaks is large enough to serve three or four. To get the caramelized brown outside without overcooking or undercooking the center, Kari starts the steaks on the stove top in a heavy skillet then pops them in the oven to finish cooking.

PREP **30 min.** COOK **30 min.**
BAKE **20 min.3** OVEN **350°F**

1   cup chopped onion
1   Tbsp. olive oil
1   lb. fresh tomatillos (about 12), husks removed and coarsely chopped
4   cloves garlic, minced
1   Tbsp. packed brown sugar
2   tsp. chili powder or ground chipotle chili pepper
1   tsp. coarse kosher salt
2   bone-in beef strip (top loin) steaks, cut 1½ inches thick (about 3 lb. total)
     Nonstick cooking spray
2   medium avocados, halved, seeded, peeled, and chopped
¼   cup chopped cilantro
1   Tbsp. red wine vinegar
1   red or green jalapeño pepper, sliced (see note, page 11) (optional)

1. Preheat oven to 350° F. In a large skillet cook onion in oil over medium heat until tender, about 5 minutes. Add tomatillos and garlic. Cook, covered, for 10 minutes, stirring occasionally. Uncover; cook 5 minutes more or until slightly thickened. Cool mixture to room temperature.
2. Meanwhile, combine brown sugar, chili powder, and ½ teaspoon of the salt. Rub evenly over steaks. Coat a 10-inch cast-iron skillet or other oven-proof skillet with non-stick spray. Heat skillet over medium-high heat. Add steaks. Cook steaks for 5 minutes on each side or until nicely browned. Bake in preheated oven for 20 minutes or until desired doneness (145°F for medium-rare or 160°F for medium), turning once.
3. Stir avocados, cilantro, red wine vinegar, jalapeño, and remaining ½ teaspoon salt into tomatillo mixture. Serve with steaks. Makes 6 to 8 servings.
EACH SERVING *646 cal, 47 g fat, 138 mg chol, 393 mg sodium, 14 g carb, 5 g fiber, 41 g pro.*

KID FRIENDLY

Honey-Glazed Pork Roast

This is your everyday pork loin roast with the bone removed and then tied back on to add flavor and act as a roasting rack (ask your butcher to do this). Don't toss the ribs; they're tasty sliced in two-rib portions and served to guests alongside the sliced roast. Or refrigerate them, covered, and reheat later with a little barbecue sauce.

PREP **25 min.**   ROAST **1 hr. 10 min.**
STAND **10 min.**   OVEN **350°F**

2   to 3 tsp. smoked paprika or paprika
2   tsp. coarse kosher salt
1   3- to 5-lb. bone-in pork roast, ribs removed and tied back on
     Fresh oregano sprigs
3   small red and/or yellow sweet peppers, stemmed, seeded, and quartered
1   small green pepper, stemmed, seeded, and quartered
1   Tbsp. olive oil
     Salt and pepper
⅓   cup honey
¼   cup lime juice
     Fresh oregano and/or thyme sprigs

1. Preheat oven to 350°F. In a small bowl combine paprika and coarse kosher salt.
2. Place pork in a shallow roasting pan, bone side down. Rub paprika mixture all over pork, pressing in lightly. Tuck sprigs of fresh oregano under the kitchen string, tying the roast to the bone. Roast, uncovered, in the preheated oven for 20 to 25 minutes per pound (1 hour 10 minutes to 2 hours).
3. Meanwhile, place sweet pepper pieces on a baking sheet. Drizzle peppers with oil and sprinkle lightly with salt and pepper; toss to coat. Spread peppers on baking sheet. Place in oven with pork the last 40 to 45 minutes of roasting until peppers are tender and begin to brown. When roast reaches 155°F internal temperature, remove to a cutting board and cover with foil. Let stand 10 minutes.
4. While roast stands, in a small saucepan combine honey and lime juice. Bring to boiling, stirring occasionally. Boil gently, uncovered, for 2 minutes. Remove from heat and cool slightly. Season with salt and pepper.
5. Remove string from roast. Using tongs, turn roast on its side and pull bone away. Turn roast topside up and slice. Serve with peppers, honey glaze, and fresh herbs. Makes 8 servings.
EACH SERVING *282 cal, 14 g fat, 65 mg chol, 620 mg sodium, 15 g carb, 1 g fiber, 23 g pro.*

BAKED HAM WITH
MUSTARD-PLUM GLAZE

ROSEMARY-GARLIC
LAMB LOIN CHOPS

Baked Ham with Mustard-Plum Glaze

PREP 20 min. BAKE 1¾ hr.
STAND 10 min. OVEN 350°F

1   3- to 4-lb. small smoked bone-in ham
1   10-oz. jar plum jam (1 cup)
¼   cup pomegranate juice
⅛   tsp. ground cloves (optional)
1   Tbsp. Dijon-style mustard
6   medium leeks
     Salt and pepper
½   cup finely shredded Parmesan cheese
½   cup soft bread crumbs
2   Tbsp. butter, melted
     Fresh sage leaves (optional)

1. Preheat oven to 350°F. Place ham on a rack in a foil-lined roasting pan. Roast, uncovered, for 45 minutes.
2. For sauce, in small saucepan stir together jam, pomegranate juice, and ground cloves. Heat over low until melted. Spoon half the sauce over ham. Tent with foil. Roast for 1 to 1½ hours more or until internal temperature of ham is 140°F. Remove and let stand, covered, for 10 minutes. Stir mustard into remaining sauce and heat through.
3. For leeks, trim root ends and tough green tops. Halve leeks lengthwise. Remove and discard tough outer layers. Rinse well. Arrange leek halves in a 2-quart rectangular baking dish. Add 2 tablespoons *water*. Sprinkle leeks lightly with salt and pepper and ¼ cup of the cheese. Cover

with foil. Bake in the oven with ham for 35 minutes. Uncover; sprinkle with bread crumbs and remaining cheese. Drizzle with melted butter. Bake, uncovered, for 15 minutes more or until leeks are tender and topping is brown.
4. To serve, lightly spoon some of the remaining sauce over the ham. Slice ham and serve with remaining sauce and leeks. Garnish with sage leaves. Makes 12 servings.
EACH SERVING *310 cal, 13 g fat, 69 mg chol, 1,001 mg sodium, 25 g carb, 1 g fiber, 24 g pro.*

Rosemary-Garlic Lamb Loin Chops

PREP 20 min. BROIL 18 min.

1   recipe Tomato-Balsamic Rice (optional)
4   lamb loin chops, cut 1½ to 2 inches thick (1¾ to 2 lb. total)
1   Tbsp. snipped fresh rosemary
3   cloves garlic, minced
½   tsp. salt
½   tsp. ground black pepper
1   Tbsp. olive oil
2   cups cherry tomatoes
1   tsp. balsamic vinegar
     Rosemary sprigs (optional)

1. Prepare Tomato-Balsamic Rice. Meanwhile, arrange oven rack so that the top of the chop surface is 4 to 5 inches from the heat when placed on a broiler pan. Make sure to account for the height of broiler pan and chops. Preheat broiler.

2. Coat the top of broiler pan with *nonstick cooking spray*. Rub both sides of the chops with half of each of the snipped rosemary, garlic, salt, and pepper. Broil chops for 18 to 20 minutes or until an instant-read thermometer inserted in chops registers 145°F (medium-rare doneness), turning occasionally to brown evenly.
3. Meanwhile, in a large skillet heat oil over medium heat. Add tomatoes and remaining half of the snipped rosemary, garlic, salt, and pepper. Cook about 5 minutes or until the tomatoes just begin to soften. Stir in vinegar.
4. Serve chops with tomatoes and Tomato-Balsamic Rice. Top with rosemary sprigs. Makes 4 servings.
Tomato-Balsamic Rice In a medium saucepan combine 2 cups water, 1 cup uncooked jasmine or long grain rice, and ¼ teaspoon salt. Bring to boiling; reduce heat. Simmer, covered, for 18 to 20 minutes or until rice is tender and liquid is absorbed. Stir in one 14.5-ounce can diced tomatoes with basil, garlic, and oregano, drained; ½ cup frozen peas; and 1 tablespoon balsamic vinegar. Cover; let stand 5 minutes to heat through. Makes about 4 cups.
EACH SERVING *484 cal, 39 g fat, 111 mg chol, 388 mg sodium, 5 g carb, 1 g fiber, 28 g pro.*

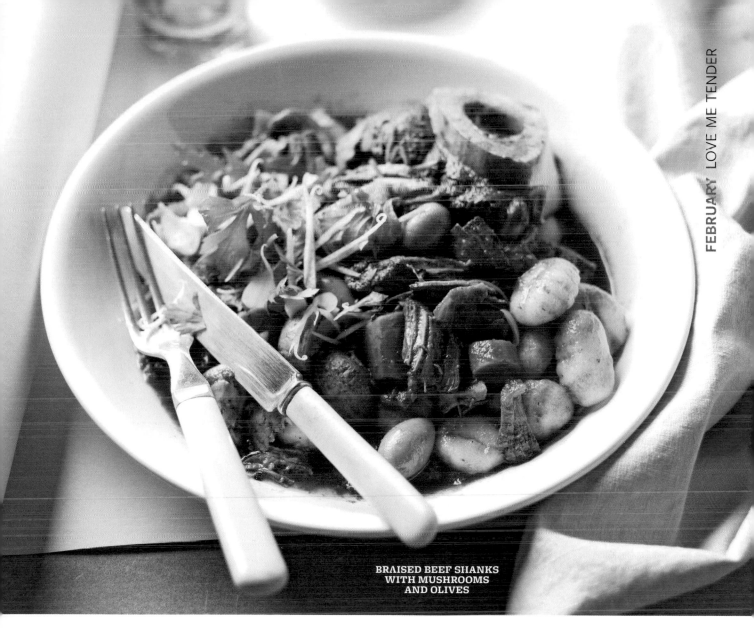

BRAISED BEEF SHANKS
WITH MUSHROOMS
AND OLIVES

Braised Beef Shanks with Mushrooms and Olives

Braising—a cooking method in which meat or vegetables are browned then slow-cooked in a little liquid—turns this tough cut into a tender dish. During cooking the meat and bone infuse the vegetables with flavor. Serve with gnocchi, small new potatoes, or rice to soak up the flavorful cooking liquid.

PREP **20 min.** BAKE **2 hr.**
COOK **15 min.** OVEN **325°F**

2	Tbsp. olive oil
4	bone-in beef shanks, about 1¼ inches thick (about 4 lb.)
	Salt and ground black pepper
2	large onions, chopped (2 cups)
2	medium carrots, coarsely chopped (1 cup)
3	cloves garlic, minced
¾	cup dry red wine or beef broth
1	14½-oz. undrained can diced tomatoes with basil, garlic, and oregano
1	cup beef broth
12	oz. cremini or button mushrooms, quartered or halved
1	recipe Fresh Herb Topping
¾	cup pitted assorted olives
	Hot cooked gnocchi (optional)

1. Preheat oven to 325°F. In a Dutch oven heat olive oil over medium-high heat. Add beef shanks and brown on both sides. Remove beef shanks from Dutch oven. Sprinkle with salt and pepper.

2. Add onions, carrots, and garlic to Dutch oven. Cook and stir for 5 minutes or until softened. Add wine and deglaze pan by scraping up browned bits from the bottom. Add undrained tomatoes, beef broth, and beef shanks to pan. Bring to boiling.

3. Cover and bake 2 to 3 hours, or until beef is tender, adding mushrooms the last 20 minutes of cooking time. Meanwhile, prepare Fresh Herb Topping.

4. Remove beef shanks to a serving platter. Strain vegetables from cooking liquid. Stir olives into vegetables and spoon over beef shanks. Skim fat from cooking liquid and drizzle over beef shanks, vegetables, and gnocchi. Sprinkle with Fresh Herb Topper. Makes 8 servings.

Fresh Herb Topper In a small bowl combine ¼ cup chopped fresh Italian (flat-leaf) parsley, 2 teaspoons finely shredded lemon peel, and 3 cloves minced garlic. Makes ¼ cup.

EACH SERVING *387 cal, 20 g fat, 66 mg chol, 666 mg sodium, 13 g carb, 2 g fiber, 34 g pro.*

Home Cooking

Nothing marks a special day quite like cake. These two three-layer beauties with mix-and-match frostings and quick decorating ideas are sure to make any celebration delightfully sweet.

KID-FRIENDLY
Classic Vanilla Cake

STAND 30 min. PREP 25 min.
BAKE 30 min. COOL 10 min. OVEN 350°F

6	eggs
3	cups all-purpose flour
1½	tsp. baking powder
¾	tsp. baking soda
¾	tsp. salt
¾	cup butter, softened
2⅔	cups sugar
2	tsp. vanilla
2	cups buttermilk
1	recipe Vanilla-Sour Cream Frosting or Chocolate-Cream Cheese Frosting

1. Separate eggs. Allow egg whites to stand at room temperature for 30 minutes (reserve yolks for another use). Meanwhile, grease three 8×1½-inch round cake pans. Line bottoms of pans with parchment paper. Grease parchment paper and lightly flour pans; set aside. In medium bowl stir together flour, baking powder, baking soda, and salt; set aside.
2. Preheat oven to 350°F. In large mixing bowl beat butter with electric mixer on medium to high speed for 30 seconds. Add sugar and vanilla; beat until well combined. Add egg whites all at once; beat on medium-high 3 minutes. Alternately add flour mixture and buttermilk to butter mixture, beating on low after each addition just until combined (batter may look slightly curdled). Divide batter among prepared pans. (If you do not have three pans, refrigerate remaining batter until ready to use.)
3. Bake in preheated oven 30 to 35 minutes or until a wooden toothpick inserted near centers comes out clean. Cool cakes in pans on wire racks 10 minutes. Remove layers from pans. Cool thoroughly on racks.
4. Frost with desired frosting. Store, covered, in refrigerator. Makes 16 servings.
EACH SERVING (*with frosting*) *641 cal, 20 g fat, 52 mg chol, 378 mg sodium, 113 g carb, 1 g fiber, 5 g pro.*

KID-FRIENDLY
Vanilla-Sour Cream Frosting

PREP 10 min.

¾	cup butter, softened
¾	cup sour cream
1½	tsp. vanilla
8	cups powdered sugar
	Buttermilk or milk

In large mixing bowl combine butter, sour cream, and vanilla. Beat with electric mixer on medium speed for 30 seconds. Gradually beat in powdered sugar. Thin with buttermilk or milk to desired consistency. Makes about 4½ cups.

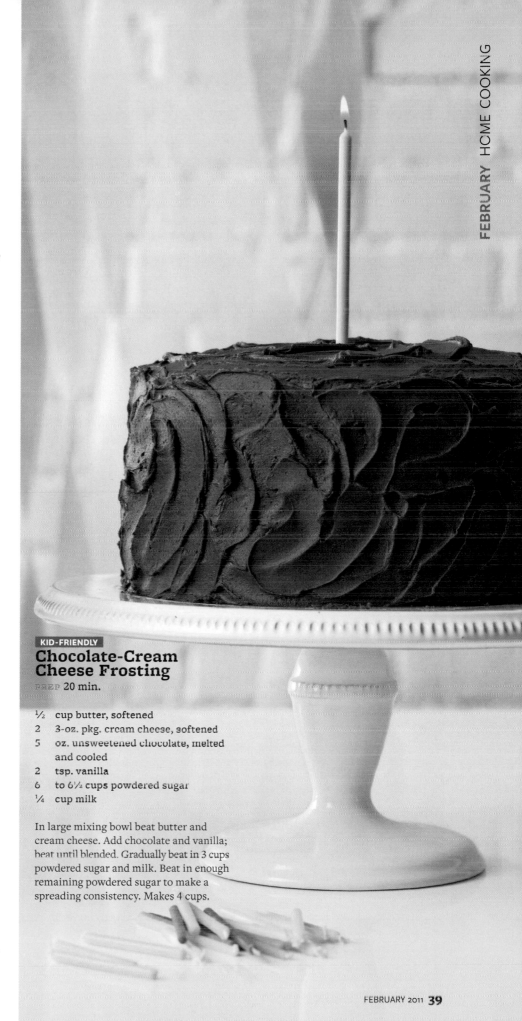

Double-Chocolate Cake

STAND 30 min. PREP 30 min.
BAKE 30 min. COOL 10 min. OVEN 350°F

3	eggs
2	cups all-purpose flour
¾	cup unsweetened cocoa powder
1	tsp. baking soda
¾	tsp. baking powder
½	tsp. salt
¾	cup butter, softened
2	cups sugar
2	tsp. vanilla
1½	cups milk
3	oz. dark or bittersweet chocolate, grated
1	recipe Chocolate-Cream Cheese Frosting or Vanilla-Sour Cream Frosting

1. Allow eggs to stand at room temperature 30 minutes. Meanwhile, grease three 8×1½-inch round cake pans. Line bottoms of pans with parchment paper. Grease parchment paper and lightly flour pans; set aside. In medium bowl stir together flour, cocoa powder, baking soda, baking powder, and salt; set aside.

2. Preheat oven to 350°F. In large mixing bowl beat butter with electric mixer on medium to high speed for 30 seconds. Gradually add sugar, ¼ cup at a time, beating on medium until well combined. Scrape sides of bowl; beat 2 minutes more. Add eggs, one at a time, beating after each addition. Beat in vanilla. Alternately add flour mixture and milk to butter mixture, beating on low after each addition just until combined. Beat on medium to high 20 seconds more. Stir in grated chocolate. Divide batter among prepared pans. (If you do not have three pans, refrigerate remaining batter until ready to use.)

3. Bake 30 to 35 minutes or until a wooden toothpick inserted near centers comes out clean. Cool cakes in pans on wire racks 10 minutes. Remove layers from pans. Cool thoroughly on wire racks.

4. Frost with desired frosting. Store, covered, in refrigerator. Makes 16 servings.

EACH SERVING (*with frosting*) *605 cal, 26 g fat, 92 mg chol, 334 mg sodium, 92 g carb, 4 g fiber, 7 g pro.*

Chocolate-Cream Cheese Frosting

PREP 20 min.

½	cup butter, softened
2	3-oz. pkg. cream cheese, softened
5	oz. unsweetened chocolate, melted and cooled
2	tsp. vanilla
6	to 6½ cups powdered sugar
¼	cup milk

In large mixing bowl beat butter and cream cheese. Add chocolate and vanilla; beat until blended. Gradually beat in 3 cups powdered sugar and milk. Beat in enough remaining powdered sugar to make a spreading consistency. Makes 4 cups.

Frosting brings the yum factor while also keeping cakes moist and adding flavor and texture.

No Rushing—Let It Cool
When the cake comes out of the oven, let it cool slightly in the pan, then turn it out onto a cooling rack. Peel the parchment paper, then allow the cake to cool completely. A cool cake is easier to frost because it has a chance to set up and won't crumble. A cool cake also won't melt the frosting.

Crumb-Free Frosting
To avoid crumbs in frosting, brush cake layers with a pastry brush before assembling. Spread about ½ cup of frosting on the first layer, then carefully top with the next layer. Repeat to assemble cake. Next, add a "crumb coat" by spreading a very thin layer of frosting on the sides and top of the cake. This does not have to be perfect—its purpose is to keep crumbs out of the finished frosting. Let stand for 30 minutes to set up before adding the final frosting.

Finishing Touch
Using an offset spatula or butter knife, generously spread remaining frosting on the top and along sides of the cake, swirling frosting. Once the cake is frosted, go back and add swirls as desired.

These tried-and-true cake recipes and easy frostings are the only ones you'll ever need— they're that good.

Playing Dress Up

Here are four fun ways to decorate these cakes— no piping bag required.

BANANA SPLIT
Top the cake with toasted coconut, sliced bananas (brush the slices with a little lemon juice to keep them from turning brown), whipped cream, and cherries.

DAISY CHAIN
Attach small candies to the center of flower-shape cookies (about 9 to 12) with a little dab of frosting. Press the cookies into the frosting along the bottom of the cake to create a border.

ROCKY ROAD
Top the cake with crushed waffle cones, mini marshmallows, peanuts, and chocolate syrup.

BERRIES & COOKIES
Top the cake with three whole Oreo cookies and a strawberry. Halve additional cookies and slice 7 or 8 strawberries and press into the sides of the cake at an angle. Slice with a sharp serated knife and serve within 2 hours.

Chill and Grill

Barbecue expert Elizabeth Karmel shares her tips for making the perfect steak: a great rub, a delicious sauce, and a New York strip steak.

FAST **LOW FAT**

Chicago Steakhouse Sauce

START TO FINISH 42 min.

In a large heavy bottom saucepan over medium heat stir together 2 tablespoons olive oil, ½ cup chopped onion, and 1 tablespoon brown sugar. Add 1 tablespoon each of sweet smoked Spanish paprika, sweet Hungarian paprika, and dry mustard. When onions are soft and spices are fragrant, stir in 2 tablespoons Worcestershire sauce, 1 cup each of cola and Spicy Hot V8 juice, ¾ cup ketchup, ¼ cup bourbon, ¼ cup rice vinegar, and 1 tablespoon reduced-sodium soy sauce. Bring to boiling; reduce heat to medium-low and simmer 15 minutes or until thick. Makes about 3½ cups sauce.

FAST **LOW FAT**

Chicago Steakhouse Rub

START TO FINISH 5 min.

Stir together 1 tablespoon of dry mustard, 2 teaspoons each of granulated garlic and coarsely ground black pepper, 1 teaspoon sweet smoked Spanish paprika, and ½ teaspoon each of dried thyme and cayenne pepper. To use, cover both sides of steak generously with rub; allow to stand 30 minutes at room temperature before grilling.

Everyday Easy

Keep your resolution to eat well. These quick-to-make dishes are healthful, colorful, and filling.

OPEN-FACE ITALIAN
BEEF SANDWICHES

FAST

Open-Face Italian Beef Sandwiches

START TO FINISH 20 min.
BUDGET $3.17 per serving

¼	cup white wine vinegar or cider vinegar
1	tsp. sugar
½	tsp. ground black pepper
1	17-oz. pkg. refrigerated cooked Italian-style herbed beef roast au jus
1	cup sliced baby or regular size red or yellow sweet peppers
2	square whole grain ciabatta rolls or buns
4	slices provolone cheese
2	Tbsp. snipped fresh Italian (flat-leaf) parsley

1. Preheat broiler. In a large microwave-safe bowl combine vinegar, sugar, and pepper. Stir in undrained beef and sliced peppers. Cover and cook on high (100% power) for 4 minutes.
2. Meanwhile, split rolls and then place cut sides up on baking sheet. Broil 3 to 4 inches from heat for 1 minute or until lightly toasted. Top each roll with cheese; broil 1 to 2 minutes until cheese is melted.
3. Using a fork, coarsely shred beef. Stir in parsley. With slotted spoon, mound beef mixture on rolls. Sprinkle with additional snipped parsley. Serve with any remaining cooking liquid. Serves 4.

EACH SERVING *341 cal, 15 g fat, 78 mg chol, 774 mg sodium, 22 g carb, 2 g fiber, 31 g pro.*

GREEN CHILE PORK STEW

FAST LOW FAT

Green Chile Pork Stew

START TO FINISH 30 min.
BUDGET $2.75 per serving

1	lb. pork tenderloin
	Salt and ground black pepper
1	Tbsp. olive oil
3	7-oz. pkg. frozen yellow carrots, spinach, and white bean medley in garlic herb sauce, thawed
1	4.5-oz. can diced green chiles
1	tsp. ground cumin
	Fresh cilantro
	Lime wedges (optional)

1. Cut pork in ¾-inch pieces; sprinkle lightly with salt and pepper. In Dutch oven heat olive oil over medium-high heat. Add pork; cook 4 to 5 minutes or until browned. Stir in two packages of the thawed vegetables, the chiles, and the cumin.
2. In a blender combine remaining thawed vegetables and 1 cup *water*. Process until smooth. Add pureed vegetables to Dutch oven. Bring to a simmer. Cook, covered, over medium heat about 15 minutes or until pork is cooked through, stirring occasionally. Ladle into soup bowls. Top with cilantro and a squeeze of lime juice. Makes 4 servings.

EACH SERVING *297 cal, 11 g fat, 74 mg chol, 823 mg sodium, 21 g carb, 7 g fiber, 30 g pro.*

EGGPLANT PARMESAN HEROES

MOROCCAN MEAT LOAF

FAST LOW FAT

Eggplant Parmesan Heroes

START TO FINISH **30 min.**
BUDGET **$1.92 per serving**

1   medium eggplant (about 1 lb.)
1   cup bottled marinara sauce
1   cup seasoned croutons, crushed
⅓   cup shredded Parmesan cheese
4   hero or hoagie buns, split
     Fresh basil leaves (optional)

1. Preheat oven to 400°F. Lightly coat a baking sheet with *nonstick cooking spray.* Peel eggplant (optional); cut in ¼-inch slices.
2. Place marinara in a shallow dish. In a second shallow dish add croutons and half the cheese. Dip eggplant in marinara then crouton mixture; press to coat. Place eggplant on prepared baking sheet. Lightly coat with cooking spray. Bake 15 minutes or until breading is browned and eggplant is tender. Remove from oven.

3. On baking sheet toast buns for 2 minutes or until lightly toasted. Meanwhile, transfer remaining marinara to small microwave-safe bowl; heat for 30 seconds. Place eggplant on toasted buns; top with marinara and cheese. Sprinkle basil leaves. Makes 4 servings.
EACH SERVING *423 cal, 9 g fat, 7 mg chol, 1,011 mg sodium, 73 g carb, 9 g fiber, 13 g pro.*

FAST LOW FAT

Moroccan Meat Loaf

START TO FINISH **35 min.**
BUDGET **$2.51 per serving**

1½ cups raisins
1   small red onion, chopped
½   cup couscous, uncooked
1   tsp. salt
1   tsp. curry powder
1   tsp. ground cinnamon
1   lb. ground turkey
1   egg, lightly beaten
1   pint grape tomatoes

1. Preheat oven to 425°F. In a large mixing bowl combine 1 cup of the raisins, half the onion, the couscous, salt, curry powder, and ½ teaspoon of the cinnamon. Pour ¾ cup boiling *water* over mixture; cover. Let stand 2 minutes. Add turkey and egg; mix well. Pat mixture into a foil-lined greased 8×8×2-inch baking pan. Bake in the top third of oven for about 20 minutes or until cooked through (165°F).
2. Meanwhile, for chutney, in saucepan combine the remaining ½ cup raisins, remaining onion and cinnamon, tomatoes, and ¼ cup *water.* Cook, covered, over medium-high until tomato skins pop. Lift meat loaf from pan using foil. Slice and serve with tomato chutney. Makes 4 servings.
EACH SERVING *487 cal, 11 g fat, 142 mg chol, 721 mg sodium, 73 g carb, 5 g fiber, 27 g pro.*

Saucy BBQ Chicken

START TO FINISH 30 min.
BUDGET $2.08 per serving

8   small chicken drumsticks
1   large onion, cut in 6 slices
1   cup ketchup
¼   cup molasses
3   to 4 Tbsp. cider vinegar
2   Tbsp. packed brown sugar
1   tsp. smoked paprika
    Several dashes bottled hot
    pepper sauce
    Fresh Italian (flat-leaf) parsley

1. Preheat broiler. Broil chicken on unheated rack of broiler pan, 4 to 5 inches from heat, for 10 minutes.
2. Lightly brush onion slices with *olive oil*. Remove pan from oven. Turn and move chicken to one end of pan. Place onion slices, in single layer, on opposite end of pan. Broil 15 minutes or until chicken is no longer pink and juices run clear (180°F).
3. Meanwhile, in saucepan combine ketchup, molasses, vinegar, brown sugar, paprika, and pepper sauce. Bring to boiling over medium heat. Remove from heat; keep warm. Remove onions. Broil chicken 2 minutes more; brush with sauce during last minute.
4. Chop 2 onion slices; stir into sauce. Serve chicken with onion slices and parsley. Makes 4 servings.
EACH SERVING 426 cal, 16 g fat, 118 mg chol, 801 mg sodium, 40 g carb, 1 g fiber, 30 g pro.

SAUCY BBQ CHICKEN

GET CREATIVE Combine pantry staples—canned tomatoes, olives, go-to seasonings, and pasta—for fresh meals. Plus, learn from a pro the delicious art of topping a hot dog.

52

55

60

**CHICKEN AND PASTA
FRITTATA WITH
SIMPLE SPINACH SALAD**

**CHICKEN AND
VEGETABLE SAUTÉ**

LEMON-BASIL PASTA

Knockout Meals

Dazzle the family with meals made from scratch in 30 minutes or fewer.

FAST LOW FAT

Chicken and Vegetable Sauté

PREP 15 min. COOK 16 min.

2 cups broccoli florets
4 medium carrots, cut lengthwise into strips
1 Tbsp. olive oil
4 medium boneless skinless chicken breasts (1¼ lb. total), cut lengthwise into thirds
½ a medium red onion, cut in thin wedges
1 15-oz. can great Northern beans, rinsed and drained
½ cup reduced-sodium chicken broth
1 Tbsp. finely shredded lemon peel

1. Fill a 3-quart saucepan about two-thirds full of water; add ½ teaspoon *salt*. Bring to boiling; add broccoli and carrots. Boil 3 minutes or until crisp-tender. Drain vegetables and place in bowl of ice water to stop cooking. When cool, drain; set aside.
2. Heat oil in a very large nonstick skillet over medium-high heat. Season chicken with *salt* and *pepper*. Cook over medium-high heat until browned and cooked through, about 10 to 12 minutes, turning occasionally to brown evenly. Remove from skillet; set aside.
3. Reduce heat to medium-low. Add onion and season with *salt* and *pepper*. Cook and stir for 2 minutes. Increase heat to medium-high. Add beans, broth, lemon peel, vegetables, and chicken. Cook and stir 1 minute or until heated through. Makes 4 servings.
EACH SERVING 356 cal, 6 g fat, 82 mg chol, 587 mg sodium, 33 g carb, 8 g fiber, 43 g pro.

FAST

Chicken and Pasta Frittata

START TO FINISH 30 min. OVEN 400°F

1 cup broccoli florets
1 medium onion, chopped (½ cup)
2 Tbsp. olive oil
1¼ cups cooked penne or desired pasta
1 cup chopped cooked chicken
2 Tbsp. chopped fresh basil
8 eggs, lightly beaten
½ cup shredded mozzarella cheese

1. Preheat oven to 400°F. In large oven-going skillet cook broccoli and onion in hot oil over medium heat 5 minutes or until tender. Stir in penne, chicken, basil, and ¼ teaspoon each *salt* and *black pepper*.
2. Pour eggs over mixture in skillet. Cook over medium heat. As mixture sets, run a spatula around edge of skillet, lifting egg mixture so uncooked portion flows underneath. Continue cooking and lifting until egg mixture is almost set. Top with cheese. Bake 5 minutes or until puffed. Sprinkle with pepper. Makes 4 servings.
EACH SERVING 415 cal, 23 g fat, 462 mg chol, 421 mg sodium, 23 g carb, 2 g fiber, 30 g pro.

FAST LOW FAT

Simple Spinach Salad

START TO FINISH 5 min.

1 Tbsp. lemon juice
1 Tbsp. olive oil
1 to 2 tsp. honey
4 cups baby spinach

In a large bowl whisk together the lemon juice, olive oil, and honey. Add spinach, tossing to coat. Season with *salt* and *pepper*. Makes 4 servings.
EACH SERVING 50 cal, 3 g fat, 0 mg chol, 116 mg sodium, 4 g carb, 1 g fiber, 1 g pro.

FAST LOW FAT

Lemon-Basil Pasta

START TO FINISH 25 min.

10 oz. dried linguine or desired pasta
1 19-oz. can white kidney (cannellini) beans, rinsed and drained
½ a lemon
3 Tbsp. olive oil
1 cup packed fresh basil leaves
½ tsp. salt
¼ tsp. black pepper

1. Cook pasta according to package directions, adding beans the last 2 minutes of cooking time. Remove ½ cup of the cooking liquid; set aside. Drain pasta and beans; cover to keep warm.
2. Meanwhile, finely shred peel from the lemon half (about 2 teaspoons). In a small skillet heat 1 tablespoon of the oil over medium heat. Add lemon peel; cook and stir 1 minute, or until lightly golden.
3. In food processor combine cooked lemon peel, basil, the remaining 2 tablespoons olive oil, the juice from the lemon half, salt, and pepper. Cover and process until smooth. Add reserved cooking liquid, 1 tablespoon at a time, until desired consistency, processing mixture after every addition.
4. To serve, toss hot cooked pasta mixture with lemon-basil mixture. Makes 4 servings.
EACH SERVING 452 cal, 10 g fat, 0 mg chol, 648 mg sodium, 75 g carb, 9 g fiber, 18 g pro.

What's on your list? These super-flexible recipes allow plenty of wiggle room to swap in your family's must-have ingredients.

MEAT LOAF SANDWICH

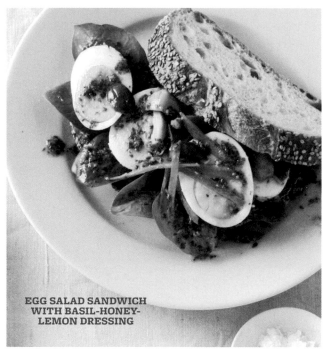

EGG SALAD SANDWICH WITH BASIL-HONEY-LEMON DRESSING

KID-FRIENDLY
Meat Loaf Sandwich

PREP 20 min. BAKE 22 min. OVEN 375°F

5 ciabatta buns or sandwich rolls
1 egg
1 14½-oz. can diced tomatoes with basil, garlic, and oregano, drained
2 Tbsp. snipped fresh basil
1 lb. lean ground beef or ground turkey
4 oz. cheddar cheese, sliced
1 cup fresh spinach leaves

1. Preheat oven to 375°F. In a food processor, process one of the buns until coarse crumbs form. Measure ¾ cup of the crumbs; set aside remaining crumbs for another use.
2. In a bowl combine egg, 1 cup of the tomatoes, the ¾ cup bread crumbs, and basil. Add beef and mix well. Divide into four portions and shape each into a 4-inch square. Place on unheated rack of broiler pan. Bake 20 minutes (160°F). Top with cheese. Bake 2 minutes more. Serve meat loaves on buns with spinach and remaining tomatoes. Makes 4 sandwiches.
EACH SANDWICH *531 cal, 25 g fat, 153 mg chol, 598 mg sodium, 40 g carb, 8 g fiber, 37 g pro.*

FAST
Egg Salad Sandwich with Basil-Honey-Lemon Dressing

START TO FINISH 20 min.

½ cup coarsely shredded carrot
½ a small red onion, cut into very thin wedges
⅓ cup pitted Kalamata olives, halved
8 slices crusty bread
1 cup baby spinach
6 hard-cooked eggs, thickly sliced lengthwise
¼ cup olive oil
¼ cup fresh basil leaves
2 Tbsp. finely shredded Parmesan cheese
2 Tbsp. lemon juice
2 tsp. honey

1. In bowl toss together carrot, red onion, and olives. Layer 4 bread slices with spinach. Top with sliced eggs and carrot mixture.
2. In blender or food processor combine oil, basil, Parmesan, lemon juice, honey, ⅛ teaspoon *salt*, and a dash of *pepper*. Process until blended and slightly thickened. Drizzle over carrot mixture and eggs. Top with remaining bread. Makes 4 sandwiches.
EACH SANDWICH *452 cal, 26 g fat, 319 mg chol, 692 mg sodium, 38 g carbo, 3 g fiber, 16 g pro.*

Veggie Burgers
PREP 25 min. COOK 8 min.

1   19-oz. can cannellini beans, rinsed and drained
1½ cups soft bread crumbs
¼   cup shredded carrot
¼   cup finely chopped onion
1   egg
2   Tbsp. snipped fresh parsley
3   Tbsp. olive oil
1   cup packed fresh baby spinach
4   slices country Italian bread, toasted
¼   cup Easy Tomato Sauce, *page 56*

1. In a medium bowl mash beans with a fork or potato masher. Stir in half the bread crumbs, carrot, onion, egg, half the parsley, 1 tablespoon of the olive oil, and ¼ teaspoon each *salt* and *pepper*. Combine remaining bread crumbs and the parsley in a shallow dish.
2. Shape bean mixture into 4 patties (mixture will be soft). Dip both sides of patties into crumb mixture to coat.
3. Heat remaining 2 tablespoons oil in a large skillet over medium heat. Cook patties for 4 minutes per side or until browned.
4. Arrange spinach and patties on bread. Top with Easy Tomato Sauce. Makes 4 servings.
EACH SERVING *353 cal, 13 g fat, 53 mg chol, 873 mg sodium, 48 g carb, 9 g fiber, 15 g pro.*

Apple-Onion Salad
START TO FINISH 15 min.

2   medium Granny Smith or tart green and/or red apples, cored
1   Tbsp. lemon juice
1   Tbsp. olive oil
1   Tbsp. honey
½   small red onion, sliced

Slice apples; set aside. In a bowl whisk together lemon juice, olive oil, honey, and ¼ teaspoon *salt*. Add apple and onion slices; toss. Makes 4 servings.
EACH SERVING *98 cal, 4 g fat, 0 mg chol, 147 mg sodium, 18 g carb, 2 g fiber, 0 g pro.*

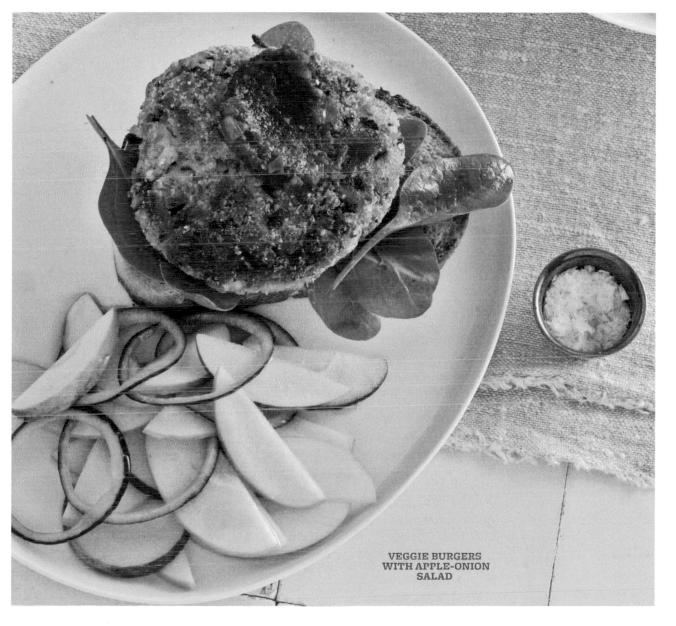

VEGGIE BURGERS WITH APPLE-ONION SALAD

SLOPPY JOE
PIZZA

CARROT SOUP WITH
CHILI-SPICED
CROUTONS

HUMMUS-CRUSTED
CHICKEN
WITH CHILI CARROTS

EGG SANDWICH WITH
SWEET-SOUR CARROTS
AND ONIONS

Hummus-Crusted Chicken

PREP 15 min. COOK 12 min.

1   15- to 16 oz. can navy beans, rinsed
    and drained
3   Tbsp. olive oil
3   Tbsp. lime or lemon juice
4   skinless, boneless chicken breast
    halves
    Salt and ground black pepper
2   cups coarse soft bread crumbs
2   to 3 Tbsp. olive oil
    Lime or lemon wedges

1. For hummus, in a blender or food
processor combine beans, the 3 tablespoons
olive oil, and the lime juice; process until
smooth. Set aside ⅓ cup of hummus for
another use.
2. Sprinkle chicken with salt and pepper.
Spread chicken with remaining hummus;
roll in bread crumbs.
3. Heat the 2 tablespoons oil in a skillet over
medium heat. Add chicken; cook 12 minutes
or until no pink remains (170°F), turning
once. Add more oil, if needed. If crumbs
brown too quickly, reduce heat. Serve with
lime wedges. Makes 4 servings.
EACH SERVING *491 cal, 20 g fat, 82 mg chol,
676 mg sodium, 35 g carb, 6 g fiber, 43 g pro.*

FAST   LOW FAT

Chili Carrots

PREP 15 min. COOK 11 min.

4   medium carrots, peeled and
    bias-sliced in 1-inch pieces
1   Tbsp. olive oil
1   Tbsp. honey
½   to 1 tsp. chili powder

In saucepan cook carrots in boiling salted
water 8 minutes or until crisp-tender; drain.
In same saucepan combine oil, honey, and
chili powder; cook and stir 1 minute. Add
carrots; cook 2 minutes more or until
glazed. Season with *salt* and *pepper*. Makes
4 servings.
EACH SERVING *72 cal, 4 g fat, 0 mg chol,
46 mg sodium, 10 g carb, 2 g fiber, 1 g pro.*

FAST   KID-FRIENDLY

Sloppy Joe Pizza

PREP 25 min. BAKE 8 min. OVEN 400°F

1   lb. ground beef or ground turkey
1   large onion, chopped (1 cup)
5   medium carrots, thinly sliced
1   tsp. chili powder
1   14.5 oz. can diced tomatoes with
    roasted garlic
1   13.8-oz. pkg. refrigerated pizza dough
¼   to ½ cup shaved Parmesan cheese

1. Preheat oven to 400° F. In a large skillet
cook ground beef, onion, and carrots until
beef is browned. Drain off fat. Stir in chili
powder; cook 1 minute. Add tomatoes;
bring to boiling. Reduce heat and simmer,
uncovered, 10 minutes or until desired
consistency.
2. Meanwhile, unroll pizza dough on a lightly
floured surface. Cut into four pieces (about
6×8-inches each). Lightly *oil* a baking sheet;
place dough rectangles on sheet. Build up
edges slightly; prick centers with a fork.
Bake 8 to 10 minutes or until golden brown.
3. Place 1 square on each plate; top with
ground beef mixture and sprinkle with
cheese. Makes 4 servings.
EACH SERVING *647 cal, 37 g fat, 89 mg chol,
921 mg sodium, 49 g carb, 5 g fiber, 27 g pro.*

FAST   LOW FAT

Egg Sandwich with Sweet-Sour Carrots and Onions

PREP 15 min. CHILL 1 hr.

¼   cup white wine vinegar
2   tsp. sugar
1   tsp. chili powder
1   medium carrot, cut in very thin strips
½   cup thin onion wedges
1   baguette, cut crosswise into
    4 sections
4   eggs
1   Tbsp. olive oil
    Fresh cilantro sprigs and/or
    parsley sprigs

1. In a bowl stir together vinegar, sugar,
1 teaspoon *salt*, and chili powder until sugar
is dissolved. Stir in carrot and onion. Cover;
set aside.
2. Cut baguette sections in half horizontally;
set aside.

3. In a bowl beat together eggs and a pinch
of *salt*. In a 12-inch skillet heat oil over
medium-high heat. Add eggs. Cook, without
stirring, 1 to 2 minutes or until set. Divide
egg into four pieces. Place an egg portion on
bottom half of baguette sections, folding
to fit. Top with drained carrot mixture and
cilantro. Makes 4 sandwiches.
EACH SANDWICH *457 cal, 11 g fat, 211 mg
chol, 1,444 mg sodium, 70 g carb, 4 g fiber,
20 g pro.*

FAST   LOW FAT

Carrot Soup with Chili-Spiced Croutons

PREP 15 min. COOK 35 min.

3   Tbsp. olive oil
4   cups sliced onions
4   cups sliced carrots
32 oz. reduced-sodium chicken broth
1   recipe Chili-Spiced Croutons

1. In Dutch oven or large saucepan heat
oil over medium heat. Add onions and
season with *salt*. Cook 10 minutes, stirring
occasionally.
2. Add carrots; cook for 10 minutes more,
stirring occasionally. Add broth; bring to
a simmer. Simmer, covered, 15 minutes.
Remove from heat. Cool slightly.
3. In a blender or food processor blend
soup, one-third at a time, until smooth.
Return to pot; heat through. Serve with
Chili-Spiced Croutons. Makes 4 servings.
Chili-Spiced Croutons Preheat oven to
450°F. Cut 2 ounces crusty bread into
½-inch cubes. Toss with 1 teaspoon olive
oil and ¼ teaspoon chili powder. Spread
cubes on baking sheet. Bake for 5 to
7 minutes.
EACH SERVING *250 cal, 12 g fat, 0 mg chol,
927 mg sodium, 32 g carb, 6 g fiber, 7 g pro.*

FAST **LOW FAT** **KID-FRIENDLY**

Vegetable-Beef Pot Pie

PREP 18 min. BAKE 15 min. OVEN 400°F

1   lb. lean ground beef or ground turkey
1½ cups chopped carrots
1   cup chopped onion
1   Tbsp. chili powder
1   14.5-oz. can diced tomatoes
1   13.8-oz. pkg. refrigerated pizza dough
1   egg, lightly beaten
1   Tbsp. water

1. Preheat oven to 400°F. In a 10-inch skillet cook ground beef, carrots, and onion about 8 minutes or until beef is browned and carrots are tender. Drain off fat. Stir in chili powder, ½ teaspoon *salt*, and ⅛ teaspoon *pepper*. Add tomatoes; bring to boiling. Simmer, uncovered, 5 minutes or until liquid is nearly evaporated.
2. Meanwhile, unroll pizza dough. Cut into 1-inch strips. In a small bowl combine egg and water.
3. Spoon meat mixture into individual 16-ounce casseroles. Top with strips of pizza dough; trim to fit. Brush dough with egg mixture. Bake for 15 to 20 minutes or until golden brown. Makes 4 servings.
EACH SERVING *526 cal, 23 g fat, 130 mg chol, 903 mg sodium, 50 g carb, 6 g fiber, 30 g pro.*

FAST **LOW FAT** **KID-FRIENDLY**

Scrambled Egg Stromboli

PREP 30 min. BAKE 15 min. OVEN 400°F

8   eggs
3   Tbsp. olive oil
1½ cups chopped broccoli florets
½   cup chopped onion
1   13.8-oz. pkg. refrigerated pizza dough
1½ cups baby spinach leaves
¼   cup chopped fresh basil
¼   cup grated Parmesan cheese
1   recipe Easy Tomato Sauce

1. Preheat oven to 400°F. In a bowl whisk together the eggs, ¼ teaspoon *salt*, and ⅛ teaspoon *pepper*; set aside.
2. In a large skillet heat 2 tablespoons of the oil over medium heat. Add broccoli and onion. Cook and stir for 3 to 4 minutes or until tender. Add egg mixture to skillet. Cook without stirring until mixture begins to set around edges and on bottom. With a large spatula, lift and fold the partially cooked egg mixture so the uncooked portion flows underneath. Continue cooking just until egg mixture is cooked through but still glossy. Remove skillet from heat.
3. On a work surface unroll pizza dough, pressing dough to an even thickness

(14×9-inch rectangle), stretching slightly. Arrange spinach on dough. Sprinkle with basil and 2 tablespoons of the Parmesan cheese. Spoon egg mixture evenly on dough. Carefully roll up dough around filling, starting from a long side. Pinch ends to seal. Place roll, seam side down, on a large greased baking sheet. Brush roll with remaining olive oil and sprinkle with remaining Parmesan cheese. Using a sharp knife, make diagonal slashes in top of roll at about 1½-inch intervals.
4. Bake for 15 to 20 minutes or until golden brown. Cool slightly. Cut into slices and top with Easy Tomato Sauce. Makes 6 servings.
Easy Tomato Sauce Place one 14.5-ounce can diced tomatoes in a blender or food processor. Cover and blend or process to desired consistency. Pour into a bowl and stir in 2 tablespoons snipped fresh basil. Season with salt and pepper. Makes 1½ cups.
EACH SERVING *335 cal, 17 g fat, 285 mg chol, 649 mg sodium, 31 g carb, 3 g fiber, 15 g pro.*

FAST **LOW FAT** **KID-FRIENDLY**

Carrot Ribbon Salad

START TO FINISH 15 min.

1   Tbsp. drained juice from a jar of pitted ripe olives, or lemon juice
1   Tbsp. olive oil
4   yellow and/or orange carrots, peeled
⅓   cup sliced green onions

For dressing, in a medium bowl whisk together olive liquid, olive oil, and ⅛ teaspoon each *salt* and *pepper*; set aside. Using a vegetable peeler, peel carrots lengthwise into long strips, or coarsely shred them. Add to dressing mixture along with sliced green onions. Makes 4 servings.
EACH SERVING *59 cal, 4 g fat, 0 mg chol, 116 mg sodium, 7 g carb, 2 g fiber, 1 g pro.*

VEGETABLE-BEEF
POT PIE

SCRAMBLED EGG
STROMBOLI
WITH
CARROT RIBBON SALAD

PASTA, RED BEAN, AND
PARSLEY TOSS

FAST **LOW FAT** **KID-FRIENDLY**

Pasta, Red Bean, and Parsley Toss

PREP 15 min. COOK 15 min.

8   oz. dried medium shell pasta
    or desired pasta
3   cups broccoli florets
1   Tbsp. olive oil
1½ cups chopped onion
1   15-oz. can red beans, drained,
    reserving ¼ cup of liquid
½ cup chicken broth
1½ tsp. chili powder
½ cup finely shredded pecorino or
    Parmesan cheese
¼ cup snipped Italian (flat-leaf) parsley

1. Cook pasta according to package
instructions, adding broccoli during the
last 3 minutes; drain.
2. Meanwhile, in a 12-inch skillet heat
olive oil over medium high heat. Add
onion and ½ teaspoon *salt*. Reduce heat
to medium; cook about 5 minutes more
or until onion is tender.
3. Increase heat to high; add pasta,
broccoli, beans, chicken broth, reserved
bean liquid, and chili powder to pan.
Cook over high heat for 2 minutes, stirring
occasionally. Add cheese and parsley.
Cook and stir until cheese is melted.
Makes 4 servings.
EACH SERVING *422 cal, 8 g fat, 11 mg chol,
796 mg sodium, 70 g carb, 11 g fiber, 19 g pro.*

CANNED TOMATOES
Canned tomatoes work
in a variety of recipes—
diced tomatoes can be
stirred into a meat loaf
or burger mixture, and
whole plum tomatoes
can be whirled into a
quick sauce. Change
the flavor of a recipe by
using spicy tomatoes
with green chiles. Or
go Italian and use diced
tomatoes with garlic,
basil, and oregano.

Start with everyday staples. End up with an amazing array of delicious dinner sensations. They're easy beyond belief.

Egg and Wilted Spinach Salad

PREP 30 min. COOK 11 min.

1	5- to 6-oz. bag baby spinach
2	medium Granny Smith apples, cored and sliced
3	Tbsp. olive oil
2	Tbsp. balsamic vinegar
1	Tbsp. honey
8	eggs
4	oz. blue cheese, crumbled (½ cup)

1. In a large serving bowl place spinach; set aside.
2. In a very large skillet cook apple slices in 2 tablespoons of the olive oil for 3 to 4 minutes or until tender. Stir in balsamic vinegar and honey. Bring just to boiling. Add to spinach in bowl; toss to combine and slightly wilt.
3. In the same skillet heat remaining 1 tablespoon olive oil over medium heat. Break 4 eggs into skillet. Sprinkle with half of the blue cheese, ⅛ teaspoon each *salt* and *pepper*. Reduce heat to low; cook 4 to 5 minutes or until whites are set. For more doneness, cover the last 2 minutes. Repeat with remaining eggs and cheese. Place two eggs on each serving. Makes 4 servings.
EACH SERVING *412 cal, 28 g fat, 444 mg chol, 686 mg sodium, 21 g carb, 3 g fiber, 20 g pro.*

LOW FAT
Feta-Stuffed Chicken Breasts

PREP 25 min. COOK 18 min.

4	skinless, boneless chicken breast halves
½	cup crumbled feta cheese
1	tsp. finely shredded lemon peel
1	Tbsp. olive oil

1. Using a sharp knife, cut a pocket in each chicken breast by cutting horizontally through the thickest portion to, but not through, the opposite side. In a small bowl combine ¼ cup of the feta cheese and the lemon peel. Spoon cheese mixture into each pocket. Sprinkle chicken with *salt* and *pepper*.
2. In a large skillet heat oil over medium heat. Add chicken. Cook for 18 to 20 minutes or until chicken is no longer pink (170°F), turning once. Sprinkle with remaining feta cheese. Makes 4 servings.
EACH SERVING *236 cal, 9 g fat, 99 mg chol, 447 mg sodium, 1 g carb, 0 g fiber, 35 g pro.*

FAST LOW FAT
White Bean and Olive Salad

START TO FINISH 15 min.

3	cups baby spinach leaves, coarsely chopped
1	cup canned white beans, rinsed and drained
1	cup halved cherry tomatoes or one 14.5-oz. can plum tomatoes, chopped
¼	cup pitted Kalamata olives, quartered
1	tsp. shredded lemon peel

In a medium bowl combine spinach, beans, tomatoes, olives, and lemon peel. Toss to combine. Makes 4 servings.
EACH SERVING *118 cal, 1 g fat, 0 mg chol, 333 mg sodium, 21 g carb, 6 g fiber, 7 g pro.*

Meatballs with Balsamic-Apple Chutney

PREP 40 min. COOK 35 min. BROIL 8 min.

1	lb. lean ground beef or ground turkey
½	cup soft bread crumbs
1	egg, lightly beaten
2	Tbsp. minced onion
	Crusty bread slices
3	oz. crumbled blue cheese
	Italian (flat-leaf) parsley
1	recipe Balsamic-Apple Chutney

1. Line a 15×10×1-inch baking pan with foil and lightly coat with *nonstick cooking spray*; set aside. In a medium bowl combine ground beef, bread crumbs, egg, onion, 1 teaspoon *salt*, and ⅛ teaspoon *pepper*. Mix to combine. Shape meat mixture into a 8×4-inch rectangle on waxed paper. Cut into 1-inch squares. Roll each portion into a ball and place in prepared pan.
2. Broil meatballs 4 to 5 inches from heat for 8 to 10 minutes or until internal temperature of meatballs reaches 160°F.
3. Gently toss meatballs with Balsamic-Apple Chutney. Serve with crusty bread slices. Sprinkle with blue cheese and parsley. Makes 4 servings.
Balsamic-Apple Chutney In a large nonstick skillet heat 2 tablespoons olive oil over medium heat. Add 1½ cups chopped onions and ½ teaspoon kosher salt. Cook over medium to medium-high heat for 10 minutes, stirring frequently, just until golden. Add 3 Granny Smith apples, peeled, cored, and chopped; ⅓ cup balsamic vinegar; and 2 tablespoons honey to skillet. Cook over medium heat, uncovered, until most of the liquid has evaporated. Add ⅔ cup water to skillet; simmer, covered 20 minutes or until apples are tender.
EACH SERVING *678 cal, 33 g fat, 33 mg chol, 1,336 mg sodium, 66 g carb, 3 g fiber, 31 g pro.*

FETA-STUFFED CHICKEN BREASTS WITH WHITE BEAN AND OLIVE SALAD

EGG AND WILTED SPINACH SALAD

MEATBALLS WITH CHUTNEY

Chill and Grill

Topping hot dogs is an art form in Chicago, a city known for its famous "Dawg" style. Here, grilling expert Jamie Purviance shares his own ideas for the delicious mainstay.

FAST KID-FRIENDLY

Chicago-Style Hot Dogs

Don't forget the celery salt—it brings all the flavors together. The recipe can be doubled or tripled for big picnics or family gatherings. Wrap each dressed hot dog in foil for a true ballpark feel.
START TO FINISH 20 min.

2   medium ripe tomatoes
16   pepperoncini peppers
     Yellow mustard
½   cup finely chopped white onion
½   cup sweet pickle relish
     Celery salt
8   ¼ lb. all-beef hot dogs, grilled;
     (see Basic Hot Dog Grilling, *below*)
8   hot dog buns, preferably poppy seed

1. Cut each tomato crosswise into ¼-inch slices, then cut each slice in half to make half moons.
2. Prepare remaining toppings.
3. Place a grilled hot dog in each bun. Tuck 2 tomato slices between each hot dog and bun. Add 2 peppers, 1 on each side of each hot dog. Spread a generous amount of mustard on top and scatter about one tablespoon each of chopped onion and pickle relish over each hot dog, or to taste. Finish with a generous dash of celery salt. Makes 8 hot dogs.
EACH HOT DOG WITH TOPPINGS *534 cal, 36 g fat, 60 mg chol, 2,097 mg sodium, 35 g carb, 2 g fiber, 18 g pro.*

Basic Hot Dog Grilling

With a sharp knife, make a few shallow slashes in each hot dog. On gas or charcoal grill, grill hot dogs directly over medium heat with lid closed, until lightly marked on outside and heated through—5 to 7 minutes—turning occasionally. During last minute of grilling, toast buns.

CHICAGO-STYLE HOT DOG

Chipotle Chili Cheese Dogs

PREP **10 min.** COOK **21 min.** GRILL **5 min.**

- 2 slices bacon, finely chopped
- 1 medium white onion, finely chopped, divided
- 1 Tbsp. minced jalapeño chile pepper (see note, page 11)
- 2 tsp. minced garlic
- 1 lb. ground sirloin
- 1 canned chipotle pepper in adobo sauce, chopped, or 1 tsp. ground chipotle chile powder
- 1 tsp. smoked paprika
- ½ tsp. ground cumin
- ¼ tsp. kosher salt
- 1 can (8 oz.) tomato sauce
- ½ cup lager beer, beef broth, or water
- 8 ¼ lb. all-beef hot dogs, grilled; (see Basic Hot Dog Grilling, *opposite*)
- 8 hot dog buns
- 1 cup shredded sharp cheddar cheese

1. In a skillet over medium heat cook bacon and half the onion until bacon is crisp, about 5 minutes.
2. Add jalapeño and garlic to skillet; cook 1 minute. Add ground beef; cook and stir 5 minutes, breaking up chunks with side of spoon. Drain off fat. Stir in seasonings, tomato sauce, and beer. Bring to boiling; reduce heat and simmer, stirring occasionally until thickened, about 10 minutes. Set aside; keep warm.
3. Top grilled hot dogs with chili, cheese, and remaining chopped onion. Makes 8 hot dogs.

EACH HOT DOG WITH TOPPINGS *733 cal, 52 g fat, 108 mg chol, 1,917 mg sodium, 31 g carb, 2 g fiber, 34 g pro.*

FAST
Dogs with Avocado and Chips

START TO FINISH **20 min.**

- 2 ripe Hass avocados
- 1 Tbsp. lime juice
- 8 ¼ lb. all-beef hot dogs, grilled; (see Basic Hot Dog Grilling, *opposite*)
- 8 hot dog buns
- 1 small white onion, cut into slivers
- 2 ripe plum tomatoes, seeded and chopped
- 1 cup crushed regular potato chips

1. In bowl mash together avocados, lime juice, ½ teaspoon *kosher salt*, and ¼ teaspoon *ground pepper*. Cover surface with plastic wrap; refrigerate.
2. Top grilled hot dogs with avocado mixture, slivered onions, tomatoes, and crushed potato chips. Makes 8 hot dogs.

EACH HOT DOG WITH TOPPINGS *633 cal, 46 g fat, 60 mg chol, 1,741 mg sodium, 5 g fiber, 19 g pro.*

Tube Steaks with Pickled Onion Topping

PREP **10 min.** MARINATE **2 to 3 hr.** GRILL **5 min.**

- 1 small white or sweet yellow onion
- 1 small red onion
- ½ cup cider vinegar
- ½ cup distilled white vinegar
- ½ cup granulated sugar
- 2 tsp. celery seeds
- 1 tsp. crushed red pepper flakes
- 8 ¼ lb. all-beef hot dogs, grilled; (see Basic Hot Dog Grilling, *opposite*)
- 8 hot dog buns

1. Cut onions into thin slices and place in a shallow glass dish. In bowl whisk together vinegars, sugar, 1 tablespoon *kosher salt*, celery seeds, and red pepper flakes until sugar and salt are dissolved. Pour vinegar mixture over onions; stir to evenly coat. Cover and set aside at room temperature for 2 to 3 hours, stirring occasionally.
2. Top grilled hot dogs with mustard, ketchup, and drained, pickled onions. Makes 8 hot dogs.

EACH HOT DOG WITH TOPPINGS *525 cal, 36 g fat, 60 mg chol, 1,794 mg sodium, 33 g carb, 1 g fiber, 17 g pro.*

TUBE STEAK WITH PICKLED ONION TOIPPING

AVOCADO AND CHIPS

CHIPOTLE CHILI CHEESE

AVOCADO AND CHIPS

GET CRACKIN' Spring brings out a lighter side of comfort food. Stir, knead, or whisk your way to tender brunch breads perfectly suited for Sunday mornings and special occasions. Plus, chef Jamie Oliver plants a bushel of fresh recipes.

65

67

72

CARROT BREAD WITH CREAM CHEESE ICING

Sweet Spot

Whether you have just a little time to bake or a lot, bring fresh-from-the-oven goodness to any spring celebration with these luscious breads.

Carrot Bread with Cream Cheese Icing

PREP 20 min.   BAKE 55 min.   OVEN 350°F

2   cups all-purpose flour
⅔   cup packed brown sugar
2   tsp. baking powder
1   tsp. ground cinnamon
½   tsp. ground cardamom or nutmeg
¼   tsp. baking soda
¼   tsp. salt
2   cups shredded carrots
2   beaten eggs
⅔   cup milk
⅓   cup canola oil
1   recipe Cream Cheese Icing
1   recipe Candied Carrots

1. Preheat oven to 350°F. Grease the bottom and ½ inch up the sides of an 8×4×2-inch loaf pan or three 4¾×2½×2-inch loaf pans; set aside.
2. In a large bowl stir together flour, brown sugar, baking powder, cinnamon, cardamom, soda, and salt. In another bowl combine carrots, eggs, milk, and oil; add to dry ingredients, stirring just until moistened.
3. Pour batter into prepared pan(s). Bake for 55 to 60 minutes for the large loaf or 30 to 35 minutes for the small loaf pans or until a toothpick inserted near center comes out clean (check the loaf 10 minutes before the end of baking time. If it is browning too quickly, cover loosely with foil). Cool in pan 10 minutes; remove and cool completely on a rack. Wrap in foil; store overnight before slicing. Store up to 3 days at room temperature or freeze up to 3 months. Glaze with Cream Cheese Icing and top with Candied Carrots just before serving. Makes 16 servings.
Cream Cheese Icing Whisk together 1 ounce (2 tablespoons) cream cheese, ¾ cup powdered sugar, and a little milk (3 to 4 teaspoons) until smooth and glazelike. Drizzle over Carrot Bread.
Candied Carrots In a skillet melt 2 tablespoons butter over medium heat. Add 1 cup shaved carrots and 2 to 3 tablespoons honey. Cook and stir 2 to 3 minutes or until carrots are glazed and tender. Spread on paper towel to cool.
EACH SERVING 205 cal, 7 g fat, 33 mg chol, 148 mg sodium, 32 g carb, 1 g fiber, 3 g pro.

PINEAPPLE UPSIDE-
DOWN COFFEE CAKE

KID FRIENDLY

Pineapple Upside-Down Coffee Cake

PREP **25 min.** BAKE **35 min.**
OVEN **350°F**

½   cup (1 stick) butter
1   cup packed brown sugar
12 canned pineapple rings in juice*
2   cups all-purpose flour
2   tsp. baking powder
½   tsp. salt
½   tsp. ground nutmeg
½   cup (1 stick) butter, softened
½   cup granulated sugar
½   cup packed brown sugar
2   eggs
½   cup milk
1   tsp. vanilla
      Vanilla Greek yogurt or sweetened
      whipped cream (optional)
12 maraschino cherries (optional)

1. Heat oven to 350°F. Butter the bottom and sides of a 13×9×2-inch baking pan. Line bottom of pan with parchment paper; set pan aside. For pineapple topping, melt ½ cup butter in a medium saucepan over low heat. Stir in 1 cup brown sugar. Bring to boiling over medium heat, stirring frequently. Pour into prepared pan. Drain pineapple rings, reserving ½ cup juice. Fit 12 rings into bottom of pan.

2. In a bowl whisk together flour, baking powder, salt, and nutmeg. In a large mixing bowl beat softened butter, granulated sugar, and ½ cup brown sugar with electric mixer on medium speed for 2 minutes, scraping sides of bowl occasionally. Add eggs; beat until combined. On low speed, beat in half the flour mixture. Pour in reserved ½ cup pineapple juice and the milk; beat until combined. Beat in remaining flour mixture and vanilla.

3. Carefully spread batter over pineapple slices in pan. Bake 35 to 40 minutes or until toothpick inserted near center comes out clean. Cool in pan on wire rack 10 minutes. (If you invert the coffee cake too soon, the pineapple rings may stick to pan.) Place a serving tray or baking sheet over coffee cake; carefully invert. If any pineapple sticks to pan, gently replace on cake top.

4. Serve warm topped with yogurt and maraschino cherries. Makes 12 servings.
*You will need one 20-ounce can plus one 8-ounce can of pineapple slices for 12 rings. Reserve remaining pineapple for another use.
EACH SERVING *396 cal, 17 g fat, 77 mg chol, 290 mg sodium, 60 g carb, 1 g fiber, 4 g pro.*

DOUBLE-STRAWBERRY SCONES

APRICOT-RAISIN HOT CROSS BUNS

KID FRIENDLY
Double-Strawberry Scones

These flaky scones boast both fresh and freeze-dried strawberries. Basil adds a touch of bright, snappy herb flavor that complements the berries.

PREP 25 min. BAKE 16 min. OVEN 400°F

2½ cups all-purpose flour
2 Tbsp. sugar
1 Tbsp. baking powder
¼ tsp. salt
½ cup (1 stick) butter, cut into chunks
¾ cup chopped fresh strawberries
½ cup freeze-dried strawberries (optional)
2 Tbsp. snipped basil
2 eggs, lightly beaten
½ cup half-and-half
   Half-and-half or milk
   Sugar

1. Preheat oven to 400°F. In a large bowl stir together flour, the 2 tablespoons sugar, baking powder, and salt. Using a pastry blender or two knives, cut in butter until mixture resembles coarse crumbs. Gently toss in fresh and freeze-dried strawberries and basil. Make a well in center of flour mixture; set aside.
2. In a medium bowl stir together eggs and the ½ cup half-and-half. Add egg mixture to flour mixture all at once. Using a large spoon, gently stir just until moistened.
3. Turn dough out onto a generously floured surface. Knead dough by folding and gently pressing it five to seven times, turning dough a quarter turn after each fold. Transfer to a lightly floured parch-ment-lined baking sheet. Pat or lightly roll dough into a ¾-inch-thick circle. Cut circle into wedges and pull apart slightly.
4. Brush wedges with additional half-and-half and sprinkle with sugar. Bake about 16 minutes or until golden. Serve warm. Refrigerate leftover scones; reheat 15 seconds in microwave. Makes 12 scones.
EACH SCONE *209 cal, 10 g fat, 60 mg chol, 211 mg sodium, 26 g carb, 1 g fiber, 4 g pro.*

FAST   KID FRIENDLY
Apricot-Raisin Hot Cross Buns

PREP 35 min. RISE 2 hr. 15 min. BAKE 12 min. OVEN 375°F

4 to 4½ cups all-purpose flour
1 pkg. active dry yeast
¼ cup warm water (110°F)
⅛ tsp. sugar
¾ cup milk
½ cup (1 stick) butter
⅓ cup sugar
½ tsp. salt
2 eggs
½ cup finely snipped dried apricots
½ cup raisins, coarsely chopped
1 egg white, beaten
1 Tbsp. water
   Dried apricots, cut into strips (optional)

1. In a large mixing bowl place 2 cups of the flour; set aside. In a bowl combine the yeast, the warm water, and ⅛ teaspoon sugar. Stir until yeast is dissolved; set aside. In a medium saucepan heat and stir the milk, butter, ⅓ cup sugar, and salt until warm (120°F to 130°F) and butter is almost melted. Add to flour mixture along with yeast mixture and eggs. Beat with an electric mixer on low speed for 30 seconds, scraping sides of bowl constantly. Beat on high speed for 3 minutes. Stir in apricots, raisins, and as much of the remaining flour as you can with a wooden spoon.
2. Turn dough out onto a lightly floured surface. Knead in enough remaining flour to make a moderately soft (not sticky) dough that is smooth and elastic (3 to 5 minutes total). Shape dough in a ball. Place dough in a lightly greased bowl, turning once to grease surface of dough. Cover and let rise in a warm place until double in size (about 1½ hours).
3. Punch down dough. Turn out onto a floured surface. Cover and let rest for 10 minutes. Grease two baking sheets; set aside. Divide dough into 20 portions; shape each into a smooth ball. Place balls 2 inches apart on prepared baking sheets. Cover; let rise until nearly double (45 to 60 minutes).
4. Preheat oven to 375°F. Make a crisscross slash across top of each bun with a sharp knife or scissors. In a small cup combine beaten egg white and the water; brush on buns. Bake for 12 to 15 minutes or until golden brown, rotating baking sheets half-way through baking. Top with apricot strips. Serve warm. Store remaining buns in an airtight container in the refrigerator up to 3 days. To reheat, place 1 or 2 buns at a time on a microwave-safe plate and heat for 15 to 20 seconds. Makes 20 buns.
EACH BUN *177 cal, 6 g fat, 34 mg chol, 106 mg sodium, 28 g carb, 1 g fiber, 4 g pro.*

Everyday Easy

Feed your family something homemade with these weeknight-friendly dishes.

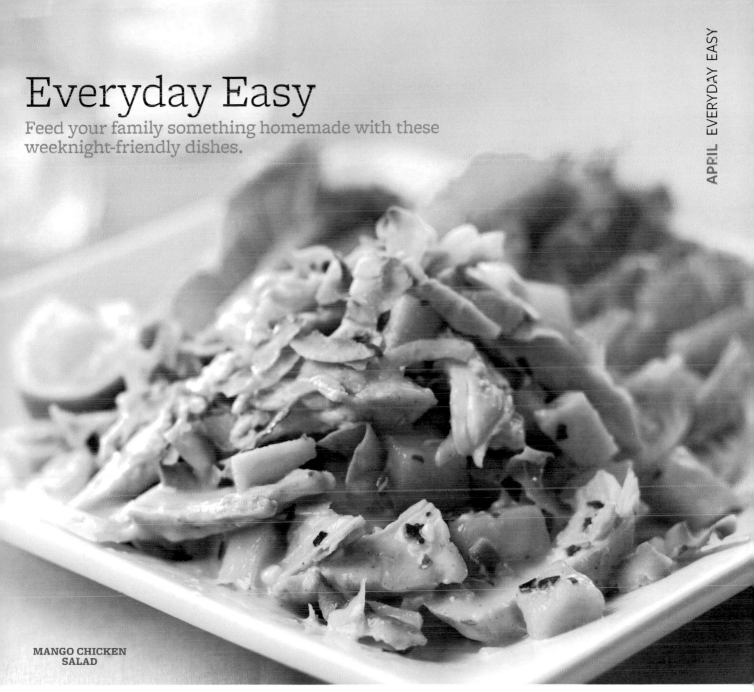

MANGO CHICKEN
SALAD

FAST LOW FAT Mango Chicken Salad

START TO FINISH 30 min.
BUDGET $2.86 per serving

3   skinless, boneless chicken breast halves
2   limes
1   cup unsweetened coconut milk
1   Tbsp. soy sauce
½   tsp. crushed red pepper
½   cup flaked unsweetened coconut
2   mangoes, seeded, peeled, and chopped
    Lettuce leaves (optional)

1. Preheat oven to 350°F. Cut chicken into bite-size chunks. Squeeze juice from 1 lime (2 tablespoons); cut remaining lime into wedges.

2. In a large saucepan combine the coconut milk, the lime juice, soy sauce, and crushed red pepper. Add chicken and bring to boiling; reduce heat and cook, covered, for 12 to 15 minutes or until chicken is cooked through, stirring occasionally.

3. Meanwhile, spread coconut in a shallow pan. Bake, uncovered, for 4 to 5 minutes or until golden, stirring once.

4. Remove chicken and cooking liquid to a bowl. Add mangoes; toss to coat. Sprinkle with toasted coconut. Spoon onto lettuce leaves to serve. Pass lime wedges.

EACH SERVING 303 cal, 10 g fat, 62 mg chol, 381 mg sodium, 29 g carb, 4 g fiber, 27 g pro.

ON THE SIDE Accompany this spring-fresh salad with crisp cracker bread.

BEEF AND
NOODLE TOSS

FISH TACOS
WITH LIME
SAUCE

Beef and Noodle Toss

START TO FINISH **25 min.**
BUDGET **$3.99 per serving**

- 8   oz. lasagna noodles
- 12   oz. boneless beef sirloin, cut into bite-size pieces
- 2   Tbsp. all-purpose flour
- 1   Tbsp. olive oil
- 1   pint grape tomatoes (2 cups)
- 8   oz. sliced cremini or button mushrooms
- 4   cloves garlic, minced (2 tsp.)
- 1   14-oz. can beef broth

1. Break noodles in half; cook according to package directions. Drain (do not rinse).
2. Meanwhile, season beef with ½ teaspoon each *salt* and *pepper*. Toss with flour. Heat oil in a 12-inch skillet over medium-high heat. Add meat, any remaining flour, and the tomatoes to skillet. Cook 3 to 4 minutes or until beef is well browned, stirring often. Add mushrooms and garlic. Cook 5 minutes more. Add broth; cook 3 to 4 minutes more or until beef is done and liquid is slightly thickened.
3. Add cooked noodles to skillet; stir gently to coat. Heat through. Spoon into pasta bowls to serve. Makes 4 servings.
EACH SERVING *468 cal, 16 g fat, 40 mg chol, 712 mg sodium, 52 g carb, 3 g fiber, 28 g pro.*

Fish Tacos with Lime Sauce

START TO FINISH **50 min.**
BUDGET **$2.63 per serving**

- 1   lb. fresh tilapia or catfish fillets
- 3   limes
- ½   cup mayonnaise
- 1   tsp. chili powder
- ⅓   cup all-purpose flour
- 8   small (6- to 7-inch) flour tortillas
- 1   cup shredded cabbage
- 2   small carrots, peeled and shredded (½ cup)
- 1   jalapeño or serrano pepper, thinly sliced (see note, page 11)

1. Rinse fish and pat dry. Cut into 1-inch pieces.
2. For Lime Sauce, juice two of the limes into a bowl (cut remaining lime into wedges for serving). Stir mayonnaise and chili powder into juice. Remove ⅓ cup sauce and toss fish in it.
3. In large skillet heat 2 tablespoons *cooking oil* over medium heat. In shallow dish combine flour and ½ teaspoon *salt*. Working with a third of the fish at a time, lightly toss in flour mixture and add to hot oil. Cook 2 to 4 minutes or until fish flakes, turning to brown evenly and adding additional oil as needed. Drain on paper towels.
4. Wrap tortillas in paper towels; heat in microwave 30 seconds. Top tortillas with fish, cabbage, carrots, and jalapeño. Drizzle with Lime Sauce. Pass lime wedges. Makes 4 servings.
EACH SERVING *652 cal, 39 g fat, 67 mg chol, 557 mg sodium, 41 g carb, 2 g fiber, 31 g pro.*

FAST LOW FAT KID FRIENDLY

Potato-Cheddar Soup

START TO FINISH 30 min.
BUDGET $2.79 per serving

1 28-oz. pkg. frozen diced hash brown potatoes with onions and peppers
1 cup chopped miniature sweet peppers
3 cups fat-free half-and-half
½ tsp. salt
½ tsp. curry powder
⅛ to ¼ tsp. cayenne pepper
6 oz. cheddar cheese, shredded
   Miniature sweet peppers, sliced (optional)
   Snipped Italian (flat-leaf) parsley (optional)

1. In a 4-quart Dutch oven combine potatoes, sweet peppers, half-and-half, salt, curry powder, cayenne, and ½ cup *water*. Bring just to boiling. Reduce heat. Simmer, covered, over medium heat 10 minutes or until potatoes are tender, stirring occasionally. Cool slightly.
2. Carefully transfer about half the soup to a blender; add ½ cup *water* and blend until nearly smooth. Return to Dutch oven; stir to combine. Cook and stir over low heat until heated through. Stir in cheese until melted.
3. Top servings with sliced sweet peppers and parsley. Makes 4 (2-cup) servings.

EACH SERVING *438 cal, 17 g fat, 54 mg chol, 883 mg sodium, 53 g carb, 5 g fiber, 19 g pro.*

FAST KID FRIENDLY

Mustard-Glazed Pork Chops

START TO FINISH 25 min.
BUDGET $2.05 per serving

4 ½-inch-thick bone-in pork chops
2 tsp. olive oil
1 large onion, cut in thin wedges
½ cup apricot preserves
1 Tbsp. Dijon-style or spicy mustard
1 tsp. paprika
½ tsp. ground nutmeg
   Fresh sage leaves (optional)

1. Season pork chops with *salt* and *pepper*. In a 12-inch skillet heat olive oil over medium-high heat. Add pork and onion to skillet. Cook 3 minutes; turn pork and onions. Cook 3 minutes more.
2. Meanwhile, in a small microwave-safe bowl combine preserves, mustard, ¼ cup *water,* paprika, and nutmeg. Heat in microwave for 1 to 2 minutes or until melted. Pour over pork in skillet. Reduce heat to medium. Cook, covered, for 10 minutes or until pork is cooked through (slightly pink in center).
3. Divide pork and onion mixture among serving plates; top with sage. Makes 4 servings.

EACH SERVING *503 cal, 32 g fat, 89 mg chol, 313 mg sodium, 31 g carb, 1 g fiber, 20 g pro.*

POTATO-CHEDDAR SOUP

MUSTARD-GLAZED
PORK CHOPS

Jamie Oliver

Jamie Oliver is all about improvising in the kitchen. He takes a relaxed approach to cooking, leaving room for playing and swapping out what is fresh and on hand in the garden or kitchen. These recipes are some of his garden-fresh favorites.

Meet Jamie

According to chef Jamie Oliver, the key to eating well—and getting kids to eat well—is engagement. "It's all about getting involved, whether that means starting a garden at your kids' school or in your own backyard. When you get kids involved in the garden, in growing and picking the food—they'll eat it."

Food and cooking have always been a way of life for Jamie. As a kid, he helped out in the kitchen of his parents' restaurant/pub in rural England. He became so fascinated with food and cooking that he went on to train at a catering college and became a chef.

He landed his own show, *The Naked Chef,* which is all about stripping recipes to food's basic goodness. His laid-back demeanor and hands-on approach were a hit with people hesitant to delve into cooking, and Jamie has been encouraging everyday cooks ever since.

His TV series *Jamie's Kitchen* filmed the operation of a training restaurant he created for young people who were not employed or in school full-time. In 2004, he used the power of television to improve a school cafeteria's lunch fare, launching an online petition for healthier food. This petition led the government to put $1 billion toward the school food system.

Jamie's work includes a string of TV shows, restaurants, and books, including *Jamie at Home,* describing fruit and vegetable gardening at his Essex farmhouse, with recipes inspired by the harvests. The second season of *Jamie Oliver's Food Revolution* is paired with a companion cookbook. Both continue his campaign to use cooking skills and fresh food to help end the obesity crisis in America.

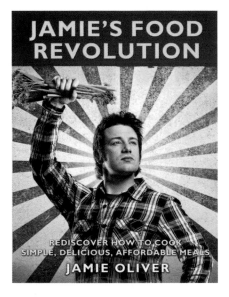

LOW FAT **KID-FRIENDLY**

Cup-of-Garden Soup

"This soup is all about using whatever vegetables happen to be springing up in your garden."

PREP 30 min. COOK 1 hr.

1 Tbsp. olive oil
2 strips of smoked bacon, finely chopped
1 clove garlic, peeled and finely chopped
1 medium red onion, peeled, halved, and finely chopped
2 carrots, washed and finely chopped
2 stalks of celery, finely chopped
1 zucchini, finely chopped
1 small leek, washed and finely chopped
½ tsp. dried oregano
1 bay leaf
2 14.5-oz cans chopped plum tomatoes
1 large potato, scrubbed and diced
1 cup Romanesco cauliflower or cauliflower florets
1 15.5-oz. can chickpeas, drained and rinsed
4 cups (one 1-qt. container) reduced-sodium vegetable broth, preferably organic
  Large handful curly kale, stalks removed, and chopped (about 2 cups)
½ cup mixed small pasta shapes or broken spaghetti
  Small bunch of fresh basil (optional)
  Sea salt and freshly ground black pepper
5 Tbsp. freshly grated Parmesan cheese

1. Heat a large saucepan over medium heat and add the olive oil. Add the bacon and fry it gently until it starts to turn golden. Add the chopped garlic, onion, carrots, celery, zucchini, leek, oregano, and bay leaf. Cook slowly for about 15 minutes, stirring now and then, until the vegetables have softened.
2. Add the cans of tomatoes, the chopped potato, cauliflower, drained chickpeas, and vegetable broth. Cover and bring to a boil. Turn down the heat and simmer for about 30 minutes, or until the potatoes are tender and cooked through (check by sticking one with a small knife).
3. Add 2 cups of *water* to the pan and return to boil. Once boiling, add kale and pasta and cook for 10 minutes more, or until the pasta is tender. If soup is too thick, thin it out with a little more broth or water.
4. If using the basil, tear the larger leaves into the soup and reserve the baby leaves for garnish. Season with a little pinch of salt and black pepper. Taste to check the flavors. Remove bay leaf and discard. Divide soup among serving bowls and sprinkle with the reserved basil leaves. Serve the Parmesan in a small bowl alongside to sprinkle over servings. Makes 8 servings.
EACH SERVING *245 cal, 8 g fat, 9 mg chol, 760 mg sodium, 36 g carb, 6 g fiber, 9 g pro.*

CUP-OF-GARDEN
SOUP

**GARDEN SALAD WITH
BALSAMIC DRESSING
AND HERB FETA**

Garden Salad with Balsamic Dressing and Herb Feta

"The dressing will make twice as much as you will need, so the rest can be refrigerated for up to a week and used on other salads."

START TO FINISH **40 min.**

For the dressing

2 Tbsp. balsamic vinegar
6 Tbsp. extra virgin olive oil
   Juice from half a lemon
   A few sprigs of fresh mint, leaves picked and finely chopped
   Sea salt
   Freshly ground black pepper

For the salad

1 head of Boston lettuce or small heart of romaine lettuce
3 small carrots, peeled
½ a cucumber
6 radishes
1 cup cherry or grape tomatoes, halved
¼ a head of broccoli, broken into florets
2 Candy Cane beets or other beets, scrubbed, trimmed, and thinly sliced
   A few sprigs of mixed soft herbs, such as mint, chives, and flat-leaf parsley
1 lemon
6 oz. block of feta cheese
   Sourdough bread, sliced lengthwise into long pieces

1. Put all dressing ingredients into a small screw-top jar with a tight-fitting lid, adding a pinch of salt and pepper. Shake well and set aside.
2. Remove any wilted or bruised outer leaves on the lettuce. Separate the rest of the leaves, tearing out any thick stems; tear leaves into bite-size pieces. Wash the leaves, spin dry in a salad spinner, and transfer to a serving bowl.
3. Slice the carrots thickly on an angle. Halve the cucumber lengthwise and cut into half-moon slices. Slice the radishes as thinly as you can, and halve the tomatoes (or leave whole, if you like). Break up the broccoli florets into small bite-size pieces and add to bowl of lettuce along with the sliced beets. Gently toss together. Set aside.
4. Finely chop the herbs on a cutting board. Grate lemon zest over the herbs and use your knife to sweep everything into the middle of the board. Place the block of feta on top to coat it with the herbs. Drizzle with a little *olive oil*. Sprinkle with a pinch of *salt* and *pepper*; turn it over and coat the other side of the cheese with the herbs.

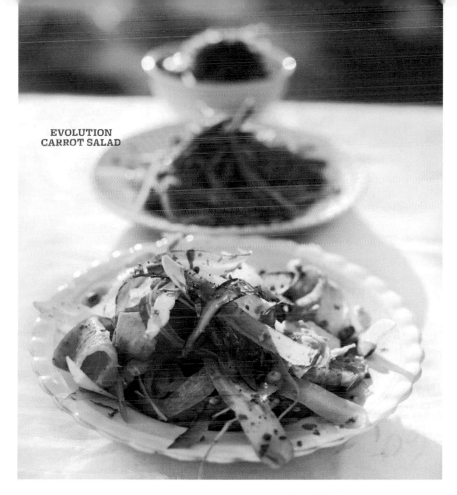

EVOLUTION CARROT SALAD

5. Toast the long slices of sourdough on a hot grill pan for a few minutes until golden with grill marks on both sides. When ready to serve, quickly dress the salad with half of the dressing and toss together. Serve the salad on the toasted bread with the herbed feta crumbled on top. Makes 4 servings.
EACH SERVING *339 cal, 20 g fat, 38 mg chol, 754 mg sodium, 32 g carb, 6 g fiber, 12 g pro.*

FAST
Evolution Carrot Salad

"You can prepare the carrots in one of several ways: Grate them on the coarse side of a box grater into a small bowl, use a Y peeler to slice them into thin ribbons, or halve and quarter the carrots lengthwise and slice into matchsticks."

START TO FINISH **30 min.**

4 large carrots, peeled and thinly chopped as desired (see above)
   A few sprigs of fresh mint, leaves picked and finely chopped
   A few sprigs of fresh cilantro, leaves picked and finely chopped
   A few fresh chives, finely chopped (optional)
   Sea salt and freshly ground black pepper

6 Tbsp. extra virgin olive oil
½ a lemon
   A good handful of mixed seeds such as sunflower seeds, pumpkin seeds, and/or poppy seeds
2 or 3 small clementines
   Crispy flatbread, pappadams, or crackers

1. Place the carrots in a bowl. Add the chopped herbs and a pinch of salt and pepper. Toss together well. Pour in the extra virgin olive oil, squeeze in the juice from the lemon half, and toss again so everything is well coated.
2. Place the mixed seeds in a hot, dry frying pan. Toss and toast them for a minute. Once toasted, sprinkle the seeds on the salad.
3. Peel clementines and cut into thick slices. Either toss them into the salad or lay a few slices on a serving platter and pile the salad on top.
4. Break the flatbread in small pieces. Toss into the salad or sprinkle over the top. Makes 6 servings.
EACH SERVING *188 cal, 17 g fat, 0 mg chol, 120 mg sodium, 10 g carb, 3 g fiber, 2 g pro.*

STIR-FRY
VEGETABLES
WITH STEAK

LOW FAT

Broccoli and Anchovy Orecchiette

"Broccoli is wonderful with orecchiette pasta, but If you can't find it in your grocery store, penne or rigatoni will also work well. "

START TO FINISH **45 min.**

2   large heads broccoli
2   pats butter (about 1 tsp. each)
2   large cloves garlic, peeled and finely sliced
4   anchovy fillets
2   small dried red chiles such as bird chiles (see note, page 11)
1   lb. dried orecchiette pasta
     Sea salt and freshly ground black pepper
     Freshly grated Parmesan cheese, to taste
     Extra virgin olive oil

1. Use a small knife to remove broccoli florets from the main stalks and set aside. Peel the remaining stalks. Trim and discard the dry end and finely slice the stalks. In a saucepan or very large 14-inch skillet melt a pat of butter and add the sliced stalks, the garlic, and anchovies. Crumble in the dried chiles (these can be pretty hot so don't go overboard). Cover and cook slowly for 8 to 10 minutes, stirring occasionally until the stalks start to soften.
2. Meanwhile, cook the pasta in a large pot of boiling salted water according to package directions. Add the broccoli florets to the pasta for the last 4 minutes. This makes them tender enough to eat but leaves them with great color and texture.
3. Drain the pasta and broccoli florets, reserving a little of the starchy pasta cooking water. Add the pasta and broccoli florets to the pan of cooked broccoli stalks. Add the remaining pat of butter and quickly toss everything together. Remove the pan from the heat. Season to taste with a pinch of salt and pepper and sprinkle in half of the Parmesan cheese. Mix well. Add a little of the cooking water if necessary to loosen the pasta. Serve immediately, drizzled with a little extra virgin olive oil and sprinkled with the rest of the Parmesan cheese.
Makes 4 to 6 servings.
EACH SERVING *394 cal, 10 g fat, 18 mg chol, 387 mg sodium, 62 g carb, 4 g fiber, 15 g pro.*

FAST

Stir-Fry Vegetables with Steak

"After a long day of work, this is one of the quickest and tastiest dinners you can make. As long as you've got a good mixture of crunchy vegetables to contrast with the soft texture of the noodles and steak, it will be lovely."

START TO FINISH **30 min.**

For the steak
1   tsp. Szechuan peppercorns or peppercorns
6   oz. sirloin steak, 1½ to 2 inches thick
     Olive oil
     Sea salt and freshly ground black pepper
2   Tbsp. yellow mustard
7   to 8 oz. dried noodles such as medium egg noodles or Thai rice noodles
For the vegetables
1   Tbsp. toasted sesame oil
     Thumb-size piece of fresh ginger, peeled and finely sliced
1   clove of garlic, peeled, finely sliced
1   to 2 red chiles, such as Thai chiles, halved, seeded, and finely sliced*
6   scallions (green onions), trimmed and sliced
1   green or yellow zucchini, trimmed, halved lengthways and finely sliced
1   carrot
     Small handful of torn kale or baby spinach
     Soy sauce
     Small bunch of cilantro

1. Lightly crush the Szechuan peppercorns with a mortar and pestle until coarsely ground. Drizzle the steak with olive oil. Sprinkle with a pinch of salt, pepper, and the crushed peppercorns; rub all over the steak. Use a vegetable peeler to peel the carrot into long ribbons; set aside.
2. Preheat a grill pan over high heat until really hot. Cook the steak for 7 to 8 minutes, or until browned and caramelized on the outside and pink inside, turning it every minute or so. Brush some of the mustard on the steak toward the end of cooking. Once cooked to your liking, move the steak to a cutting board to rest.
3. Cook the noodles according to package directions. Drain and set aside.
reheat a large wok or frying pan over high heat. Once really hot, add the sesame oil and the sliced ginger, garlic, and vegetables, except for the carrot and kale. Cook for a few minutes, stirring constantly, then add the carrot and kale and continue to cook and stir. Season with a splash or two of soy sauce and toss in the cooked noodles.
4. Take wok off heat. Divide vegetable mixture between serving bowls. Slice the steak thinly and divide between bowls; drizzle the resting juices from the meat all over everything. Sprinkle with the cilantro leaves. Makes 2 servings, plus leftover vegetables and noodles.
*Chiles contain oils that may burn skin and eyes. Wear plastic gloves and wash hands after handling.
EACH SERVING *524 cal, 21 g fat, 81 mg chol, 869 mg sodium, 55 g carb, 5 g fiber, 31 g pro.*

BROCCOLI AND
ANCHOVY
ORECCHIETTE

EASY ORANGE-CARROT CAKE

Easy Orange-Carrot Cake

"We all love a little treat once in awhile, and a slice of this cake will definitely put a smile on your face."

PREP 30 min. BAKE 50 min.
COOL 10 min. OVEN 350°F

For the cake
¾ cup vegetable oil, plus a little more for greasing pan
1¾ cups light brown sugar
4 large eggs (preferably free-range or organic)
Grated zest and juice of 1 orange (approximately 1 tsp. zest and ⅓ cup juice)
2 cups all-purpose flour
1 Tbsp. baking powder
½ tsp. sea salt
½ cup walnuts, roughly chopped
1 heaping tsp. ground cinnamon
Pinch of ground cloves
½ tsp. ground nutmeg
½ tsp. ground ginger
10 oz. carrots, peeled and coarsely grated

For the icing
2 cups low-fat sour cream
2 to 3 Tbsp. powdered sugar
2 oranges

1. Preheat oven to 350°F. Grease a 9-inch square or 10-inch round cake pan with a little vegetable oil. Line the bottom of the pan with a piece of parchment or waxed paper; cut to fit. In a large mixing bowl use an electric mixer to mix the oil and sugar. Beat in the eggs, orange zest, and juice. Stir in the flour, baking powder, and salt. Add the chopped walnuts, cinnamon, cloves, nutmeg, ginger, and grated carrots. Mix just until combined (don't overmix, because this will affect how the cake rises).
2. Spoon the batter into the prepared cake pan. Bake 50 minutes, or until golden. Check doneness by poking a skewer or toothpick into the center of the cake. If it comes out clean, the cake is cooked; if it's still slightly sticky, put it back in the oven for a few more minutes.
3. Cool the cake in the pan for 10 minutes. Turn it out onto a rack to cool completely before icing.

4. For the icing, place the sour cream in a mixing bowl. Sift in the powdered sugar and grate in the zest of 1 orange. Halve the orange and squeeze in the juice from one half. Whisk everything together until glossy. It will be a fairly loose consistency. Spread thinly over the top of the cake. Grate a little more orange zest on top of the cake. Slice the remaining orange and serve on the side. Makes 16 servings.
EACH SERVING *341 cal, 16 g fat, 63 mg chol, 180 mg sodium, 63 g carb, 2 g fiber, 5 g pro.*

Braised Peas with Scallions and Lettuce

"I tend to serve this as a side dish—it's nice with grilled white fish, served on croatini, or blitzed up in the blender with some stock for a soup."

START TO FINISH 20 min.

A pat of butter (about 1 tsp.)
Olive oil
6 scallions (green onions), trimmed, outer leaves discarded, and finely sliced
1 head romaine lettuce, washed and sliced
2 16-oz. pkg. frozen peas
Sea salt and freshly ground black pepper
1 heaping tsp. all-purpose flour
1 to 1½ cups reduced-sodium chicken or vegetable stock
A few sprigs of fresh mint
Juice from half a lemon
Extra virgin olive oil

1. Melt the butter in a medium skillet over medium heat. Add about 1 tablespoon olive oil and the sliced scallions. Cook for a few minutes, or until the scallions are softened. Meanwhile, slice the lettuce leaves, saving a few tender inner leaves to add at the end. Turn the heat up and add the peas, sliced lettuce, and a pinch of salt and pepper. Cook for 1 minute, then sprinkle in the flour and stir until everything is lightly coated. Slowly pour in the stock, then cover and turn the heat up to high. Cook for 4 minutes or until the peas are tender.
2. Taste and add another pinch of salt or pepper if needed. Pick the mint leaves, finely chop, and sprinkle into the pan. Add the lemon juice. Slice the reserved lettuce leaves, then scatter those on top and serve immediately with a tiny drizzle of extra virgin olive oil. Makes 8 servings.
EACH SERVING *142 cal, 5 g fat, 4 mg chol, 207 mg sodium, 19 g carb, 6 g fiber, 7 g pro.*

BRAISED PEAS WITH SCALLIONS AND LETTUCE

TAKE IT OUTSIDE Warm spring days mean it's time to entertain on the patio. Soak up a sunny afternoon with good friends.

83

88

93

The New Mexican Kitchen

Joanne Weir—author, teacher, and PBS star—guides you through the fresh flavors of Mexican cooking. "I'm no purist, I take chances, speed things up, and add my own twists to traditional dishes."

STACKED SWEET CORN, BEAN, AND BEEF CASSEROLE

Stacked Sweet Corn, Bean, and Beef Casserole

PREP 45 min. BAKE 20 min.
STAND 10 min. OVEN 375°F

2 ears fresh corn on the cob
8 oz. lean ground beef
7 oz. uncooked chorizo sausage
1 15-oz. can pinto beans, rinsed and drained
1 Tbsp. extra virgin olive oil
1 small yellow onion, chopped
1 large yellow sweet pepper, chopped
2 cloves garlic, minced
¾ cup bottled chunky green salsa
1 Tbsp. chili powder
2 tsp. ground cumin
¼ tsp. cayenne pepper
4 8- to 9-inch flour tortillas
1½ cups shredded cheddar or Monterey Jack cheese
   Sour cream (optional)
   Chopped tomatoes and cilantro (optional)

1. Preheat oven to 375°F. Cut corn from cobs; set aside. Grease a 9-inch springform pan, large oven-going platter, or 12-inch pizza pan; set aside.
2. In a large skillet cook beef and chorizo until brown and cooked through, breaking up any large pieces with a spatula; drain fat. Add beans to beef mixture and heat through. Cover and keep warm.
3. In another large skillet heat olive oil over medium heat. Add onion, sweet pepper, and garlic. Cook, stirring occasionally until tender, about 10 minutes. Add corn, salsa, chili powder, cumin, and cayenne. Cook 5 minutes, stirring occasionally.
4. Place two of the tortillas in prepared pan. Top with meat mixture. Reserve ¼ cup of cheese. Divide the remaining 1¼ cups of cheese in half; sprinkle one half on the meat mixture. Add another tortilla, vegetable mixture, and remaining half of cheese. Add final tortilla. Cover loosely with foil. Bake 10 minutes. Uncover and sprinkle with reserved ¼ cup of cheese. Bake 10 minutes more. Let stand 10 minutes. Remove sides if using springform pan. Top with sour cream, tomatoes, and cilantro. Slice with a serrated knife. Makes 6 servings.
EACH SERVING 514 cal, 30 g fat, 82 mg chol, 890 mg sodium, 33 g carb, 6 g fiber, 30 g pro.

Grilled Pork Tenderloin

PREP 30 min. MARINATE 30 min.
GRILL 30 min. STAND 15 min.

2 1-lb. pork tenderloins
3 tsp. olive oil
2 tsp. chili powder (hot-style, if desired)
1 tsp. ground ancho chile pepper
1 tsp. ground cumin
1 tsp. dried oregano, crushed
1 recipe Pineapple and Papaya Salsa
2 Tbsp. pumpkin seeds (pepitas), toasted
   Cilantro sprigs

1. Trim fat from pork. Rub pork with the olive oil. In a small bowl combine the chili powder, ancho chile pepper, cumin, oregano, 1 teaspoon *black pepper*, and 1 teaspoon *salt*. Rub mixture all over pork until well coated. Let stand at room temperature for 30 minutes or cover and refrigerate up to 2 hours.
2. For a charcoal grill, arrange medium-hot coals around a drip pan. Place pork on greased grill rack over drip pan. Cover; grill 30 to 35 minutes or until slightly pink in the center (155°F). (For a gas grill, preheat grill. Reduce heat to medium. Adjust for indirect cooking. Place pork on greased rack on unheated side of grill. Cover; grill as above.) Remove pork from grill; tent with foil and let rest 15 minutes.
3. To serve, cut pork into very thin slices and place on a platter. Top with Pineapple and Papaya Salsa, pumpkin seeds, and cilantro sprigs. Makes 6 servings.
EACH SERVING 267 cal, 9 g fat, 98 mg chol, 584 mg sodium, 11 g carb, 2 g fiber, 34 g pro.

Pineapple and Papaya Salsa

START TO FINISH 20 min.

8 oz. fresh pineapple, cut in ½-inch dice (about 1½ cups)
8 oz. papaya, peeled and cut in ½-inch dice (about 1½ cups)
2 green onions, trimmed and thinly sliced
¼ cup chopped fresh cilantro
1 tsp. finely shredded lime peel
1 Tbsp. freshly squeezed lime juice
1 Tbsp. olive oil

In a large bowl gently toss together all ingredients. Season to taste with *salt*.

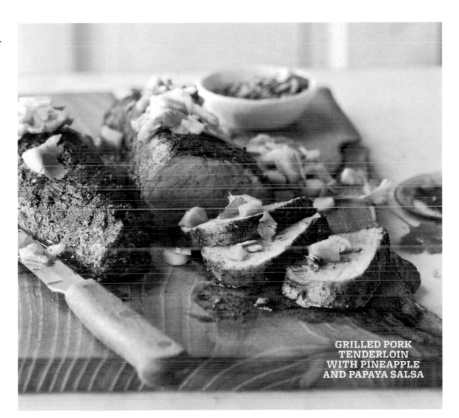

GRILLED PORK TENDERLOIN WITH PINEAPPLE AND PAPAYA SALSA

CHORIZO-PEPPER
HAND PIES

Chorizo-Pepper Hand Pies

PREP 45 min. COOK 17 min.
BAKE 12 min. OVEN 400°F

1 Tbsp. extra virgin olive oil
¼ cup finely chopped red onion
2 cloves garlic, minced
½ a yellow sweet pepper, seeded and finely chopped
5 oz. uncooked chorizo sausage
½ cup chopped tomato, fresh or canned
1 tsp. dried oregano, crushed
½ tsp. ground cumin
4 oz. grated queso fresco (¾ cup)
1 17.3-oz. pkg. frozen puff pastry sheets (2 sheets), thawed
1 egg yolk, lightly beaten
1 Tbsp. milk
1 recipe Sweet Pepper Topper (optional) Taco sauce or salsa (optional)

1. For filling, in a large skillet heat oil over medium heat. Add onion, garlic, and sweet pepper. Cook 7 minutes or until tender, stirring occasionally. Add chorizo. Cook 5 minutes or until no longer pink, breaking up sausage and stirring occasionally. Drain fat. Return to heat; add tomato, oregano, and cumin. Simmer, uncovered, 5 to 8 minutes or until liquid is evaporated. Season with *salt* and *black pepper*. Let cool. Add the queso fresco and stir to combine.
2. Preheat oven to 400°F. On a floured surface with a floured rolling pin, roll puff pastry to ⅛-inch thickness. With a 3½-inch round cookie cutter, cut 24 circles. Place 1 tablespoon filling in center of each circle. Combine beaten egg yolk with milk. Brush edges of half the circle with egg wash. Fold circle over to enclose filling; pinch edges together to seal. Brush tops with egg wash. Place on an ungreased baking sheet; bake 12 minutes or until golden brown.
3. Serve warm with Sweet Pepper Topper and taco sauce for dipping. Makes 24 hand pies.
Sweet Pepper Topper In small bowl combine 1 cup chopped yellow and/or orange sweet pepper, ⅓ cup chopped pitted ripe olives, and ¼ cup chopped fresh Italian (flat-leaf) parsley.
Make Ahead Unbaked or baked hand pies can be made well in advance and frozen. Remove from freezer; place on ungreased baking sheets in single layer. For frozen unbaked pies, bake 17 to 19 minutes. If baked before freezing, reheat 5 to 6 minutes on top rack of a 400°F oven.
EACH HAND PIE *164 cal, 11 g fat, 16 mg chol, 234 mg sodium, 12 g carb, 1 g fiber, 4 g pro.*

LOW FAT
Fish Tacos

These tacos are seasoned with shredded orange and lime peel. Reserve the citrus juices for the slaw.
PREP 25 min. BAKE 10 min. OVEN 400°F

1½ lb. fresh or frozen cod or halibut fillets, thawed and cut into 1-inch pieces
2 fresh tomatillos, cut into ½-inch pieces (2 cups)
2 tsp. olive oil
1 clove garlic, minced
½ tsp. finely shredded orange peel
½ tsp. finely shredded lime peel
12 6-inch corn tortillas
1 recipe Cabbage and Chile Pepper Slaw

1. Preheat oven to 400°F. In bowl toss together fish, tomatillos, oil, garlic, orange peel, and lime peel. Season with *salt* and *black pepper*; set aside.
2. Cut six 12-inch-square sheets of foil. Place one-sixth (about ⅔ cup) fish mixture in center of each square. Fold diagonally in half in a triangle. Fold edges two or three times to make a packet. Place packets in single layer on a large baking sheet.
3. Bake fish 10 to 12 minutes, until packets puff slightly (carefully open a packet to check fish doneness; fish should flake easily with a fork). Meanwhile, in dry skillet warm tortillas over medium-high heat until soft, about 15 seconds per side.
4. To serve, divide fish mixture between 2 tortillas. Top with Cabbage and Chile Pepper Slaw. Serve immediately. Makes 6 servings.
EACH SERVING *341 cal, 13 g fat, 36 mg chol, 293 mg sodium, 30 g carb, 5 g fiber, 28 g pro.*

FAST LOW FAT
Cabbage and Chile Pepper Slaw

START TO FINISH 15 min.

5 oz. green cabbage, thinly shredded (1¼ cups)
½ cup thinly sliced red onion
1 poblano or pasilla pepper, halved crosswise, seeded, and thinly sliced (see note, page 11)
1 carrot, peeled and shredded
¼ cup chopped fresh cilantro
3 Tbsp. olive oil
2 Tbsp. freshly squeezed lime juice
1 Tbsp. freshly squeezed orange juice

In a medium bowl combine cabbage, red onion, poblano pepper, carrot, and cilantro. For dressing, in small bowl combine olive oil, lime juice, and orange juice. Season with *salt*. Toss with slaw.

FISH TACOS WITH CABBAGE AND CHILE PEPPER SLAW

SPARKLING
MARGARITAS

HOT AND CHUNKY
GUACAMOLE

Hot and Chunky Guacamole

START TO FINISH 25 min.

1¼ cups fresh or frozen shelled peas
2 ripe avocados, halved, seeded, and peeled
1 to 2 Tbsp. lime juice
¼ cup finely chopped red onion
1 clove garlic, minced
2 Tbsp. chopped cilantro
1 small jalapeño pepper, seeded and thinly sliced (see note, page 11)
Tortilla chips

1. Bring a medium saucepan of salted water to boiling. Add peas; simmer fresh peas 5 minutes or simmer frozen peas 1 minute. Drain; rinse with cold water. Drain again and cool.
2. Place avocados and lime juice in medium bowl. With a fork, mash avocados. Add peas, onion, garlic, cilantro, and jalapeño. Season to taste with *salt*. Place guacamole in a serving bowl. Serve immediately or cover surface with plastic wrap and chill up to 2 hours. Drizzle with *olive oil* if desired; serve with tortilla chips. Makes 9 servings.
EACH ¼-CUP SERVING *69 cal, 5 g fat, 0 mg chol, 69 mg sodium, 6 g carb, 3 g fiber, 2 g pro.*

Sparkling Margaritas

START TO FINISH 20 min.

1 cup blanco (white) tequila
⅔ cup lime juice
⅓ cup agave nectar
Sparkling wine or champagne (about 1½ cups)
Lime peel strips or very thin lime slices

In a cocktail shaker combine half the tequila, lime juice, and agave nectar with plenty of *ice*. Shake for 5 seconds and strain mixture into three glasses. Repeat with remaining tequila, juice, and agave nectar. Top each serving with sparkling wine. Add a lime peel strip. Add additional lime juice to taste. Makes 6 servings.
EACH SERVING *188 cal, 0 g fat, 0 mg chol, 1 mg sodium, 18 g carb, 1 g fiber, 0 g pro.*

HASS AVOCADOS
Hass avocados have greenish-black skins and soft, buttery flesh and are best for making guacamole. Select avocados that give slightly when gently pressed at the stem end. Avoid overly soft ones. Hard, under-ripe avocados will continue to ripen at room temperature for 2 to 4 days.

LOW FAT | **KID FRIENDLY**

Chicken and Tortilla Soup

PREP **35 min.** COOK **1 hr.**

- 6 cups water
- 1 3½-lb. whole roasting chicken, cut in 8 pieces
- 1 large yellow onion, chopped (1 cup)
- 1 medium carrot, peeled and chopped (½ cup)
- 1 stalk celery, chopped (½ cup)
- 8 sprigs cilantro
- 1½ tsp. ground cumin
- 1 tsp. chili powder
- ½ tsp. ground ancho chile pepper
- ½ tsp. dried oregano
- 2 bay leaves
  Corn oil
- 8 6-inch corn tortillas, cut into ½-inch strips
- 1 32-oz. box reduced-sodium chicken broth

- 2 medium carrots, peeled and cut in ¼-inch slices
- 2 cups sugar snap peas, sliced diagonally
- 2 small zucchini, cut in ¼-inch slices (2 cups)
- 1 cup chopped fresh or canned tomato
- ½ a jalapeño pepper, seeded and finely chopped (See note, page 72)
- 1 cup sharp cheddar cheese, coarsely shredded
  Cilantro leaves

1. In a 6 quart Dutch oven combine the water, chicken, onion, ½ cup chopped carrot, celery, 8 cilantro sprigs, cumin, chili powder, ancho chile pepper, oregano, and bay leaves. Bring to boiling, reduce heat and simmer, uncovered, until the chicken is very tender, 1 to 1½ hours.

2. Meanwhile, heat ½ inch of corn oil in a large heavy saucepan to 375°F. Add tortilla strips, about one-fourth at a time, and cook until crispy and light golden, 30 to 60 seconds. Remove from saucepan with a slotted spoon. Drain strips on paper towels. Season with *salt*.

3. Using tongs, remove chicken from liquid; cool chicken. Strain remaining liquid and discard solids. Return to Dutch oven along with chicken broth. Bring to a simmer over medium heat.

4. Remove meat from bones and discard bones. Tear chicken in 1-inch pieces. Add to broth along with the 2 sliced carrots. Simmer for 3 minutes. Add the sugar snap peas, zucchini, tomato, and jalapeño. Simmer 3 minutes or until tender. Season to taste with *salt* and *black pepper*.

5. Ladle soup into bowls. Top with cheddar cheese, tortilla strips, and cilantro. Makes 6 to 8 servings.

EACH SERVING 375 cal, 14 g fat, 89 mg chol, 618 mg sodium, 29 g carb, 6 g fiber, 34 g pro.

CHICKEN AND
TORTILLA SOUP

Home Cooking

Build a triple-decker sandwich like never before with these cool new variations.

Classic Club Tweak the basic turkey club by layering on thin apple or radish slices in place of tomato, or replace cheddar with pimiento cheese.

To make a Turkey, Bacon, and Apple Club, in a bowl combine mayonnaise, a little Dijon mustard, and a pinch of snipped fresh thyme leaves; spread on three slices of toasted bread. On one slice layer cheddar cheese, sliced turkey, and lettuce. Top with another slice of bread, spread side up, then layer bacon and apple. Top with the remaining bread slice, spread side down. Skewer with long picks and cut in half to serve. Chips are optional, but highly recommended.

TURKEY, BACON,
AND APPLE CLUB

PB AND J CLUB

MEAT LOAF AND
POTATOES CLUB

FAST KID-FRIENDLY

PB and J Club

This sandwich has smashed fresh berries
plus a sprinkling of granola for crunch.
Serve a whole sandwich for dinner or a half
sandwich for breakfast.

START TO FINISH 15 min.

12 slices 12-grain or other whole grain
    bread, lightly toasted
1   cup natural peanut butter
1   pint fresh raspberries
¼   cup honey
½   cup granola with peanuts (break up
    large clusters)

1. Spread 8 slices of toast with peanut butter. In a small bowl lightly mash
raspberries with a fork. Divide mashed
berries among peanut butter-topped
toasts. Drizzle with honey and sprinkle
with granola.
2. Stack one berry-topped toast on
another, top with plain toast. Repeat with
remaining toast slices. Slice to serve.
Makes 4 sandwiches (8 servings).

EACH SERVING *420 cal, 19 g fat, 0 mg chol,
289 mg sodium, 45 g carb, 10 g fiber, 17 g pro.*

FAST LOW FAT KID-FRIENDLY

Meat Loaf and Potatoes Club

Stacks of meat loaf with spicy ketchup, crisp
french fries, and melted American cheese
make this generous sandwich an instant hit.

START TO FINISH 15 min.

½   cup ketchup
½   tsp. hot (Madras) curry powder
8   slices cooked purchased or leftover
    meat loaf
12 slices Italian bread topped with
    sesame seeds
4   slices American cheese
8   green onions, sliced
    Watercress or arugula (optional)
2   cups hot cooked french fries or
    1 cup potato sticks or potato chips

1. Stir together the ketchup and curry
powder; set aside. Heat a large skillet over
medium heat. In skillet heat meat slices,
turning once, until lightly browned and
heated through.
2. Meanwhile, broil bread on a very large
baking sheet to toast. Turn bread then top
4 slices with American cheese; sprinkle

with onions. Continue broiling until
toasted, cheese is melted, and onions are
slightly cooked.
3. Layer 4 slices of bread with watercress,
meat loaf, and some of the curry ketchup.
Top with cheese toast, cheese side up.
Add a layer of french fries. Spread the
remaining 4 bread slices with spicy
ketchup; place on fries. Skewer with
sandwich picks and cut to serve. Makes
4 sandwiches (8 servings).

EACH SERVING *333 cal, 13 g fat, 47 mg chol,
968 mg sodium, 41 g carb, 3 g fiber, 16 g pro.*

GREEK SALAD CLUB

CUBAN CLUB

Greek Salad Club

Also try the salad fillings for this pita sandwich layered between slices of toasted whole grain bread.

START TO FINISH **25 min.**

6   flat pita bread rounds, halved horizontally and toasted*
1   7-oz. container purchased hummus
4   romaine lettuce leaves
1   large tomato, sliced
1   yellow sweet pepper, seeded and sliced
½   an English cucumber, sliced
2   oz. feta cheese, crumbled
¼   cup lightly packed fresh oregano leaves
¼   cup purchased Greek vinaigrette dressing

1. Spread 8 pita halves with hummus. Layer 4 of the spread slices with romaine, tomato, and sweet pepper slices. Top with 4 spread pita halves, hummus side up.

2. Layer cucumber, feta cheese, and fresh oregano. Drizzle with dressing. Top with remaining pita halves. Makes 4 sandwiches (4 servings).

*To toast: Preheat broiler. Lay pita halves, cut sides up, on two baking sheets. One baking sheet at a time, broil pita halves 3 to 4 inches from heat for 1 minute until toasted.

EACH SERVING *454 cal, 14 g fat, 13 mg chol, 975 mg sodium, 66 g carb, 7 g fiber, 16 g pro.*

Cuban Club

For a spicy kick, sprinkle chopped jalapeño peppers along with the cilantro on the mustard-topped bread.

PREP **15 min.** COOK **6 min.**

12   slices sourdough bread
¼   cup Dijon-style mustard
2   Tbsp. chopped fresh cilantro
8   lengthwise sandwich pickle slices
8   oz. cooked pork, shredded (about 2½ cups)*
6   oz. sliced ham (8 slices)
4   oz. sliced Swiss cheese (8 slices)
1   to 2 Tbsp. butter

1. Spread 8 slices of bread with mustard. Sprinkle with cilantro. Layer pickle slices and shredded pork on four of the slices. Top each with a plain bread slice. Layer ham and Swiss, then remaining bread slices, mustard side down. Press sandwiches together.

2. In a 12-inch skillet melt butter over medium heat. Place sandwiches in skillet. Weight with another large skillet. Cook for 3 to 5 minutes. Turn sandwiches, adding more butter if needed. Weight with skillet and cook 3 to 5 minutes more or until toasted and cheese is melted. Cut in half to serve. Makes 4 sandwiches (8 servings).

* Use leftover roast pork loin, shredded pork, or purchased packaged pork roast au jus).

EACH SERVING *267 cal, 10 g fat, 52 mg chol, 955 mg sodium, 23 g carb, 1 g fiber, 19 g pro.*

Everyday Easy

The outdoors beckons. Whip up these fast and fresh suppers, then go for a stroll to smell the lilacs.

Garden Veggie Linguine with Cilantro Pesto

START TO FINISH 30 min.
BUDGET $1.76 per serving

- 8   oz. dry linguine or fettuccine
- 8   oz. baby zucchini, halved lengthwise, or 1 small zucchini, sliced
- 8   oz. pkg. peeled fresh baby carrots, halved
- 2   seedless oranges
- ½   cup olive oil
- 1   cup fresh cilantro leaves
- 1   tsp. dry mustard
- 1   tsp. minced garlic or dried garlic
- ½   tsp. crushed red pepper
       Cilantro and/or finely shredded orange peel (optional)

1. Cook pasta according to package directions, adding zucchini and carrots the last 5 minutes. Drain; reserve ¼ cup pasta water. Return pasta to pan.
2. For pesto, peel and quarter 1 orange. In processor combine orange, olive oil, cilantro, pasta water, 1 teaspoon *salt*, mustard, garlic, and red pepper. Peel and chop remaining orange. Toss all together; top with cilantro and orange peel. Makes 4 servings.
EACH SERVING *518 cal, 28 g fat, 0 mg chol, 644 mg sodium, 58 g carb, 6 g fiber, 10 g pro.*

SEASONAL TASTES
Substitute a variety of fresh in-season vegetables and herbs—asparagus, snap peas, spinach or mustard greens, tarragon, basil, or other colorful ingredients that catch your eye at the market.

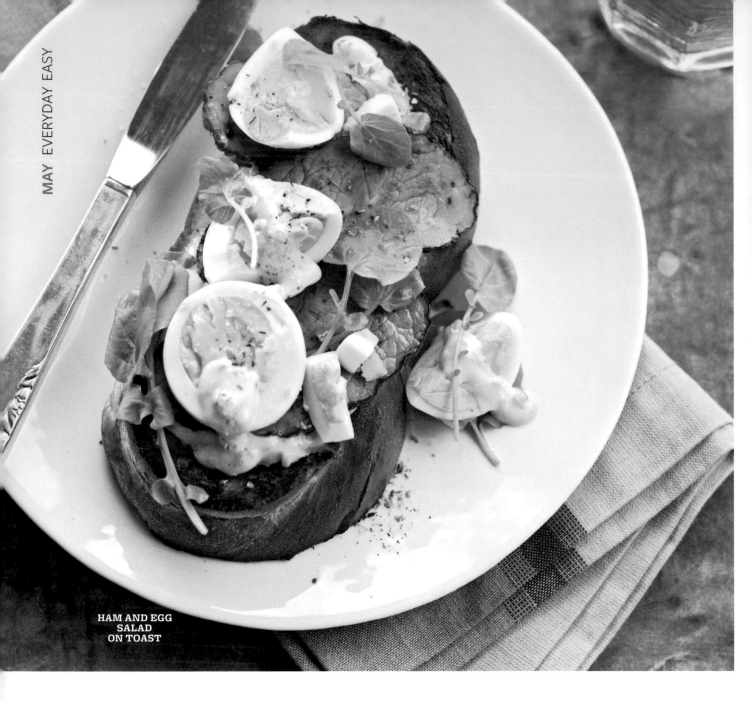

HAM AND EGG
SALAD
ON TOAST

FAST

Ham and Egg Salad on Toast

START TO FINISH 30 min.
BUDGET $1.06 per serving

6   eggs
⅓   cup mayonnaise
2   Tbsp. sweet pickle relish
1   Tbsp. Dijon-style mustard
6   oz. ham, sliced
4   thick slices challah, sweet Hawaiian,
     or French bread, toasted
½   bunch watercress, trimmed

1. Place eggs in saucepan. Cover with 1 inch of water and bring to rolling boil over high heat. Remove from heat; cover and let stand 15 minutes.
2. Meanwhile, in a small bowl combine mayonnaise, relish, and mustard; set aside. Heat a large skillet over medium-high. Cook ham 1 to 2 minutes per side until heated through.
3. Drain eggs; rinse in cold water. Peel under running water. Slice or coarsely chop eggs. Spread some mayonnaise mixture on toast. Top with ham, eggs, watercress, and any remaining mayonnaise mixture. Serve immediately. Makes 4 servings.
EACH SERVING *467 cal, 29 g fat, 363 mg chol, 1,052 mg sodium, 30 g carb, 1 g fiber, 21 g pro.*

FAST

Chicken Jambalaya

START TO FINISH 23 min.
BUDGET $3.34 per serving

8   oz. skinless, boneless chicken breast
    halves
2   tsp. Cajun seasoning
8   oz. fully cooked spicy or mild link
    sausage, sliced
1   small red onion, cut in thin wedges
2   yellow, green, and/or orange sweet
    peppers, cut in bite-size strips
2   14½-oz. cans no-salt-added stewed
    tomatoes
    Coarsely chopped fresh parsley
    (optional)

1. Cut chicken in 1-inch pieces; place in a small bowl and toss with Cajun seasoning.
2. Heat a 12-inch skillet over medium-high heat. Add chicken and sausage to skillet; cook 3 to 4 minutes or until chicken begins to brown. Add onion and sweet peppers to chicken mixture. Cook, stirring frequently, for 2 minutes. Add stewed tomatoes. Cover and cook 5 to 7 minutes or until chicken is no longer pink. Break up tomatoes with a spoon, if necessary.
3. Ladle jambalaya into shallow soup/salad bowls and top with fresh parsley. Makes 4 servings.
EACH SERVING *355 cal, 18 g fat, 81 mg chol, 637 mg sodium, 23 g carb, 3 g fiber, 29 g pro.*

CHICKEN
JAMBALAYA

CRISP CATFISH WITH
APPLE-CELERY SLAW

FAST

Crisp Catfish with Apple-Celery Slaw

START TO FINISH 25 min.

BUDGET $2.12 per serving

1	lemon
⅓	cup mayonnaise
1	Tbsp. honey
3	stalks celery, thinly sliced
1	Granny Smith apple, thinly sliced
1	cup shredded red cabbage
1	to 1½ lb. catfish fillets
⅓	cup yellow cornmeal
1	tsp. chili powder

1. Cut half of lemon in slices or wedges; set aside. Juice remaining half into large bowl. For slaw, combine mayonnaise and honey with juice; reserve 2 tablespoons juice mixture. Stir celery, apple, and cabbage in to juice mixture in bowl; set aside.

2. Sprinkle fish with ½ teaspoon *salt* and brush with reserved juice mixture. In shallow dish combine cornmeal and chili powder; coat fish with mixture.

3. In 12-inch skillet heat 2 tablespoons *oil* over medium heat. Cook fish in hot oil 3 to 4 minutes per side until golden and fish flakes easily with a fork. Serve fish with slaw and lemon. Makes 4 servings.

EACH SERVING *446 cal, 31 g fat, 60 mg chol, 488 mg sodium, 25 g carb, 4 g fiber, 19 g pro.*

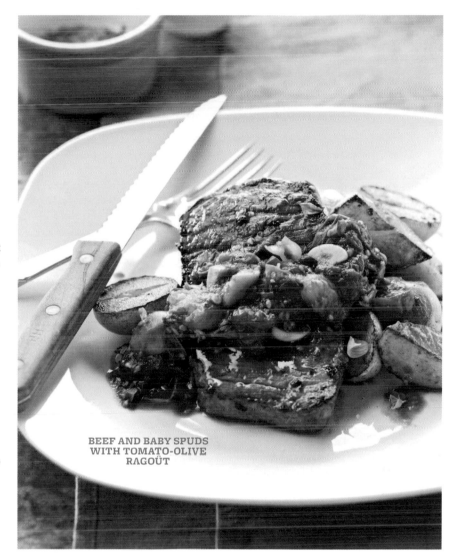

BEEF AND BABY SPUDS WITH TOMATO-OLIVE RAGOÛT

FAST

Beef and Baby Spuds with Tomato-Olive Ragout

START TO FINISH 22 min.

BUDGET $3.66 per serving

1	lb. baby Yukon gold or new potatoes, halved and/or quartered
4	4-oz. beef steaks, ½ inch thick (flat iron, strip, sirloin, or rib eye)
8	oz. cherry tomatoes
3	cloves garlic, sliced
3	teaspoons olive oil
¼	cup pitted green olives, coarsely chopped
1	tsp. snipped fresh oregano or ½ tsp. dried oregano

1. Cook potatoes, covered with vented plastic wrap, in microwave-safe bowl for 5 minutes, stirring once.

2. Meanwhile, season steaks with *salt* and *pepper*. Heat 12-inch skillet over medium-high heat; add 1 teaspoon oil. Add steaks; cook 3 to 4 minutes per side. Transfer to platter; cover. For sauce, in the same skillet, cook tomatoes and garlic in 1 teaspoon of the oil until softened. Stir in olives and oregano; cook 3 minutes more.

3. In a nonstick skillet cook potatoes over medium-high heat in the remaining 2 teaspoons hot olive oil for 4 minutes. Season with *salt* and *pepper*. Serve steaks and potatoes with sauce. Makes 4 servings.

EACH SERVING *409 cal, 23 g fat, 53 mg chol, 643 mg sodium, 24 g carb, 4 g fiber, 26 g pro.*

American Classics

"Get extra flavor with minimal effort when you bake this go-anywhere fresh-fruit dessert," says chef Scott Peacock.

KID FRIENDLY

Fresh Raspberry Bars

PREP 20 min. BAKE 45 to 50 min.
COOL 1 hr. CHILL 2 hr. OVEN 350°F

1   cup unsalted butter cut into 1-inch chunks (2 sticks)
¼   cup packed light brown sugar
½   tsp. kosher salt
2   cups unbleached all-purpose flour
      Softened butter
¾   cup seedless raspberry jam or preserves
1   pint (2 cups) fresh raspberries
½   an 8-oz. pkg. cream cheese, softened
4   oz. goat cheese (chèvre) or cream cheese
½   cup granulated sugar
1   Tbsp. unbleached all-purpose flour

1   large egg
1   large egg yolk
2   Tbsp. finely shredded lemon peel
2   Tbsp. freshly squeezed lemon juice
½   tsp. pure vanilla
      Powdered sugar

● Preheat oven to 350°F. Line a 13×9×2-inch baking pan with a 24-inch-long sheet of aluminum foil, extending extra foil over ends; set aside. In a large bowl beat the butter with an electric mixer on medium to high speed just until it begins to blend and soften slightly, about 30 seconds.
● Add brown sugar and salt; beat on low speed until incorporated, 30 seconds to 1 minute. With mixer off, add the 2 cups flour. Beat on low speed until flour is

FRESH
RASPBERRY BARS

incorporated. Increase speed to medium, mix until ingredients form an even, cohesive dough (*photo 1*).

• Break dough into small chunks and distribute in prepared pan; with your fingers press dough into an even layer (*photo 2*). Bake 20 minutes or until dough has begun to puff and is set. Cool on wire rack 5 minutes.

• Lightly brush exposed sides of foil with softened butter to keep filling from sticking (*photo 3*). Spread jam evenly over crust (*photo 4*).

• Sprinkle evenly with raspberries (*photo 5*).

• With a lemon zester, remove peel from lemon, making sure to avoid bitter white pith (*photo 6*).

• For custards, in a large bowl beat cream cheese and goat cheese with an electric mixer on medium to high speed for 30 seconds. Mix in granulated sugar and 1 tablespoon flour until blended. With mixer running, add egg, egg yolk, lemon zest, lemon juice, and vanilla. Beat until smooth.

• Pour custard batter evenly over berries (*photo 7*). Tilt pan back and forth to distribute evenly (*photo 8*). Bake at 350°F for 25 to 30 minutes or until barely set. Transfer to a wire rack until completely cool, about 1 hour; cover and transfer to refrigerator.

Chill 2 hours. Top will crack slightly as it cools.

• Use foil to lift the bars from pan. With a knife or metal spatula, support the sides of the bars while you gently peel the foil downward and away from sides of the bars (*photo 9*).

• Cut into long bars (*photo 10*), peel foil from bottom, and transfer to cutting board using side of a long knife or a spatula (*photo 11*). Cut into 24 squares.

• Sprinkle very lightly with powdered sugar (*photo 12*). Makes 24 bars.

EACH BAR *209 cal, 12 g fat, 48 mg chol, 88 mg sodium, 23 g carb, 1 g fiber, 3 g pro.*

food life

IDEAS AND INSPIRATION FOR SHARING TIME AROUND THE TABLE

Natural Beauties

At this hands-on spring gathering, flowers, friends, creativity—
and something special to sip—are the main ingredients.

As a professional crafter, Suzonne Stirling is always dreaming up inventive ways to make everyday items special. When she threw a centerpiece-making party in time for Mother's Day, she looked no farther than her New Orleans home and garden for objects to use as vases and for flowers for the arrangements.

The real fun begins when guests jump in and play. To get creative juices flowing, Suzonne set out a variety of embellishments to use on the containers. One guest swirled glass paint inside a juice glass and filled it with hellebores, dusty miller, and roses. Another decoupaged lace onto a white vessel to mimic the look of textured fabrics and created a bouquet of peonies, hydrangea, camellias, and quince branches. And another dressed up a dessert cup with paper and patterned tape and filled it with narcissus.

As if the gorgeous flowers and fixings for centerpiece making weren't enough, Suzonne sweetened the deal by serving a couple of cocktails for sipping as the women socialized and worked on their projects. (See page 103 for the recipes.)

Above: **Simple twists breathe new life into containers. A guest arranges fresh-cut flowers. Think outside the vase when choosing containers and ephemera to have on hand. Suzonne included buttons, colored twine and ribbon, scrapbooking paper, and rubber stamps to use on various papers.** *Opposite:* **Fresh blooms and a bounty of craft supplies set the table for a refreshing afternoon of floral centerpiece creation. Suzonne, lower right, encouraged her friends to bring cuttings from their gardens to share.**

"Some people are intimidated by the idea of crafting," Suzonne says. "But it's more a learned skill than a talent, and when you get a group of women together, they inspire one another and walk away having learned something new."

Fiore per Mamma Cocktail

Fresh spring flavors mix in this enticingly light cocktail you can serve at your party.

1   oz. Grey Goose L'Orange vodka
½   oz. St. Germain elderflower liqueur
¼   oz. Aperol
¼   oz. fresh lemon juice
1   tsp. elderflower syrup
     Prosecco (one bottle is enough for
     10 to 12 drinks)

Stir all the ingredients in an ice-filled cocktail shaker. Strain into champagne flute. Top with prosecco. Makes 1 drink. **To Make Ahead:** Mix all the ingredients except the prosecco in a pitcher and chill. Stir before serving, pour into glasses, and top with the prosecco.

Gran Gala Fizz Cocktail

Enjoy this refreshing orange liqueur-based cocktail at your spring party.

1½   oz. Gran Gala orange liqueur (don't
     substitute other orange liqueurs)
¾   oz. Plymouth Gin (don't substitute
     gins; others won't have the soft taste
     of this gin)
½   oz. fresh lemon juice
½   oz. fresh lime juice
½   oz. simple syrup
1   egg white
2   dashes Fee Bros. Grapefruit Bitters

Shake all ingredients with ice. Strain into coupe. Garnish with an *orange twist*. Makes 1 drink.
Cocktail recipes by Michael Glassberg

Sweet Floral Invitation

Extend an invitation for a spring party by including a "blooming" branch inside your guests' invitations. To create the envelope, cut a strip of brown paper and use a bone folder to make creases. Fold the bottom part up to form the envelope's pocket. Use a glue stick and decorative paper to line the envelope. Secure with double-sided tape along the edges.

Use decorative tape to secure the invitation note and a real branch. Pretty folded flowers enhance the mood. Once everything is enclosed, fold the top edge down.

Tip: Use a traditional origami fold to create the flower, as shown above, or use purchased flower embellishments.

june

JUST PICKED The flavors of summer are here. Make the most of garden-fresh vegetables with an impromptu gathering around the grill.

Chill and Grill

Art Smith, Daisy Martinez, and Ted Allen are experts at effortless entertaining using summer-fresh ingredients. These cooking stars share their tips on transforming the everyday into the extraordinary.

KID-FRIENDLY

Fresh Corn Salad

PREP 25 min.   GRILL 10 min.   CHILL 2 hr.

8	ears corn, shucked
6	fresh tomatoes, chopped
2	cucumbers, peeled, seeded, and chopped
2	green onions, chopped
1	green sweet pepper, seeded and chopped
1	jalapeño, seeded and chopped (see note, page 11)
¼	cup chopped fresh cilantro
4	Tbsp. white balsamic vinegar
3	Tbsp. extra virgin olive oil

1. Preheat grill to medium-high. Brush corn with a little *olive oil*. Grill corn until lightly browned, turning often to cook evenly; cool. When cool enough to handle, cut corn from cobs.
2. Toss corn with tomatoes, cucumbers, green onions, sweet pepper, jalapeño, cilantro, vinegar, and the 3 tablespoons olive oil. Season with *salt* and *pepper*. Toss and marinate at least 2 hours in the refrigerator before serving. Bring to room temperature to serve. Makes 8 servings.
EACH SERVING *176 cal, 8 g fat, 0 mg chol, 96 mg sodium, 26 g carb, 4 g fiber, 5 g pro.*

KID-FRIENDLY

Brick Chicken

This is an easy method for grilling chicken for a crowd. The herbs are rubbed under the skin so all the flavor stays put during grilling.
START TO FINISH 1 hr.

1	3-lb. whole chicken, butterflied, with backbone removed
¼	cup olive oil
4	cloves garlic, minced
2	Tbsp. chopped fresh chives
2	Tbsp. chopped fresh parsley
2	Tbsp. chopped fresh oregano
2	Tbsp. chopped fresh thyme

1. Set chicken on a baking sheet and allow to come to room temperature (about 20 minutes). Season with *salt* and *pepper*. Preheat grill to high.
2. In small bowl make a paste by combining olive oil, garlic, and fresh herbs. Use your hands to loosen skin on the chicken, then spread paste under skin.
3. Place the chicken on the hot grill, skin side up. Place the baking sheet on top of the chicken and weight it down with a brick.
4. Close grill; reduce heat to medium. Begin checking doneness after 30 minutes. Chicken is done when a meat thermometer inserted in thigh reaches 170°F.
5. When done, remove the brick and carefully transfer chicken to a clean baking sheet or serving platter. Allow the chicken to rest 10 minutes before cutting and serving. Makes 4 servings.
EACH SERVING *513 cal, 33 g fat, 155 mg chol, 284 mg sodium, 2 g carb, 0 g fiber, 51 g pro.*

Sweet Potato Salad

PREP 30 min.   BAKE 1 hr.   COOL 30 min.
CHILL 1 hr.   OVEN 400°F

4	sweet potatoes
¼	cup regular or reduced-fat mayonnaise
2	Tbsp. Dijon-style mustard
4	ribs celery, cut into ¼-inch slices
1	small red sweet pepper, seeded and cut in ¼-inch dice
1	cup diced (½-inch) ripe fresh pineapple
2	scallions, white and green parts, finely chopped
½	cup coarsely chopped pecans, toasted (2 oz.)
	Chopped fresh chives

1. Preheat oven to 400°F. Wrap each potato in foil. Bake for 1 hour or until tender. Cool until easy to handle. Peel, then cut into ¾-inch chunks.
2. In large bowl mix mayonnaise and mustard. Add sweet potatoes, celery, red pepper, pineapple, and scallions; toss gently, seasoning to taste with *salt* and *pepper*. Cover and refrigerate until chilled, about 1 hour.
3. Just before serving, fold in pecans and sprinkle with the chives. Makes 8 servings.
EACH SERVING *174 cal, 11 g fat, 3 mg chol, 253 mg sodium, 18 g carb, 4 g fiber, 2 g pro.*

"Everybody loves a barbecue. When I have one, I always make too much food on purpose. People love it when you send them home with the extras."

SWEET POTATO SALAD

BRICK CHICKEN WITH FRESH CORN SALAD

GINGER-PEACH
MARGARITAS

ELECTRIC
LEMONADE

WATERMELON
MARTINIS

FAST LOW FAT

Ginger-Peach Margaritas

For the ginger syrup, simmer together equal parts sugar and water with a few slices of ginger until syrupy. Strain and chill before using.

START TO FINISH **10 min.**

12 oz. fresh peach puree or pureed frozen peaches
4 oz. ginger syrup
2 oz. lime juice
6 oz. peach juice or nectar
6 to 8 oz. tequila
3 to 4 oz. Cointreau or Triple Sec
  Lime slices for garnish

Place pureed peaches, ginger syrup, lime juice, and peach juice in a blender and mix together. Pour the mixture into a bowl and place in the freezer. When ready to serve, add tequila and Cointreau. Combine well and serve with lime slices. Makes 8 generous-size margaritas.

EACH SERVING *163 cal, 0 g fat, 0 mg chol, 2 mg sodium, 25 g carb, 1 g fiber, 0 g pro.*

FAST LOW FAT

Watermelon Martinis

START TO FINISH **20 min.**

5 cups watermelon cubes (rind and seeds removed)
¾ cup lemon vodka
6 Tbsp. lime juice
3 Tbsp. Cointreau or Triple Sec
3 Tbsp. sugar

1. Place watermelon in blender. Cover; blend until smooth. Pour puree into a pitcher and keep very cold, even a little frozen to make it icy.
2. For two martinis, add 1 cup watermelon puree, ¼ cup lemon vodka, 2 tablespoons lime juice, and 1 tablespoon each Cointreau and sugar to the blender with 3 to 6 *ice cubes.* Cover; blend until slushy. Makes 6 large martinis.

EACH SERVING *150 cal, 0 g fat, 0 mg chol, 2 mg sodium, 20 g carb, 1 g fiber, 1 g pro.*

FAST LOW FAT KID FRIENDLY

Electric Lemonade

START TO FINISH **25 min.**

1 cup fresh-squeezed lemon juice
¼ to ½ cup sugar
½ cup fresh mint leaves
1 cup sparkling mineral water
  Dash ginger ale
2 to 3 cups ice
1 cup vodka or sparkling mineral water
  Mint sprigs and lemon slices for garnish

1. Chill 4 serving glasses in the freezer. In a blender combine lemon juice, sugar, mint, mineral water, ginger ale, and ice. Slowly blend until thick.
2. Remove the glasses from the freezer and pour a jigger (¼ cup) of vodka into each. Top with frozen lemonade mixture.
3. Add a straw and garnish each glass with a fresh mint sprig and a slice of lemon. Makes 4 servings.

EACH SERVING *210 cal, 0 g fat, 0 mg chol, 8 mg sodium, 21 g carb, 2 g fiber, 1 g pro.*

KID FRIENDLY

Coconut Panna Cotta with Tropical Fruit

PREP 40 min.   CHILL 6 hr.

1   Tbsp. powdered gelatin
1   15-oz. can coconut cream (Daisy
    prefers Coco Lopez brand)
1   13.5-oz. can unsweetened coconut milk
2   cups chilled whipping cream
¼   cup confectioners' sugar
    Tropical fruits, such as kiwi, mango,
    papaya, star fruit, pineapple, or
    kumquats, peeled if necessary, and
    sliced or cut up (1½ cups total)
    Dark rum (optional)

1. Evenly sprinkle gelatin over ¼ cup cool water in a small bowl. Set aside to soften.
2. In a medium saucepan heat coconut cream and coconut milk over medium heat until the sides begin to bubble. Reduce heat and whisk in the softened gelatin, stirring until completely dissolved.
3. Fill a large bowl with ice cold water. Strain coconut mixture into a bowl that will fit easily into the bowl of cold water. Set bowl of coconut mixture into bowl of water to cool, stirring every few minutes with a rubber spatula until the mixture starts to thicken, and replacing cold water occasionally. If mixture starts to set, remove it immediately.
4. Remove bowl of coconut mixture from bowl of water. Empty water and wipe the bowl dry. In dry bowl stir cream and confectioners' sugar together until sugar is dissolved. Stir into coconut mixture. Divide among six 7- to 8-ounce custard cups. Chill until firm, at least 6 hours.
5. To serve, top with fruit and a drizzle of rum. Makes 6 servings.
EACH SERVING 686 cal, 68 g fat, 110 mg chol, 43 mg sodium, 19 g carb, 3 g fiber, 8 g pro

COCONUT PANNA
COTTA WITH
TROPICAL FRUIT

KID-FRIENDLY

Barbecued Beef Short Ribs

Flanken-style ribs need marinating to help tenderize them before grilling. Tenderness can vary from rib to rib. For a substitution, see Make with Flank Steak, *below*.

PREP 25 min. MARINATE 1 hr.
GRILL 12 min. STAND 4 min.

4   lb. beef flanken-style ribs, cut across the ribs into 1½-inch slices
2   Tbsp. red wine vinegar
1   recipe Lemon-Cilantro Gremolata

1. Trim any surface fat from ribs. Generously rub all surfaces of the ribs with *salt* and *pepper*. Put ribs in a large baking dish that fits them in a single layer. Drizzle vinegar over both sides of ribs. Marinate ribs, at room temperature up to 1 hour or in the refrigerator for up to 4 hours, turning occasionally. (Longer marinating time may make the surface of the ribs turn gray in spots. That is fine and the discoloration will disappear when they are grilled.)
2. Preheat grill to medium-high. Grill ribs, covered, about 6 minutes per side, turning once, until well browned. If ribs flare up as they grill, temporarily move them to a cooler area on the grill. The ribs should be a touch rarer than medium; anything less and they will be chewy. Let rest 4 minutes before serving. Sprinkle with Lemon-Cilantro Gremolata. Makes 8 servings.
Lemon-Cilantro Gremolata In a small bowl combine ¼ cup chopped yellow sweet pepper, 2 tablespoons snipped fresh cilantro, and 1 tablespoon finely shredded lemon peel.
EACH SERVING *265 cal, 16 g fat, 51 mg chol, 318 mg sodium, 2 g carb, 1 g fiber, 26 g pro.*
Make with Flank Steak Score 2 pounds flank steak on both sides. Sprinkle with *salt* and *pepper* and marinate as directed in main recipe. Grill directly over medium heat for 17 to 21 minutes or until medium (160°F), turning once halfway through.

FAST

Cilantro Pesto

START TO FINISH 15 min.

1   cup extra virgin olive oil
1   packed cup coarsely chopped fresh cilantro
1   packed cup fresh flat-leaf parsley
¼   cup marcona almonds or blanched almonds
2   tsp. white wine vinegar

Pour oil into blender. Add cilantro, parsley, almonds, and vinegar. Blend until herbs are finely chopped and mixture is fairly smooth. Season to taste with *salt* and *pepper*. Scrape into a storage container and press a piece of plastic wrap to the surface to prevent pesto from turning dark. Store up to 5 days in the refrigerator. Bring to room temperature to serve. Makes 12 (2-Tbsp.) servings.
EACH SERVING *181 cal, 20 g fat, 0 mg chol, 87 mg sodium, 1 g carb, 1 g fiber, 1 g pro.*

FAST **LOW FAT** **KID-FRIENDLY**

Tomatillo Salsa

PREP 15 min. COOK 15 min.

1   lb. fresh tomatillos, husks removed
1   large Spanish onion, cut into large chunks (about 2 cups)
3   cloves garlic
½   cup packed coarsely chopped fresh cilantro
½   jalapeño (see note, page 11)
    Juice of half a lime

1. Wash tomatillos under cool water until they no longer feel sticky. Cut them into quarters and place in a food processor. Add onion and garlic; process until smooth. Add cilantro, jalapeño, and lime juice then process until the jalapeño is finely chopped.
2. Scrape the mixture into a small saucepan. Season lightly with *salt* and bring to a boiling over medium heat. Cook, stirring occasionally, until most of the liquid is boiled off and the salsa has thickened, about 15 minutes. Cool before using. The sauce can be refrigerated up to 1 week. If refrigerated, you may want to add a little salt and/or lime juice to the salsa before serving. Makes 10 (¼-cup) servings.
EACH SERVING *31 cal, 1 g fat, 0 mg chol, 197 mg sodium, 7 g carb, 2 g fiber, 1 g pro.*

LOW FAT **KID-FRIENDLY**

Skillet Wrinkled Potatoes

These potatoes are best on the grill but also work well on the stove top.
PREP 5 min. COOK 40 min.
STAND 10 min.

1½   lb. small (about 1½ inch) new potatoes, scrubbed
2   Tbsp. kosher salt
     Ancho chili powder
1   recipe Cilantro Pesto

1. Place potatoes and salt in a large, deep heavy cast iron skillet in which they fit comfortably. (Pan should be as deep as the potatoes are wide and there should be room for them to roll around when pan is shaken.) Pour in enough water to cover potatoes. Bring to boiling over hot coals or high heat (adjust heat if using gas grill so water is at a steady boil) and cook, shaking the pan every few minutes, until water is almost evaporated and potatoes look ashy, about 35 minutes.
2. Move skillet to cooler part of grill or reduce heat and cook just until water is evaporated, about 2 to 3 minutes. Remove pan from heat. Cover with a clean damp kitchen towel. Let sit for 10 to 15 minutes. Dust with chili powder and brush with Cilantro Pesto. Serve right from the pan. Makes 6 servings.
EACH SERVING *105 cal, 3 g fat, 2 mg chol, 1,017 mg sodium, 19 g carb, 2 g fiber, 3 g pro.*

"For stress-free entertaining, get your prep done beforehand. Wash and dry greens, chop salad ingredients, prepare sauces and salsas, and make the dessert a day early."

GRILL For Daisy's **Barbecued Beef Short Ribs**, have your butcher cut the ribs 1½ inches thick—they'll be finished cooking and full of flavor in less than 15 minutes. Serve them with **Tomatillo Salsa** and **Skillet Wrinkled Potatoes.** The potatoes are drizzled with **Cilantro Pesto,** also ready in 15 minutes.

TOMATILLO SALSA

SKILLET WRINKLED POTATOES

CILANTRO PESTO

BARBECUED BEEF SHORT RIBS

FAST

Sangria Peach Compote with Ice Cream

START TO FINISH 25 min.

½ cup dry white wine
⅓ cup honey
2 cups peaches, peeled, pitted, and sliced, or one 10-oz. bag frozen peaches
1 Tbsp. butter
1 Tbsp. fresh lemon juice
1 tsp. finely shredded lemon peel zest
1 Tbsp. brandy
1 Tbsp. Cointreau
1 Tbsp. chopped mint or basil
   Vanilla bean ice cream and/or purchased shortbread

In saucepan bring wine, honey, and peaches to boiling; reduce heat. Simmer, uncovered, until fruit is softened and mixture is slightly thickened, about 10 minutes. Swirl in butter; remove from heat. Add lemon juice and zest, brandy, Cointreau, and mint. Serve with ice cream and/or shortbread. Makes 4 servings.
EACH SERVING 326 cal, 11 g fat, 33 mg chol, 59 mg sodium, 48 g carb, 1 g fiber, 3 g pro.

Toasted Couscous with Grilled Mango and Zucchini

PREP 20 min. COOK 23 min. GRILL 5 min.

2 cups Israeli (pearl) couscous
1 mango
1 zucchini
1 Tbsp. vegetable oil
2½ cups chicken stock, seafood stock, or vegetable stock
1 Tbsp. butter
2 Tbsp. fresh Italian (flat-leaf) parsley, chopped
½ tsp. kosher salt

1. Thoroughly preheat grill to medium high.
2. In a dry, medium saucepan over medium-low heat toast couscous, stirring frequently, until golden-brown, 8 to 10 minutes. (You can skip this step in a pinch, but it's worth it!)
3. Peel mango; stand mango on its end with a skinny edge facing you, and with knife close to the seed core, cut a 1-inch slice off each of the two sides. Then, cut each of those slices into two ½-inch-thick slices. Slice zucchini lengthwise into ⅓-inch to ½-inch slices. Brush mango and zucchini pieces with vegetable oil on all sides, season lightly with a pinch of salt, and grill until charred and tender, 5 to 8 minutes. Let cool; cut into ½-inch chunks.
4. In a medium saucepan bring chicken stock to a boiling. Add couscous, stir, cover, reduce heat to simmer, and cook about 7 minutes. Add mango, zucchini, butter, parsley, and salt. Cook another minute and taste for seasoning and doneness. Keep warm. Makes 4 (1⅓-cup) servings.
EACH SERVING 365 cal, 7 g fat, 9 mg chol, 929 mg sodium, 66 g carb, 5 g fiber, 9 g pro.

LOW FAT

Grilled Chile-Lime Shrimp

PREP 20 min. MARINATE 20 min.
GRILL 5 min.

1 tsp. finely shredded lime peel
¼ Tbsp. lime juice (about 1½ limes)
1 jalapeño, seeded and finely minced (see note, page 11)
1 Tbsp. garlic, minced
2 Tbsp. low-sodium soy sauce
3 Tbsp. olive oil
1 tsp. chili powder
¼ tsp. cayenne pepper
2 Tbsp. cilantro
1 Tbsp. honey
1½ lb. medium shrimp (about 6 per person)

1. Preheat grill to medium-high. For marinade, in medium bowl combine all ingredients except shrimp and stir well. Peel shrimp except for tail, and devein. Rinse and pat dry with paper towels.
2. Place shrimp in large resealable bag. Add marinade. Through bag, rub marinade into shrimp. Refrigerate for 20 minutes. Halfway through, turn bag and massage. (Do not marinate longer than 20 minutes, or the acidic lime juice will cook the shrimp.)
3. Place shrimp on cutting board and nestle them together in groups of six. Using two bamboo skewers for each group, skewer shrimp together (nice for presentation, keeps shrimp from falling into the grill, and makes it easy to turn).
4. Grill shrimp on an oiled grill rack 2 minutes per side, or until opaque. Serve with Toasted Couscous with Grilled Mango and Zucchini. Makes 4 servings.
EACH SERVING 211 cal, 6 g fat, 259 mg chol, 320 mg sodium, 4 g carb, 0 g fiber, 35 g pro.

SANGRIA PEACH COMPOTE WITH ICE CREAM

"Designate an old cast-iron pan as your grill skillet. You can wash the inside but not worry about all the sooty, sticky greasiness that's going to happen on the outside."

TOASTED COUSCOUS WITH GRILLED MANGO AND ZUCCHINI

GRILLED CHILE-LIME SHRIMP

Honey-Sweet Onion Ribs

PREP 40 min. CHILL 2 hr.
COOK 20 min. GRILL 1½ hr.

3 Tbsp. packed brown sugar
2 Tbsp. paprika
2 Tbsp. garlic powder
1 to 2 Tbsp. coarsely ground black pepper
2 tsp. ground cumin
2 tsp. dry mustard
1 tsp. salt
3½ to 4 lb. pork loin back ribs
1 Tbsp. vegetable oil
1 medium onion, finely chopped (½ cup)
1 8-oz. can tomato sauce
⅓ cup regular or nonalcoholic beer
¼ to ⅓ cup honey
2 Tbsp. Worcestershire sauce
2 Tbsp. vinegar

1. For rub, in small bowl stir together brown sugar, paprika, garlic powder, pepper, cumin, dry mustard, and salt. Reserve 3 tablespoons of the rub. Sprinkle remaining rub over both sides of ribs; rub in. Place in 3-quart rectangular baking dish. Cover; chill 2 to 24 hours.
2. Meanwhile, for sauce, heat oil in saucepan over medium heat. Cook and stir onion in hot oil 5 minutes or until tender. Stir in tomato sauce, beer, honey, Worcestershire sauce, vinegar and reserved 3 tablespoons rub. Simmer, uncovered, 20 minutes or until sauce is reduced to 1½ cups, stirring occasionally.
3. For charcoal grill, arrange medium-hot coals around drip pan. Test for medium heat above pan. Place ribs, bone sides down, on lightly oiled grill rack over drip pan. Cover; grill for 1½ to 1¾ hours or until ribs are tender, brushing with sauce the last 5 minutes of grilling. (For a gas grill, preheat grill. Reduce heat to medium. Adjust for indirect cooking. Place ribs in a roasting pan. Grill as above.)
4. To serve, cut ribs into portions. Pass remaining sauce. Makes 6 servings.
EACH SERVING *594 cal, 39 g fat, 131 mg chol, 772 mg sodium, 28 g carb, 3 g fiber, 28 g pro.*

HONEY-SWEET
ONION RIBS

Home Cooking

Enjoy summer's fresh produce in four delicious salads: layered, tossed, chunked, and—wiggly.

FAST
Spicy Ginger-Carrot Slaw

Layer this slaw in a straight-sided glass dish or bowl to show off the colorful vegetables.
PREP 25 min.

1   small head napa cabbage, core removed and shredded
2   medium red sweet peppers, cut into bite-size strips
4   to 6 medium carrots, shredded
1   to 2 pink grapefruit, peeled and sectioned
4   green onions, sliced
    Lime peel
1   recipe Lime Dressing

1. In a large glass bowl layer cabbage, sweet peppers, carrots, and grapefruit. (At this point, the salad can be covered and refrigerated up to 1 day.)
2. Just before serving, add green onions and lime peel. Pour over about half the Lime Dressing; toss. Pass remaining dressing. Makes 8 servings.
Lime Dressing In a small screw-top jar combine ¼ cup olive oil; 2 to 4 tablespoons tequila; ½-inch section of fresh ginger, peeled and thinly sliced; juice and peel of 1 lime (about 2 tablespoons juice); and ½ teaspoon crushed red pepper or 1 small jalapeño, seeded and diced (see note, page 11). Cover and shake to combine. Allow to stand at least 1 hour before serving. Shake again just before serving.
EACH SERVING WITH 1 TBSP. DRESSING *127 cal, 7 g fat, 0 mg chol, 101 mg sodium, 14 g carb, 3 g fiber, 2 g pro.*

SPICY GINGER-CARROT SLAW

Make a better tossed salad

Start with crisp greens. If they're a bit wilty, soak in a bowl of cool water for 20 to 30 minutes, then drain thoroughly and dry.

POTATO-CAULIFLOWER SALAD

Potato-Cauliflower Salad

All the cooking is done in the microwave making for super quick and easy prep.

PREP 25 min. MICROWAVE 13 min. CHILL 1 hr.

- 12 small fingerling or round new potatoes, scrubbed
- 1 medium head cauliflower, chopped into bite-size pieces
- 1 small onion, chopped
- 2 stalks celery, sliced
- ⅓ cup sour cream chive dip
- 2 Tbsp. lemon juice
- 2 Tbsp. salad oil
- ¼ cup blue cheese
- ¼ cup fresh Italian (flat-leaf) parsley
- 2 slices bacon, crisp cooked and crumbled
- 4 crisp breadsticks, broken
  Sea salt or salt and freshly ground pepper

1. Arrange potatoes on paper towels in a single layer in microwave. Cook on 100% power (high) for 5 minutes. Turn potatoes; cook until tender, about 3 minutes more.

2. Place cauliflower and 2 tablespoons *water* in a 1½-quart microwave-safe casserole. Cook on 100% power (high) for 5 minutes or until crisp tender, stirring once. Drain. Cool slightly.

3. In a large serving bowl combine potatoes, cauliflower, onion, and celery. In a small bowl stir together sour cream dip, lemon juice, and salad oil; gently toss with potato mixture and fold in blue cheese. Refrigerate 1 to 24 hours. Just before serving top with parsley, bacon, broken breadsticks, salt, and freshly ground pepper. Makes 8 to 10 servings.

EACH SERVING *152 cal, 7 g fat, 12 mg chol, 299 mg sodium, 18 g carb, 3 g fiber, 5 g pro.*

Chunked Think
potato salad, but better: Start with potatoes, then add lightly steamed cauliflower and crisp bacon. It's great as a main dish salad but equally compatible with other sides on a potluck spread.

LOW FAT

Watermelon Salad

PREP 25 min. CHILL 3 hr.

2   envelopes unflavored gelatin
2   cups watermelon juice*
1½ cups white grape juice
1   tsp. shredded lemon peel
1½ cups assorted chopped fruit
    (such as peeled peaches, nectarines,
    pears, and/or green grapes)
⅓   cup crumbled feta cheese
    Mint leaves

1. In a medium saucepan sprinkle gelatin over watermelon juice. Allow to stand 5 minutes. Cook and stir until gelatin is dissolved. Stir in grape juice and lemon peel.

2. With a ladle or cup, transfer half the watermelon juice mixture to a 2-quart square baking dish. Add fruit. Cover and refrigerate about 1½ hours or until thickened to the texture of egg whites to "lock in" the fruit (keep remaining watermelon juice mixture at room temperature). Carefully spoon remaining watermelon juice mixture over set mixture. Cover and refrigerate 1½ hours more or until all layers are set.

3. Top with feta and mint leaves before serving. Makes 9 servings.

*To juice watermelon, puree seeded chunks in blender; strain to remove pulp.

EACH SERVING 92 cal, 1 g fat, 5 mg chol, 68 mg sodium, 18 g carb, 1 g fiber, 3 g pro.

Gelatin Fresh fruit juice stirred into plain gelatin reinvents this easy side dish. Even better, gelatin salads are refreshing when paired with an unexpected ingredient or two, such as feta cheese and mint.

WATERMELON SALAD

Garden Three-Bean Salad with Fresh French Dressing

START TO FINISH 40 min.

2   cups green beans, trimmed if desired
8   cups mixed greens
2   cups frozen shelled sweet soybeans (edamame), thawed
1   cup canned white beans, such as cannellini, thoroughly rinsed and drained
1   cup radishes, quartered and/or sliced
    Freshly ground black pepper
1   recipe Fresh French Dressing

1. In microwave-safe bowl combine green beans with ¼ cup *water* and 1 teaspoon *salt*. Toss to distribute salt among beans. Cook, uncovered, on 100% power (high) for 3 to 5 minutes or until just tender. Set aside and allow to cool.

2. Place salad greens in a large salad bowl; add green beans, edamame, white beans, and radishes. Add about half the dressing. Sprinkle with pepper and toss gently. Pass remaining dressing. Makes 8 servings.

Fresh French Dressing In a blender combine 2 medium tomatoes, halved and seeded; ¼ cup olive oil; 2 to 3 tablespoons red wine vinegar; 2 tablespoons tomato paste; 1 tablespoon snipped fresh tarragon; and 2 teaspoons Dijon mustard. Cover and process until thoroughly blended.

Season to taste with salt and pepper. Tomatoes vary in juiciness; if dressing is too thin, blend in additional tomato paste, 1 teaspoon at a time. Refrigerate until serving time.

EACH SERVING WITH 1 TBSP. DRESSING *175 cal, 9 g fat, 380 mg sodium, 18 g carb, 7 g fiber, 8 g pro.*

Tossed This everything-goes salad makes it easy to eat local. Take the best of the garden or market then combine with a classic French dressing and fresh tomatoes.

GARDEN THREE-BEAN SALAD WITH FRESH FRENCH DRESSING

Everyday Easy

Five fast burgers make the most of summer living. Take your pick of beef, pork, fish, veggie, and turkey.

FAST

Blue Cheese-Stuffed Burger with Red Onion and Spinach

COST PER SERVING $1.97

START TO FINISH 28 minutes

1   lb. ground beef
1   Tbsp. Worcestershire sauce
1   tsp. freshly ground black pepper
⅓   to ½ cup crumbled blue cheese (2 oz.)
1   medium red onion, sliced crosswise
    Olive oil
4   hamburger buns, split
1   cup fresh baby spinach

1. In a bowl combine beef, Worcestershire sauce, and black pepper. On waxed paper, shape into eight thin 4-inch-diameter patties. Place 1 tablespoon of the blue cheese in center of four of the patties. Top with remaining four patties; pinch edges to seal.

2. Brush onion slices with olive oil; sprinkle with *salt*.

3. Place burgers and onions directly over medium-high heat. Grill 5 minutes per side or until no pink remains in burger. Brush cut sides of buns with olive oil. Grill, cut side down, the last minute of grilling.

4. Serve burgers on buns with grilled onions, spinach, and remaining cheese. Makes 4 servings.

EACH SERVING *497 cal, 31 g fat, 89 mg chol, 638 mg sodium, 26 g carb, 2 g fiber, 27 g pro.*

BLUE CHEESE-STUFFED BURGER WITH RED ONION AND SPINACH

Salmon Burgers

COST PER SERVING $3.65
START TO FINISH 30 min.

1 cup broken herb-seasoned crackers,
such as Nabisco Italian herbed crisp
flatbread crackers (8 crackers)
1 lb. skinless, boneless salmon fillets,
cut into 2-inch pieces
1 egg
3 Tbsp. Dijon-style or honey mustard
4 ciabatta buns, split
Sliced avocado and green onions
(optional)

1. Place crackers in a food processor; cover
and process until coarsely ground. Add
half the salmon, the egg, and 1 tablespoon
of the mustard. Cover and process
until salmon is ground and mixture is
thoroughly combined. Add remaining
salmon. Cover and pulse with several on/
off turns until salmon is coarsely chopped.
With damp hands, shape mixture into four
½-inch-thick patties.
2. Brush patties lightly with *olive oil*. Grill
directly on a greased grill rack over medium
heat for 3 minutes per side or until cooked
through (160°F). Grill buns, cut sides
down, the last 1 to 2 minutes of grilling.
3. Serve salmon burgers on buns with
sliced avocado and green onions. Makes
4 servings.

EACH SERVING *614 cal, 23 g fat, 120 mg chol,
968 mg sodium, 67 g carb, 3 g fiber, 36 g pro.*

THE BIG PIG

CUMIN-CRUSTED VEGGIE BURGERS WITH PINEAPPLE SALSA

SALMON BURGERS

FAST | LOW FAT

Cumin-Crusted Veggie Burgers with Pineapple Salsa

COST PER SERVING $2.30
START TO FINISH 20 min.

- 2 tsp. cumin seeds
- 4 refrigerated or frozen meatless burger patties, thawed
- 6 slices fresh or canned pineapple
- 4 pita breads or flatbreads
- 1 Tbsp. bottled pepper and onion relish
  Spiced peanuts, chopped, and fresh basil (optional)

1. In a medium skillet heat cumin seeds over medium heat until they are fragrant and starting to brown, about 3 to 4 minutes. Transfer seeds to a cutting board. Crush seeds using a mortar and pestle.
2. Brush meatless patties with *olive oil;* coat with crushed cumin seeds. Blot excess moisture from pineapple slices and lightly brush with *olive oil.*
3. Grill pineapple slices directly over medium-high heat for 3 to 4 minutes per side or until heated through. Transfer to a cutting board. Add meatless patties to grill; cook 4 minutes per side or until heated through, adding pita breads the last 3 to 4 minutes of grilling. Cover and keep warm.
4. Chop pineapple and place in a bowl; stir in relish.
5. Serve veggie patties on pita bread with pineapple mixture, chopped peanuts, and basil. Makes 4 servings.
EACH SERVING *316 cal, 5 g fat, 0 mg chol, 619 mg sodium, 52 g carb, 6 g fiber, 19 g pro.*

FAST | KID FRIENDLY

The Big Pig

COST PER SERVING $1.92
START TO FINISH 30 min.

- 1 lb. lean ground pork
- 2 cups packaged shredded cabbage with carrot (coleslaw mix)
- 2 Tbsp. mayonnaise
- 1 tsp. bottled barbecue sauce
- 8 thin ham slices (4 oz. total)
- 8 slices Texas toast
- ¼ cup bottled barbecue sauce

1. Shape pork into four 4-inch patties about ½ inch thick. Grill directly over medium-high heat for 5 to 6 minutes per side or until no pink remains (160°F), turning once.
2. Meanwhile, in a medium bowl combine shredded cabbage with carrot, mayonnaise, and barbecue sauce; set aside.
3. Add ham and bread slices to grill for 1 to 2 minutes until ham is lightly browned and bread is toasted, turning once.
4. Serve pork burgers on toast topped with ham, slaw, and barbecue sauce. Makes 4 servings.
EACH SERVING *581 cal, 28 g fat, 92 mg chol, 1,080 mg sodium, 49 g carb, 3 g fiber, 32 g pro.*

FAST **KID-FRIENDLY**

Turkey Burger with Peaches and Blueberries

COST PER SERVING $2.87

START TO FINISH 30 minutes

4   small peaches
1   lb. ground turkey
4   slices Monterey Jack cheese
½   cup blueberries
¼   tsp. chili powder
4   thick slices roasted garlic country bread or garlic bread, toasted if desired
   Fresh mint (optional)

1. Finely chop one of the peaches. In a bowl mix chopped peach with ground turkey, *salt*, and *pepper*. Shape into four ½-inch-thick patties (if sticky, use dampened hands). Grill directly over medium-high heat for 5 minutes per side or until no pink remains (165°F). Add cheese; cover and cook 1 minute more.

2. Meanwhile, coarsely chop remaining peaches; combine in a large skillet with blueberries and chili powder. Cook, stirring occasionally, over medium heat for 5 minutes or until heated through and juicy.

3. Serve turkey burgers on garlic bread topped with peach mixture and mint. Makes 4 servings.

EACH SERVING *464 cal, 25 g fat, 114 mg chol, 614 mg sodium, 28 g carb, 3 g fiber, 31 g pro.*

TURKEY BURGER WITH PEACHES AND BLUEBERRIES

Good and Healthy

Hummus, the popular dip and spread, is hearty and good for you—thanks to hunger-pleasing protein.

FAST

Creamy Hummus

START TO FINISH 15 min.

1   15-oz. can chickpeas (garbanzo beans), rinsed and drained
¼   cup tahini (sesame seed paste)
½   tsp. finely shredded lemon peel
3   Tbsp. lemon juice
4   cloves garlic, peeled
¼   tsp. salt
⅛   to ¼ tsp. cayenne pepper
¼   to ½ cup water
    Halved or quartered grape tomatoes (optional)
    Fresh chives, cut up (optional)
    Extra virgin olive oil (optional)
    Cayenne pepper (optional)
    Dippers: cracker bread, Belgian endive or baby bok choy leaves, bias-sliced cucumbers

1. In a food processor combine chickpeas, tahini, lemon peel, lemon juice, garlic, salt, and the ⅛ teaspoon cayenne pepper. Cover and process until smooth, adding enough water to reach desired consistency. Spoon into a serving bowl.
2. Refrigerate up to 48 hours. To serve, top with tomatoes and/or chives, a drizzle of olive oil, and/or a dash of additional cayenne pepper. Serve with dippers. Makes 12 to 16 servings (1¾ cups total).
EACH 2-TBSP. SERVING *75 cal, 3 g fat, 0 mg chol, 158 mg sodium, 10 g carb, 2 g fiber, 3 g pro. Daily Values: 6% vit. C, 2% calcium, 4% iron.*

CREAMY HUMMUS

HEALTH MAGNET
With its high-quality protein and fiber, hummus is a filling snack. Plus, hummus invites more healthful nibbling— it complements a variety of fresh vegetables and whole grain crackers.

BLUEBERRY ICE CREAM PIE

American Classics

"With just a few ingredients, you can make a sensational, crowd-pleasing, seasonal dessert," says chef Scott Peacock.

FAST **LOW FAT** **KID-FRIENDLY**

Blueberry Ice Cream Pie

PREP 30 min. BAKE 8 to 12 min. OVEN 350°F CHILL 2 hr. FREEZE Overnight

Make the Almond-Brown Sugar Crust

1½ cups slivered almonds
2 Tbsp. packed light brown sugar
½ tsp. kosher salt
3 Tbsp. unsalted butter, melted

• Preheat oven to 350°F. In bowl of food processor fitted with a steel blade combine almonds, brown sugar, and salt. Pulse until coarsely ground (*photo 1*). Transfer to bowl and stir in melted butter (*photo 2*). Turn into 9-inch pie plate. With fingers press onto bottom and sides to form a firm, even layer (*photo 3*).

• Bake 8 to 12 minutes until lightly golden. "Don't overbrown or the crust will have an overpowering flavor," Scott says. Allow to completely cool on a rack. Transfer to freezer until ready to use (may be made up to a week in advance and frozen, tightly wrapped).

Make the Blueberry Sauce

3 cups blueberries, rinsed, well drained, and carefully picked over for damaged berries
⅓ cup granulated sugar
1 tsp. cornstarch
¼ tsp. kosher salt
1 tsp. grated lemon zest
2 tsp. freshly squeezed lemon juice
1 Tbsp. water
A few gratings of nutmeg (about ⅛ tsp.)

• In a large, wide, nonreactive skillet combine blueberries, sugar, cornstarch, and salt (*photo 4*), stirring well with a spoon to distribute the sugar and cornstarch. Add zest (*photo 5*), lemon juice, water, and a few gratings of fresh nutmeg (*photo 6*); stir again to blend.

• Cook and stir over medium heat until blueberries begin to pop, give off juice, and come to a full simmer. Simmer, stirring gently for 1 additional minute until sauce is lightly thickened and cornstarch is well cooked (*photo 7*).

• Set aside to cool; refrigerate sauce until completely chilled before proceeding. "Otherwise you'll wind up with a blueberry milk shake," Scott says.

> "You think it's just ice cream pie, but thanks to the layering, every bite is a little bit different from the one before."
>
> Scott Peacock

Assemble and Serve

1 qt. homemade or purchased vanilla ice cream
¾ cup of the Blueberry Sauce, chilled
½ cup crème fraîche or sour cream
½ cup heavy cream
1 Tbsp. sugar
2 cups fresh blueberries, rinsed, picked over, and well dried on paper-towel-lined baking sheets
  Remaining Blueberry Sauce, heated

• Transfer ice cream to a mixing bowl and let stand in the refrigerator 30 minutes or just until softened.

• Spoon half into prepared crust (*photo 8*). Spread in even layer and top with the chilled Blueberry Sauce (*photo 9*). Spoon on remaining ice cream and spread to edges.

• Cover surface of ice cream with plastic wrap and freeze at least 8 hours or overnight until firmly set.

• To serve, in chilled mixing bowl

whisk crème fraîche, heavy cream, and sugar just until thickened to spreading consistency. Do not overbeat. "It is very easy to go from smooth to grainy," Scott says. Spread cream mixture on pie (*photo 10*); top with blueberries. Serve with heated Blueberry Sauce on the side. Makes 10 servings.

EACH SERVING *363 cal, 22 g fat, 53 mg chol, 200 mg sodium, 39 g carb, 4 g fiber, 6 g pro.*

ROADSIDE ATTRACTIONS It's peak produce time. Pull over at a farm stand or visit a farmer's market and give in to the luxury of summer's fresh produce. And be sure to buy an extra basket or two to share.

134

137

138

BLACKBERRY SALAD
WITH CREAMY FETA

Fresh and Fabulous

Erin Flynn and Skip Connett own and run Green Gate Farms, a model of community-supported agriculture (CSA) on the outskirts of Austin, Texas. A sampling of their inspired recipes appears here. Turn to page 142 to see how they share home-grown foods with good friends.

LOW FAT

Blackberry Salad with Creamy Feta

Erin serves this salad with creamy feta. You can make it following the recipe instructions or use crumbled feta drizzled with olive oil.

PREP **25 min.** STAND **1 hr.**

1	recipe Quick Pickled Onions
4	oz. feta cheese
2	Tbsp. olive oil
	Dash crushed red pepper (optional)
6	to 8 cups fresh blackberries or blueberries
⅓	cup fresh mint leaves, large leaves torn
2	Tbsp. turbinado sugar (raw sugar)
2	tsp. finely shredded lemon peel
1	Tbsp. olive oil

1. Prepare Quick Pickled Onions.
2. Meanwhile, for the creamy feta, in a food processor combine feta cheese, the 2 tablespoons olive oil, and red pepper. Cover and process until nearly smooth.
3. In a large bowl gently toss blackberries, mint, sugar, lemon peel, and drained Quick Pickled Onions. Arrange on serving platter. Serve with creamy feta; drizzle olive oil. Makes 12 servings.
Quick Pickled Onions Thinly sliver 1 small or half a large red onion. In bowl toss onion, 3 tablespoons cider vinegar, 1 teaspoon sugar, ½ teaspoon mustard seeds, and ¼ teaspoon salt. Cover; let stand at room temperature for 1 to 4 hours, stirring occasionally.
EACH SERVING *101 cal, 6 g fat, 8 mg chol, 156 mg sodium, 11 g carb, 4 g fiber, 3 g pro.*

FAST

Fresh Arugula Bruschetta

The arugula grown at Green Gate is large with a bold, peppery bite. When using baby arugula, use a few extra leaves to top the toast.

START TO FINISH **25 min.**

1	lb. baguette-style French bread (24 diagonal slices, ¼- to ½-inch thick)
	Olive oil
6	oz. goat cheese (chèvre)
1	tsp. finely shredded lemon peel
48	to 72 arugula leaves (about 2 cups)
	Coarse sea salt
	Cracked black pepper

1. Preheat broiler. Place bread in a single layer on a large baking sheet; lightly brush both sides of bread with oil. Broil 3 to 4 inches from heat for 1 to 2 minutes per side or until toasted. Cool slightly.
2. In a small bowl combine goat cheese and lemon peel. Spread toast with cheese mixture; top with 2 to 3 arugula leaves. Drizzle olive oil; sprinkle lightly with sea salt and pepper. Makes 12 (2-slice) servings.
EACH SERVING *202 cal, 9 g fat, 11 mg chol, 353 mg sodium, 22 g carb, 1 g fiber, 8 g pro.*

FRESH ARUGULA BRUSCHETTA

FAST **LOW FAT** **KID-FRIENDLY**

Farm Salad with Sweet Peppers and Sage Croutons

At Green Gate, sage leaves are sprinkled in this salad to complement the croutons. If you grow other herbs, add those; or skip them altogether.

PREP **20 min.** ROAST **20 min.**
STAND **15 min.** BAKE **10 min.**
OVEN **425°F**

4	sweet peppers
10	cups torn mixed greens
½	cup small fresh sage leaves, tear large leaves
½	cup fresh herb flowers
2	cups cherry tomatoes, halved
1	recipe Sage Croutons
1	recipe Apple Cider Vinaigrette

1. Preheat oven to 425°F.* Halve peppers lengthwise; remove stems, seeds, and veins. Place pepper halves, cut side down, on foil-lined baking sheet. Roast 20 to 25 minutes. Enclose peppers in foil; let stand about 15 minutes or until cool. Use a sharp knife to gently loosen and remove skins. Cut peppers in bite-size strips.
2. In a large salad bowl combine greens, sage, herb flowers, tomatoes, pepper strips, and Sage Croutons; toss with about half the Apple Cider Vinaigrette; pass remaining. Makes 12 servings.
Sage Croutons Preheat oven to 425°F. Tear baguette (about 8 ounces bread) in enough bite-size pieces to equal 4 cups. In a bowl toss bread with 2 to 3 tablespoons olive oil, 2 tablespoons snipped fresh sage, ½ teaspoon garlic powder, ¼ teaspoon salt, and ¼ teaspoon freshly ground pepper.

Spread in a 15×10×1-inch baking pan. Bake for 10 minutes or until browned, stirring once.
Apple Cider Vinaigrette In a screw-top jar combine ⅔ cup cider vinegar, ⅓ cup olive oil, 1 tablespoon stone ground mustard, 1 tablespoon honey, ½ teaspoon salt, and ¼ teaspoon freshly ground pepper. Shake to combine.
* To roast peppers on a gas range, place a pepper on a long-handled fork and roast directly over flame, turning to char evenly. Wrap, cool, and peel as above.
EACH SERVING *128 cal, 6 g fat, 0 mg chol, 217 mg sodium, 16 g carb, 2 g fiber, 4 g pro.*

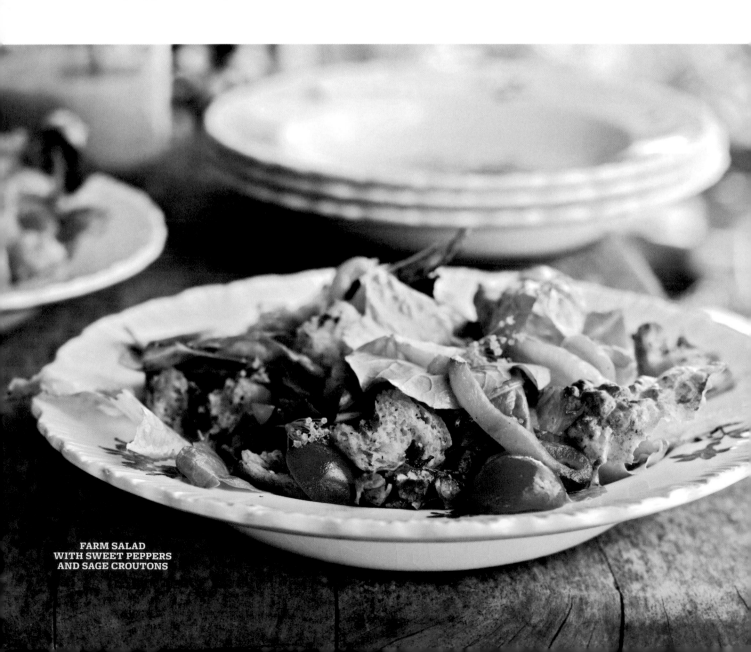

FARM SALAD
WITH SWEET PEPPERS
AND SAGE CROUTONS

FAST

Squash and Mushroom Orzo

START TO FINISH **35 min.**

- 1½ cups dried orzo
- ¼ cup olive oil
- 4 cups assorted mushrooms, halved or sliced (such as shiitake, cremini, or button)
- 3 medium yellow summer squash, chopped
- 4 cloves garlic, minced
- ½ cup whole roasted almonds, coarsely chopped
- 1 cup basil, cut into thin strips
  Salt and freshly ground black pepper

1. In a Dutch oven cook orzo according to package directions. Drain; toss with 1 tablespoon of the oil. Return to Dutch oven; cover and set aside.
2. Meanwhile, in a large skillet heat remaining oil. Add mushrooms, squash, and garlic; cook, stirring occasionally, over medium heat about 5 minutes or until crisp tender. Stir into cooked orzo along with almonds and basil. Season to taste with salt and pepper. Makes 12 servings.
EACH SERVING *187 cal, 8 g fat, 0 mg chol, 72 mg sodium, 25 g carb, 3 g fiber, 5 g pro.*

Honey-Glazed Chicken with Peppers and Goat Cheese

Bright cilantro and goat cheese blend perfectly with the spicy-sweet brush-on glaze.
PREP **15 min.** ROAST **1 hr. 10 min.**
STAND **10 min.** OVEN **375°F**

- ½ cup goat cheese
- 1 small bunch fresh cilantro, coarsely chopped (about ¾ cup)
- 3 3-lb. whole broiler-fryer chickens
- 2 Tbsp. olive oil
  Salt and freshly ground black pepper
- 6 cloves garlic
- 3 lemon halves
- 3 to 6 fresh red jalapeño peppers (see note, page 11) (optional)
- ¼ cup honey
- 1 tsp. crushed red pepper

1. Preheat oven to 375°F. In a medium bowl combine cheese and cilantro; set aside. Remove the neck and giblets, if present, from chickens. One side at a time, slip your fingers between skin and meat to loosen skin. Once your entire hand is under the skin, free skin around thigh and

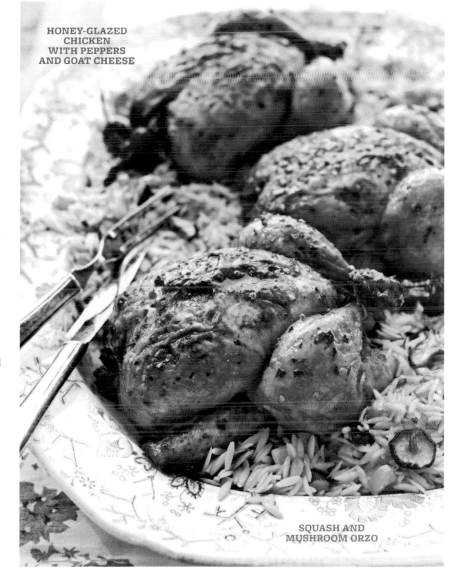

HONEY-GLAZED CHICKEN WITH PEPPERS AND GOAT CHEESE

SQUASH AND MUSHROOM ORZO

leg area. Rub cheese mixture under the skin of each chicken.
2. Brush chickens with olive oil and sprinkle with salt and pepper. Place 2 garlic cloves and half a lemon in cavities of each chicken. Fold under neck skin and skewer to back; tie legs to tail. Place, breast side up, on a rack in a shallow roasting pan. If desired, insert a meat thermometer into center of inside thigh muscle. Add jalapeño peppers to roasting pan.
3. Roast, uncovered, for 60 minutes, spooning juices over chicken occasionally. Combine honey and crushed red pepper. Brush on chickens. Roast 10 to 15 minutes longer or until drumsticks move easily in sockets and chicken is no longer pink (180°F). Remove chicken from oven.

Brush with any remaining honey mixture. Cover; let stand 10 minutes. Cut chickens in quarters. Serve with roasted jalapeños. Makes 12 servings.
Chicken Breast Option Substitute 12 small bone-in chicken breast halves for whole chickens. Stuff cheese mixture under skin and brush with oil. Omit garlic and lemons. Sprinkle with salt and pepper. Place on a rack in a shallow roasting pan. Roast at 375°F for 45 to 55 minutes (170°F), brushing with honey mixture the last 10 minutes of roasting. Brush with remaining honey mixture before serving.
EACH SERVING *468 cal, 24 g fat, 163 mg chol, 286 mg sodium, 8 g carb, 1 g fiber, 53 g pro.*

GARLIC BREAD
WITH CHARD

MELON-FRESH
HERB SORBET

HIBISCUS TEA

Garlic Bread with Chard

PREP 25 min.   BAKE 20 min.
OVEN 375°F

6   to 8 cups coarsely chopped Swiss
    chard or spinach (about 6 to 8 oz.)
2   to 3 Tbsp. olive oil
2   1-lb. ciabatta loaves
½   cup butter, softened
4   to 6 cloves garlic, peeled and finely
    chopped

1. Preheat oven to 375°F. In a large bowl
toss chard with olive oil.
2. Cut each loaf in 8 to 10 slices, cutting
to bottom but not through loaf. In a small
bowl combine butter and garlic, lightly
spread on bread slices. Spoon in chard
mixture, mounding slightly. Wrap each
loaf in foil. Place loaves on a large baking
sheet.
3. Warm 20 minutes or until heated
through. Unwrap and remound any chard
that falls out as it is served. Makes 16 to
20 slices.
EACH SLICE *199 cal, 8 g fat, 18 mg chol,
310 mg sodium, 27 g carb, 1 g fiber, 5 g pro.*

LOW FAT   KID-FRIENDLY
Melon-Fresh Herb Sorbet

Mix and match melon and herb flavors to
suit your taste—or to use what's popping
up in the garden or at the farmer's market.
PREP 20 min.   COOK 5 min.   CHILL 2 hr.

4   cups seedless melon chunks
    (watermelon, cantaloupe, or
    honeydew)
2   lemons or 3 limes, juiced
    (6 tablespoons)
4   5-inch sprigs leafy herbs (basil,
    mint, thyme, sage, tarragon, or
    other herb) or 2 teaspoons
    crushed lavender flowers
1   cup sugar
⅔   cup water
1   Tbsp. honey
⅛   tsp. salt

1. In a processor or blender combine melon
with half the citrus juice; cover and process
or blend until smooth. Transfer to bowl;
set aside.
2. In a small saucepan combine herbs,
sugar, water, remaining citrus juice, honey,
and salt. Bring to boiling over medium
heat. Reduce heat; simmer 5 minutes, stirring occasionally. Strain herb mixture into
melon puree. Place bowl over container of
ice water; stir for several minutes or until
mixture has chilled to about 40°F. Cover;
refrigerate 2 to 4 hours.
3. Transfer chilled mixture to a 1- to
2-quart ice cream freezer; freeze according
to manufacturer's instructions. Store,
covered, in freezer. Makes 8 servings.
EACH SERVING *134 cal, 0 g fat, 0 mg chol,
39 mg sodium, 36 g carb, 2 g fiber, 1 g pro.*

FAST   LOW FAT   KID-FRIENDLY
Hibiscus Tea

This bright red-purple tea will go fast in
the summer sun, so make two pitchers
when serving a crowd. Using a vegetable
peeler, thinly peel 2 oranges, being care-
ful not to remove the bitter white pith.
Squeeze and set aside juice from oranges.
In a very large bowl combine peel, 2 cups
dried hibiscus flowers,* 4 cinnamon sticks,
and ¾ cup honey. Stir in 14 cups boiling
water. Cool to room temperature (about
2 hours). Strain into a very large pitcher;
stir in orange juice. Serve at once over ice
or cover and chill up to 24 hours. Makes
12 (8-oz.) servings.
*Find hibiscus flowers in the Mexican or
Caribbean section of Latin markets and
health food stores.

Home Cooking

Cocktail expert Steve McDonagh shows how to use three time-tested methods to create new, refreshing summer cocktails.

Muddling means to crush fruits, herbs, and zests to unlock every bit of flavor. "It's imperative for herbs because it brings out the essential oils," says Steve McDonagh. "A mint julep with muddled mint (or basil! *yum!*) is a much different cocktail than when ingredients are just stirred in."

`FAST` `LOW FAT`

Celery Mary

For this drink, Steve recommends using a muddler, a tool that looks like a miniature baseball bat. "The wide base gives the best extraction. In a pinch, use the end of a large wooden spoon."

START TO FINISH **5 min.**

1	lemon
	Celery salt
3	cherry tomatoes
½	Tbsp. diced fresh green pepper
½	Tbsp. diced fresh yellow pepper
	Dash of hot pepper sauce, such as Tabasco
1.5	oz. aquavit or vodka
	Celery soda (such as Dr. Brown's Cel-Ray Soda) or substitute ginger ale with a pinch of crushed celery seeds
	Celery

1. Juice 1 tablespoon of juice from the lemon; set aside juice. Use the juiced lemon to rub the rim of a tall glass; dip rim into a shallow dish of celery salt. Fill the glass with ice.

2. In a sturdy glass or cocktail shaker use a muddling tool or end of a wooden spoon to crush and stir cherry tomatoes, green and yellow peppers, hot pepper sauce, and reserved lemon juice. Add aquavit and ice; shake well. Strain into prepared glass and top with celery soda. Garnish with a thin slice of celery stalk. Makes 1 cocktail.

EACH COCKTAIL *156 cal, 0 g fat, 0 mg chol, 239 mg sodium, 15 g carb, 2 g fiber, 1 g pro.*

CELERY MARY

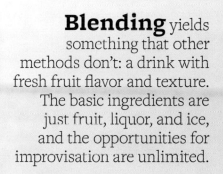

Blending yields something that other methods don't: a drink with fresh fruit flavor and texture. The basic ingredients are just fruit, liquor, and ice, and the opportunities for improvisation are unlimited.

GRILLED PEACH FRAPPÉ

FAST   LOW FAT

Grilled Peach Frappé

"I love rediscovering historic drinks and giving them a modern spin," Steve says. This recipe is based on one in the 1947 booklet "Pick Ups and Cheer Ups" from the Waring Blender. For an alcohol-free drink, substitute orange juice for the Southern Comfort.

PREP 15 min. GRILL 8 to 10 min.

2	fresh peaches, halved
3	oz. Southern Comfort
2	tsp. raw sugar
2	Tbsp. fresh lime
2	Tbsp. fresh lemon
¼	tsp. pure vanilla extract
1	cup ice
	Peach, sliced for garnish

1. Grill peach halves on the rack of an uncovered charcoal grill, directly over medium coals, for 8 to 10 minutes or until tender and lightly browned. Midway through grilling, rotate peaches one-quarter turn to create crosshatch marks, "essential for best flavor," Steve says. (For a gas grill: Preheat grill, then reduce heat to medium. Grill peaches on rack over heat. Cover; grill as above.) Remove from heat; cool. Slip off peach skins, using a peeler if necessary.

2. In a blender container combine peaches and remaining ingredients, except ice. Cover and blend on high for 20 seconds; add ice and blend until smooth. Serve at once in chilled glasses. Top each drink with a slice or two of fresh peach. Makes 4 cocktails.

EACH COCKTAIL *151 cal, 0 g fat, 0 mg chol, 1 mg sodium, 14 g carb, 1 g fiber, 1 g pro.*

Shaking does much more than simply chill the drink. "It incorporates water and softens the alcohol edge; essential for a well-balanced cocktail," Steve says.

STEVE'S MARTINI

`FAST` `LOW FAT`
Steve's Martini

This recipe uses St. Germain, a French liqueur flavored with elderflower blossoms. No St. Germain? Substitute orange liqueur and add 3 dashes of Angostura bitters.
START TO FINISH **10 min.**

¼ cup gin
1 oz. St. Germain liqueur
1 to 2 lime halves
  Lime slices

1. In a cocktail shaker combine gin and liqueur. Squeeze juice from half a lime into shaker; add squeezed lime to shaker. Add 5 ice cubes per drink. Shake well. Strain into a martini glass, garnish with lime slice, and serve. Makes 1 cocktail.
EACH COCKTAIL *217 cal, 0 g fat, 0 mg chol, 1 mg sodium, 13 g carb, 0 g fiber, 0 g pro.*

Meet Steve
Steve McDonagh is a television personality, co-owner of Chicago's Hearty restaurant, and co-author of *Talk with Your Mouth Full*.

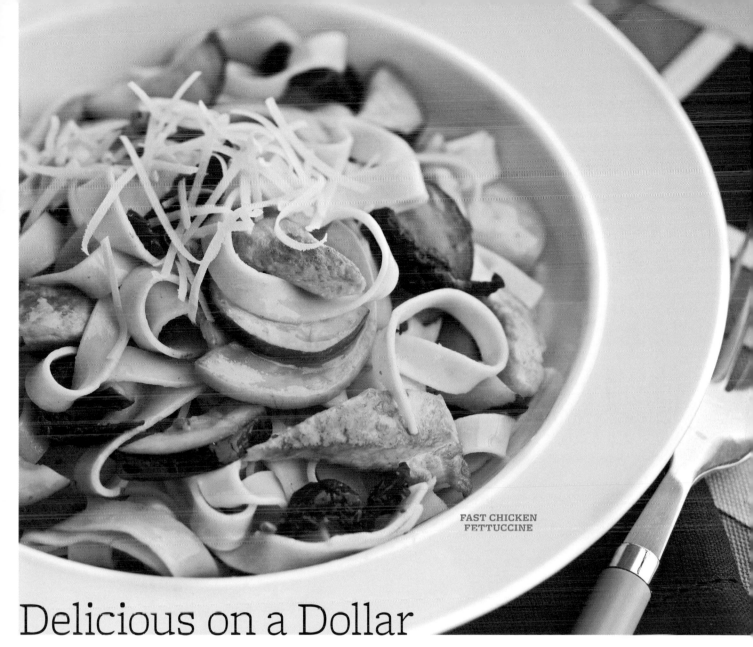

FAST CHICKEN
FETTUCCINE

Delicious on a Dollar

This family meal takes advantage of fresh summer produce to keep costs low.

FAST   KID-FRIENDLY

Fast Chicken Fettuccine

START TO FINISH: 20 min.

8   oz. dried fettuccine
¼   cup oil-packed dried tomato strips
     or pieces
1   large zucchini or yellow summer
     squash, halved lengthwise and sliced
     (about 2 cups)
8   oz. chicken breast meat, cut in cubes
½   cup finely shredded Parmesan,
     Romano, or Asiago cheese (2 oz.)
     Freshly ground black pepper

1. Cook pasta in lightly salted boiling water according to package directions; drain. Return pasta to hot pan.
2. Meanwhile, drain dried tomatoes, reserving 2 tablespoons oil from jar; set aside.
3. In 12-inch skillet heat 1 tablespoon reserved oil over medium-high heat. Add zucchini; cook and stir for 2 to 3 minutes or until crisp-tender. Remove from skillet. Add remaining reserved oil to skillet. Add chicken; cook and stir for 2 to 3 minutes or until no longer pink. Gently toss zucchini, chicken, and tomato with cooked pasta. Sprinkle each serving with cheese. Season to taste with pepper. Makes 4 servings.
EACH SERVING *381 cal, 14 g fat, 40 mg chol, 334 mg sodium, 40 g carb, 3 g fiber, 24 g pro.*

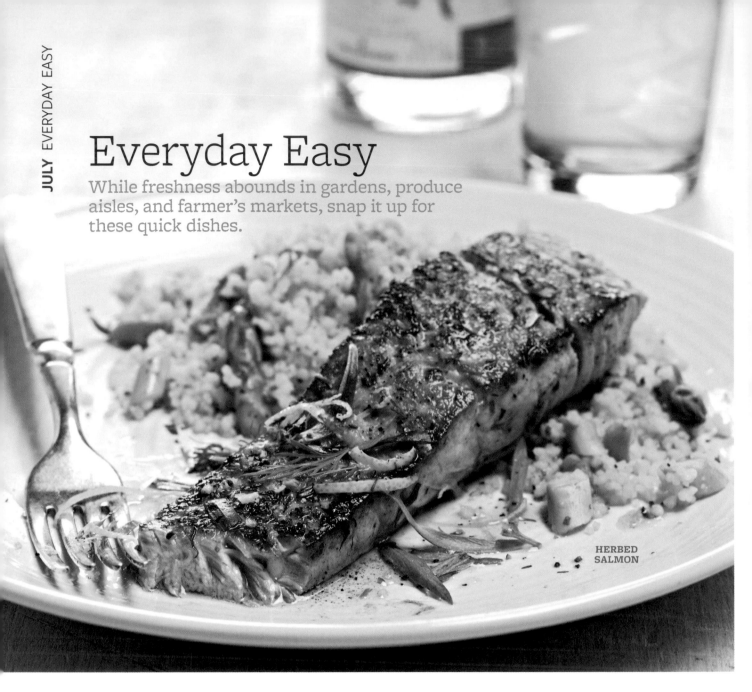

Everyday Easy

While freshness abounds in gardens, produce aisles, and farmer's markets, snap it up for these quick dishes.

HERBED SALMON

FAST

Herbed Salmon

START TO FINISH **16 minutes**
BUDGET **$2.49 per serving**

1   lb. skinless salmon fillet, cut into
    4 portions
1   lemon
1   Tbsp. snipped fresh dillweed
1   Tbsp. snipped fresh tarragon or
    lemon thyme
1   Tbsp. snipped fresh Italian (flat-leaf)
    parsley or bias-sliced chives
½   tsp salt
½   tsp. ground black pepper
2   Tbsp. butter, softened
    Lemon peel and fresh herbs
    (optional)

1. Preheat oven to 350°F. Rinse fish; pat dry. Shred 1 teaspoon of peel from lemon; set aside. Juice half the lemon. In a small bowl combine lemon peel, snipped herbs, salt, pepper, and butter; stir to combine. Spread evenly on the salmon.
2. Heat a 12-inch nonstick oven-going skillet over medium heat. Add salmon, herb side down. Cook 3 minutes or until golden brown. Turn salmon; pour lemon juice over. Place pan in oven and cook 3 to 7 minutes or until salmon flakes easily with a fork.
3. Transfer to serving plates; drizzle with pan juices. If desired, top with additional shredded lemon peel and snipped fresh herbs. Makes 4 servings.
EACH SERVING *294 cal, 21 g fat, 78 mg chol, 400 mg sodium, 3 g carb, 1 g fiber, 24 g pro.*

CHILLED TOMATO
SOUP WITH CORN
BREAD CROUTONS

FIVE-SPICE PORK
KABOBS

FAST **KID-FRIENDLY**

Chilled Tomato Soup with Corn Bread Croutons

START TO FINISH 25 minutes
BUDGET $1.45 per serving

- 1 8.5-oz. pkg. corn muffin mix
- 1 Tbsp. olive oil
- 1 tsp. chili powder
- 2 14.5-oz. cans diced tomatoes with green pepper, celery, and onion
- ½ an English cucumber, seeded and coarsely chopped
- 3 green onions, trimmed and coarsely chopped
- 1 cup ice cubes
- 1 medium avocado, halved, seeded, peeled, and sliced
    Sliced green onion, chopped cucumber, and chili powder (optional)

1. Preheat oven to 400°F. Prepare muffin mix according to package directions. Spread in lightly greased 13×9×2-inch baking pan. Bake 14 minutes or until golden brown and toothpick inserted near center comes out clean. Cool slightly. Cut in 1 inch cubes. Toss with olive oil and chili powder. Place on baking sheet and crisp in oven 5 minutes.
2. Meanwhile, for soup, in a blender combine undrained tomatoes, cucumber, onions, and ice; cover and blend until nearly smooth. Pour soup in bowls; top with avocado and half the croutons (reserve remaining for another use). If desired, sprinkle with additional green onion, cucumber, and chili powder. Drizzle with olive oil. Makes 4 servings.
EACH SERVING *482 cal, 22 g fat, 40 mg chol, 1,061 mg sodium, 66 g carb, 5 g fiber, 9 g pro.*

FAST **LOW FAT** **KID-FRIENDLY**

Five-Spice Pork Kabobs

START TO FINISH 25 minutes
BUDGET $1.96 per serving

- 2 Tbsp. ketchup
- 1 Tbsp. soy sauce
- 2 tsp. packed brown sugar
- 1 tsp. Chinese five-spice powder
- 1½ lb. pork tenderloin
- 8 bamboo or metal skewers (soak bamboo skewers in water to prevent scorching)
- ¼ cup peanuts
- ¼ cup cilantro sprigs
    Lime wedges (optional)

1. Preheat grill. For sauce, in a small bowl combine ketchup, soy sauce, brown sugar, and five-spice powder. For kabobs, trim tenderloin, slice thinly, then thread slices onto skewers. Brush skewered meat with some of the sauce.
2. Grill kabobs directly over medium-hot coals for 3 to 4 minutes. Brush with remaining sauce. Turn kabobs; grill 3 to 4 minutes more or until fully cooked. To serve, sprinkle with peanuts and cilantro. If desired, serve with lime wedges. Makes 4 servings.
EACH SERVING *280 cal, 11 g fat, 111 mg chol, 458 mg sodium, 7 g carb, 1 g fiber, 38 g pro.*

TURKEY, PEAR, AND
CHEESE SALAD

ITALIAN FRIED STEAK WITH
ROASTED PEPPER PESTO

FAST

Turkey, Pear, and Cheese Salad

START TO FINISH 25 minutes
BUDGET $3.17 per serving

1   lb. turkey tenderloin
1   Tbsp. honey mustard
¼   cup olive oil
2   pears, cored (optional) and sliced
4   slices provolone cheese, halved
5   oz. arugula (8 cups)
2   Tbsp. cider vinegar

1. Bias-slice turkey crosswise in eight
1-inch slices. Flatten slightly with palm
of hand, then season with *salt* and *pepper*.
Brush with half the honey mustard.
2. In a 12-inch skillet heat 2 tablespoons
oil over medium-high heat. Cook turkey,
in even layer, in hot oil, for 2 to 3 minutes
on each side or until browned. Layer pears
on turkey; top each with a half slice of
cheese. Reduce heat to medium-low. Cover
and cook 3 to 4 minutes or until cheese is
melted and pears are warm.

3. Divide arugula among dishes; top with
turkey slices. For sauce, whisk remaining
mustard and oil along with the vinegar
into pan juices in skillet; cook 30 seconds.
Drizzle sauce on each serving. Sprinkle with
freshly ground pepper. Makes 4 servings.
EACH SERVING 410 cal, 22 g fat, 90 mg chol,
480 mg sodium, 16 g carb, 3 g fiber, 36 g pro.

FAST   **KID-FRIENDLY**

Italian Fried Steak with Roasted Pepper Pesto

START TO FINISH 30 minutes
BUDGET $3.60 per serving

½   cup seasoned fine dry bread crumbs
½   cup grated Romano or Parmesan
     cheese
1   egg
2   Tbsp. water
1½   lb. beef cubed steak
     Olive oil
1   12-oz. jar roasted red sweet peppers,
     drained
⅔   cup fresh basil leaves

1. In a shallow dish combine crumbs and
half the cheese. In another shallow dish
beat together egg and the water. Cut meat
in 8 equal portions; lightly sprinkle with
salt and *pepper*. Dip in egg mixture, then
crumb mixture; press lightly to coat.
2. In a 12-inch skillet heat 1 tablespoon
olive oil over medium-high heat. Working
in two batches, cook steak, about 5 minutes
per side, adding more oil as needed.
Remove to a serving platter; cover to keep
warm. Carefully wipe skillet clean.
3. Meanwhile, for sauce, in blender or
processor combine drained peppers and
remaining cheese. Process until nearly
smooth. Finely chop ½ cup of the basil; set
aside. Transfer pepper mixture to hot
skillet and heat through. Remove from
heat. Stir in finely chopped basil. Pour
sauce over steaks. Sprinkle remaining
basil. Makes 4 servings.
EACH SERVING 425 cal, 21 g fat, 130 mg
chol, 645 mg sodium, 15 g carb, 2 g fiber,
43 g pro.

Good and Healthy

Blueberries and whole grains make this a nutrition-packed side dish or light lunch.

FAST

Grains and Fruit Summer Salad

START TO FINISH **35 min.**

1	cup lightly packed fresh basil
¼	cup lemon juice
¼	cup olive oil
4	cloves garlic, minced
2	cups cooked grains (quinoa*, wild rice, and/or brown rice)
½	cup sliced green onions
4	cups mixed salad greens (torn Bibb lettuce and/or spring mix)
2	cups blueberries (9–10 oz.)
1	cup cantaloupe cubes
1	cup yellow cherry tomatoes, halved
1	small zucchini, cut lengthwise in narrow ribbons
½	cup walnut pieces, toasted
4	oz. smoked salmon, flaked (optional)
⅓	cup snipped or shredded fresh herbs (dill, basil, and/or mint)

1. For basil dressing, in a blender or small food processor combine the 1 cup basil, lemon juice, olive oil, garlic, ¼ teaspoon *salt*, and ¼ teaspoon *black pepper.* Cover and blend or process until nearly smooth, stopping to scrape down sides as needed; set aside.

2. In a medium bowl stir together cooked grains and green onions. Stir in about 2 tablespoons of the basil dressing to coat.

3. For the salad, line a large bowl with greens. Top greens with grains mixture, blueberries, cantaloupe, tomatoes, zucchini, walnuts, and (if desired) salmon. Drizzle with half the remaining basil dressing; toss gently. Sprinkle with fresh herbs. Pass remaining dressing. Makes 8 side-dish or 4 main-dish servings.

* For 2 cups cooked quinoa, in a fine strainer rinse ½ cup quinoa under cold running water; drain. In a small saucepan combine 1⅓ cups water, the quinoa, and ¼ teaspoon salt. Bring to boiling; reduce heat. Cover and simmer for 15 minutes. Let stand to cool slightly. Drain off remaining liquid. Fluff with a fork.

EACH SIDE-DISH SERVING *207 cal, 13 g fat, 0 mg chol, 91 mg sodium, 21 g carb, 4 g fiber, 5 g pro.*

Sharing Summer

The door is always open at Erin Flynn and Skip Connett's farm. Here, the couple creates welcoming meals with a little help from their friends. See page 129 for recipes featuring their fresh produce.

Who hasn't dreamed of a lifestyle change? Five years ago, Skip Connett and Erin Flynn made their fantasies come true, abandoning successful careers in Atlanta for the farming life. They leased 3 acres, with a century-old yellow farmhouse, on the outskirts of Austin and now supply almost 100 local families with sunflowers, green beans, garlic, peppers, melons, and other crops that thrive despite the region's hailstorms, winds, and sometimes withering heat.

Skip and Erin's customers, shareholders in Green Gate Farms, pay at the beginning of each growing season for weekly portions of the eventual harvest. This creative model of farming, community-supported agriculture (CSA), is sweeping the country. CSA farms number in the thousands—but few CSA farmers take community as literally as Skip and Erin. Many of their shareholder-volunteers have become close friends. One shareholder teaches yoga classes in the hayloft. Others enroll their youngsters in Green Gate's weeklong summer camp, where kids get a taste of rural life—feeding goats and rare-breed chickens. Camp kids work and play alongside Skip and Erin's children, 10-year-old Avery and 9-year-old Ethan.

Opposite: Erin and Skip with kids Ethan and Avery. Above: Ethan plays outdoors with Boo, an Italian Maremma sheepdog mix. For Erin, everything at Green Gate Farms, even setting the table, is about sustainability. She uses vintage tablecloths and hand-me-down dishes and tableware. Angus Morrison provides the evening's sounddtrack on his handmade guitar.

"When I entertain, I rely on the talents of others," says Erin. "I'm blessed with creative family and friends who can make a drink, create an appetizer, or play a guitar."

"All farmers grow food, but not all of them grow community," says Erin, a former public relations professional who invites shareholders to teach canning and pickling classes in the farmhouse kitchen. "We want the farm to take on the colors of our customers."

When friends gather for a weekend dinner on the farm, the menu coalesces almost spontaneously. One local shareholder and talented caterer, Barbara Frisbie, shows up with fresh chickens for roasting and an idea for an orzo salad that she'll make with the farm's fresh herbs and peppers. Angel Young, a former Green Gate farmhand who now produces artisanal ice cream commercially, brings a trio of sorbets made with melons from the farm. Others pitch in to pick and wash salad greens or whisk a dressing.

The relaxed summer evening unfolds with no timetable, no script, just the sound of people enjoying each other's company, conversation, and music. For Skip and Erin, nights like these provide the reward for their risk, and prove the power of local food to nourish connections.

Opposite: Friends of the farm share recipes and ideas for making the most of the week's harvest. Above: Skip's daughter, Alex, takes a break from studies at the University of Texas at Austin to join family and friends. Vintage textiles, waving in the breeze, are used as tablecloths. Refreshing garnet-red Hibiscus Tea, sweetened with honey and scented with cinnamon, helps beat the heat (see page 133 for the recipe).

august

SEASON WIND DOWN The garden overflows with produce these last lazy days of summer. Simply dipped or tossed in a snappy herb dressing, fresh favorites are oh-so-easy to enjoy.

153

158

161

Growing Strong

When Michelle Obama tucked a vegetable garden into the White House lawn, she dreamed of a nation—and its children—embracing fresh, healthy food. Inspired, we packed a picnic of veggie-rich recipes for her and local schoolkids to share. The result? They ate it up.

GARDEN VEGGIE SUBS

Garden Veggie Subs

You can use any kind of whole wheat bread you prefer, but a hot dog bun makes for easy lunch toting. A little of the Fresh Herb Dressing adds extra flavor to the veggies. The dressing is also a fun dipper for the sandwich.

START TO FINISH 30 min.

6 whole wheat hot dog buns
½ cup Creamy Garden Spread, right, or soft-style cream cheese with vegetables
3 Roma tomatoes, thinly sliced
½ medium cucumber, thinly sliced
1 medium sweet pepper, seeded and thinly sliced
3 radishes, thinly sliced
1 cup mixed baby salad greens
   Fresh Herb Dressing (optional)

1. Use a table knife to spread the bottom halves of buns with Creamy Garden Spread. Layer tomatoes, cucumber, pepper, and radishes on spread. Top with salad greens. Drizzle with Fresh Herb Dressing. Add bun tops. Wrap subs in parchment paper; chill until serving time. Makes 6 sandwiches.

EACH SANDWICH *161 cal, 3 g fat, 1 mg chol, 294 mg sodium, 28 g carb, 2 g fiber, 6 g pro*

Fresh Herb Dressing

PREP 10 min.

1 cup orange juice
⅓ cup olive oil
1 Tbsp. cider vinegar
2 Tbsp. snipped fresh Italian parsley, basil, or thyme
2 tsp. yellow mustard
⅛ tsp. ground black pepper

1. In a screw-top jar combine orange juice, olive oil, vinegar, herb, mustard, and pepper. Cover and shake well. Serve immediately or cover and refrigerate up to 3 days. Stir or shake well before using. Makes about 1½ cups dressing.

Raspberry Vinaigrette Prepare as above, except substitute raspberry vinegar and add ¼ cup mashed fresh raspberries.

EACH 1-TABLESPOON SERVING *7 cal, 0 g fat, 0 mg chol, 1 mg sodium, 2 g carb, 0 g fiber, 0 g pro.*

Creamy Garden Spread

START TO FINISH 25 min.

2 6-oz. cartons plain Greek yogurt or 1 recipe Yogurt Cheese
¾ cup shredded carrot
1 tsp. finely shredded lemon peel
2 Tbsp. snipped fresh flat-leaf (Italian) parsley
¼ cup crumbled feta cheese (optional)
¼ tsp. salt (optional)

1. In a small bowl combine yogurt, carrot, lemon peel, parsley, and feta cheese, if using. (If using feta cheese, omit salt.) Cover and chill up to 24 hours. Stir before serving.
2. Use this as a pizza topper, sandwich spread, or veggie dip. Makes 1¾ cups.
Yogurt Cheese Line a yogurt strainer, sieve, or a small colander with three layers of 100%-cotton cheesecloth or a clean paper coffee filter. Suspend lined strainer, sieve, or colander over a bowl. Spoon in one 16-ounce carton plain yogurt. Cover with plastic wrap. Refrigerate at least 24 hours. Remove from refrigerator. Drain and discard liquid. Store, covered, in refrigerator up to 1 week. Makes about 1 cup.

EACH 2-TABLESPOON SERVING *18 cal, 1 g fat, 1 mg chol, 12 mg sodium, 2 g carb, 0 g fiber, 2 g pro.*

Fish Tacos with Melon Salsa

The mild melon salsa makes enough for leftovers. Serve the salsa with tortilla chips, over grilled chicken, or even as a fresh fruit salad.

START TO FINISH 30 min. OVEN 450°F

For Melon Salsa
2 cups cubed seedless cantaloupe, honeydew, and/or watermelon
1 cup chopped, seeded cucumber
½ cup chopped orange or yellow sweet pepper
1 ear fresh sweet corn, cut from the cob, or ½ cup frozen corn, thawed
3 Tbsp. chopped fresh cilantro
1 Tbsp. finely chopped red onion
   Juice of 1 lime (3 tablespoons)
1 Tbsp. honey
For Fish Tacos
12 6-inch corn tortillas
1 lb. fresh or thawed frozen skinless fish fillets, about ½ inch thick (such as tilapia or catfish)
2 Tbsp. olive oil

¾ tsp. chili powder
¼ tsp. salt
¼ tsp. ground cumin
⅛ tsp. garlic powder
2 cups shredded lettuce
1 cup sliced radishes
   Lime wedges

1. For Melon Salsa, in a medium bowl combine the melon, cucumber, sweet pepper, corn, cilantro, and onion. In a small bowl whisk together lime juice and honey, then toss with melon mixture; set aside.
2. Preheat oven to 450°F. Stack tortillas and wrap in foil. Bake for 10 minutes or until heated through.
3. Meanwhile, rinse fish; pat dry. Grease a shallow baking pan. Place fish in a single layer in the pan. Combine olive oil, chili powder, salt, cumin, and garlic powder; brush oil on fish. Bake for 4 to 6 minutes or until fish begins to flake when tested with a fork.
4. Divide fish in 12 portions. Fill tortillas with a portion of fish, lettuce, radishes, and some of the Melon Salsa. Pass remaining Melon Salsa and lime wedges. Cover and refrigerate any remaining salsa up to 2 days. Makes 6 servings (2 tacos).

EACH SERVING *260 cal, 8 g fat, 38 mg chol, 179 mg sodium, 31 g carb, 5 g fiber, 19 g pro.*

FISH TACOS WITH MELON SALSA

FAST LOW FAT KID-FRIENDLY

Chopped Green Salad

Salad has added appeal when served in small cups—no more chasing those veggies around a plate. With the lettuce chopped as well, this dish is super kid-friendly. Before chopping, wash lettuce and remove excess water from the leaves by patting dry with paper towels. Salad dressing clings better to dry lettuce.
START TO FINISH **30 min.**

4   cups chopped spinach and/or romaine
1   small cucumber, seeded and chopped
3   oz. broccoli florets, blanched and shocked*(1 cup)
3   oz. fresh green beans, blanched and shocked*(1½ cups)

¾   cup frozen edamame, thawed
1½   cups halved green grapes
1   recipe Fresh Herb Dressing, page 149, or your favorite dressing
     Lemon wedges (optional)

1. In a large salad bowl combine spinach, cucumber, broccoli, beans, edamame, and grapes. Toss gently to mix. Drizzle about one-third of the Fresh Herb Dressing over vegetables. Toss gently to coat.
2. Serve in small tumblers or cups along with lemon wedges, if desired. Pass remaining dressing. Makes 6 servings.
*Bring a saucepan half filled with water to boiling. Carefully add vegetables and cook for 3 minutes (do not wait for water to return to boiling to begin timing). Drain vegetables in colander then immediately

place in a bowl of ice water to halt cooking. Drain well before using.
Fresh Herb Dressing In a screw-top jar combine 1 cup orange juice, ⅓ cup olive oil; 1 tablespoon cider vinegar; 2 tablespoons snipped parsley, basil, or thyme; 2 teaspoons yellow mustard; and a pinch of black pepper. Cover and shake well. Serve immediately or cover and refrigerate up to 3 days. Just before serving, stir or shake well. Makes about 1½ cups dressing. For raspberry dressing, prepare as above, except substitute raspberry vinegar and add ¼ cup mashed fresh raspberries.
EACH SERVING *119 cal, 6 g fat, 0 mg chol, 32 mg sodium, 15 g carb, 3 g fiber, 4 g pro.*

CHOPPED
GREEN SALAD
WITH FRESH
HERB DRESSING

FAST LOW FAT KID-FRIENDLY
Garden Spaghetti

This dish can be served hot or at room temperature. You will need four ears of fresh corn to equal 2 cups of kernels.
PREP **20 min.** COOK **10 min.**

8   oz. dried multigrain, whole wheat, or regular spaghetti
2   cups small broccoli florets
2   cups fresh or frozen corn kernels
1   cup chopped carrots
2   Roma tomatoes, seeded and chopped
2   Tbsp. snipped fresh oregano or basil
1   tsp. finely shredded lemon peel
2   Tbsp. lemon juice
2   to 3 Tbsp. olive oil
1   recipe Fresh Tomato Sauce, below, or your favorite pasta sauce (optional)
    Lemon wedges (optional)

1. Cook spaghetti, with 1 teaspoon salt added to water, according to package directions. Add broccoli, corn, and carrots the last 3 minutes of pasta cooking time. Drain.
2. Return pasta mixture to pan. Toss in tomatoes, oregano, lemon peel, lemon juice, and enough olive oil to lightly coat ingredients. Serve with Fresh Tomato Sauce and lemon wedges. Makes 6 servings.
EACH SERVING *251 cal, 6 g fat, 0 mg chol, 38 mg sodium, 46 g carb, 7 g fiber, 9 g pro.*

FAST LOW FAT KID-FRIENDLY
Fresh Tomato Sauce
START TO FINISH **15 min.**

3   cups grape or cherry tomatoes, halved
¼   cup finely chopped onion
1   tsp. grated fresh ginger
1   Tbsp. cider vinegar
1   tsp. packed brown sugar

1. Place tomatoes, onion, and ginger in a microwave-safe bowl; sprinkle with vinegar and brown sugar. Cover loosely. Microcook on high (100% power) for 3 minutes or until skins burst and tomatoes are soft, stirring once. Serve warm or chilled. Makes (2½ cups) 5 servings.
EACH SERVING *14 cal, 0 g fat, 0 mg chol, 3 mg sodium, 3 g carb, 1 g fiber, 1 g pro.*

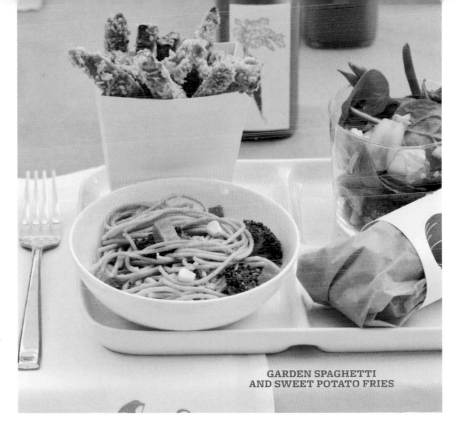

GARDEN SPAGHETTI
AND SWEET POTATO FRIES

KID-FRIENDLY
Sweet Potato Fries

The easy breadcrumb coating adds delicious crispy flavor without frying. Sweet potatoes and carrots are high in vitamin A, potassium, and fiber; either works well in this recipe.
PREP **25 min.** BAKE **20 min.**
OVEN **400°F**

    Olive oil
1   lb. sweet potatoes and/or carrots
2   tsp. olive oil
½   cup white whole wheat flour or all-purpose flour
¼   tsp. salt
2   eggs, lightly beaten
2   Tbsp. water
1   cup fine dry bread crumbs
½   cup grated Parmesan cheese
1   Tbsp. olive oil
1   recipe Baby Tomato Ketchup, right, or your favorite ketchup

1. Preheat oven to 400°F. Lightly brush a 15×10×1-inch baking pan with olive oil. Peel vegetables and cut into narrow 3- to 4-inch-long wedges. Toss vegetables with 2 teaspoons of oil. Place the vegetables on the prepared pan. Roast for 10 minutes. Remove from oven. Transfer vegetables to a tray to cool until they can be handled (about 10 minutes).
2. While vegetables are cooling, in one shallow bowl or pie plate, mix together the flour and salt. In a second dish combine the

eggs and the water. In a third dish combine the bread crumbs and Parmesan cheese.
3. Coat the same pan with 1 tablespoon oil. Dip the cooled vegetables, a few at time, in the flour mixture, then the egg mixture, then the bread crumbs, coating vegetables evenly. Arrange coated vegetables in a single layer in the pan. (You may need to do this step in two batches.)
4. Roast for 15 minutes or until vegetables are brown and crispy. Serve warm with Baby Tomato Ketchup. Makes 6 servings.
EACH SERVING *274 cal, 9 g fat, 76 mg chol, 405 mg sodium, 38 g carb, 4 g fiber, 10 g pro.*

FAST LOW FAT KID-FRIENDLY
Baby Tomato Ketchup
PREP **15 min.** ROAST **30 to 40 min.**
OVEN **400°F**

3   cups grape tomatoes
¼   cup finely chopped onion
1   Tbsp. cider vinegar
2   tsp. packed brown sugar
1   tsp. grated fresh ginger

1. Preheat oven to 400°F. Place all ingredients in a 15×10×1-inch baking pan and toss together. Roast, uncovered, for 30 to 40 minutes or until all tomato skins have burst and most of the liquid has evaporated, stirring every 10 minutes. Place in a food processor. Cover and process until smooth. Makes 1¼ cups.
EACH (1-TABLESPOON) SERVING *7 cal, 0 g fat, 0 mg chol, 1 mg sodium, 2 g carb, 0 g fiber, 0 g pro.*

GARDEN PIZZA
WITH TURKEY
MEATBALLS

I-Made-It-Myself Pizza

Let kids build pizzas to their liking with different sauces and toppers. For individual pizzas, divide the dough into six portions. Place the dough on a lightly floured work surface and use floured fingers to shape it.

PREP 20 min.　REST 10 min.
BAKE 20 min.　OVEN 425°F

2   to 2½ cups white whole wheat flour or all-purpose flour
1   pkg. pizza crust yeast* or quick-rise active dry yeast
1½   tsp. sugar
¾   tsp. salt
1   cup warm water (120°F to 130°F)
3   Tbsp. vegetable oil or olive oil
½   cup whole wheat flour
1   cup Baby Tomato Ketchup, page 151 or Creamy Garden Spread, page 149
1   to 2 cups toppings, such as chopped sweet pepper, chopped fresh spinach, thinly sliced tomatoes, sautéed onion, sautéed zucchini, and/or Mini Turkey Meatballs
1   cup shredded mozzarella cheese, ½ cup grated Parmesan cheese, or 4 oz. fresh mozzarella cheese, sliced

1. In a large mixing bowl combine 1¼ cups of the white whole wheat flour, the yeast, sugar, and salt; add the warm water and oil. Stir until combined, then stir vigorously for 1 minute. Stir in whole wheat flour and ½ cup of the remaining white whole wheat flour. Using a wooden spoon, stir in as much of the remaining flour as you can.
2. Turn dough out onto a lightly floured surface. Knead in enough remaining flour to make a dough that is smooth and elastic (about 4 minutes). Divide dough into 3 equal portions. Cover; let rest for 10 minutes. Preheat oven to 425°F.
3. Press or roll out dough to form 3 oval pizza crusts. Grease two large baking sheets. Transfer dough to baking sheets. Prick crusts with a fork. Bake crusts 8 minutes or until light brown.
4. Spread baked crusts with sauce. Add toppings and cheese. Bake for 12 to 14 minutes more or until bubbly. Makes 6 servings (½ pizza each).
*Pizza crust yeast is specially formulated so no rising time is necessary. Find it in the baking aisle.

EACH SERVING 336 cal, 13 g fat, 15 mg chol, 490 mg sodium, 44 g carb, 6 g fiber, 14 g pro.

Mini Turkey Meatballs

For easy shaping, turn the turkey mixture onto waxed paper, pat it into a 9×8-inch rectangle, then cut 36 equal-size squares. Roll the squares into balls. Or shape meatballs by using a small cookie scoop, occasionally dipping the scoop in water to prevent the meat from sticking. The meatballs can be baked then frozen to use another time.

PREP 30 min.　CHILL 2 hr.　BAKE 8 min.
OVEN 450°F

1   egg
½   cup unsweetened applesauce
½   cup shredded sweet potato or carrot
¼   cup finely chopped green onions
½   tsp. salt
½   tsp. ground black pepper
1   lb. lean ground turkey or beef
½   cup soft whole wheat bread crumbs

1. In a small bowl stir together the egg, applesauce, sweet potato, green onions, salt, and pepper.
2. In a large bowl combine ground turkey and bread crumbs. Fold the egg mixture into turkey mixture; mix well. Cover and refrigerate for 2 to 24 hours (this length of time is important for the bread crumbs to absorb moisture and flavor).
3. Heat oven to 450°F. Shape turkey mixture in ¾-inch diameter balls. Place meatballs on a foil-lined 15×10×1-inch baking pan. Bake for 8 to 10 minutes or until no pink remains (170°F).
4. Serve meatballs with spaghetti and sauce or as a pizza topper. Makes 6 servings.
Make Ahead Prepare a batch of meatballs, bake them all, then freeze some for later. To freeze meatballs, place them in a single layer on a baking sheet. Freeze for several hours, then pack them in resealable freezer bags, squeezing out excess air. Label and date the bags. Use frozen meatballs within 2 months. To serve, heat thawed meatballs in a nonstick skillet over medium heat for 5 to 8 minutes.

EACH SERVING 132 cal, 2 g fat, 72 mg chol, 299 mg sodium, 8 g carb, 1 g fiber, 20 g pro.

MINI TURKEY
MEATBALLS

EASY FRUIT POCKET PIES

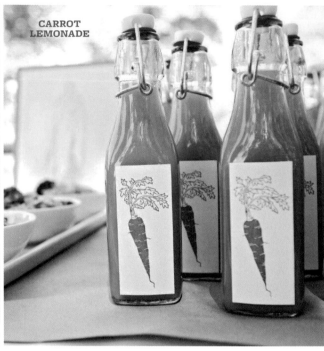

CARROT LEMONADE

KID-FRIENDLY

Easy Fruit Pocket Pies

Select soft whole grain bread for these pies. The moistness of fresh bread works to seal in the fruit. Use a spatula to lift the pies and peek at the undersides—they are done when the bottoms are evenly toasted.
PREP **20 min.** BAKE **18 min.**
COOL **30 min.** OVEN **350°F**

¾ cup fresh raspberries and/or blueberries
2 Tbsp. sugar
¼ tsp. ground cinnamon
6 Tbsp. Smashed Apples, or apple butter
12 slices soft whole grain white or whole wheat bread
¼ cup vegetable oil

1. Preheat oven to 350°F. Wash berries and spread to dry on paper towels. Meanwhile, stir together sugar and cinnamon; set aside.
2. For each pie, spoon 1 tablespoon Smashed Apples in the center of bread slice. Top with 3 to 4 berries and a slice of bread. Gently press top slice around fruit. Trim crusts from bread using a serrated knife.
3. With a fork, press edges of bread together to seal in the filling. Lightly brush the top slice of bread with some of the oil. Pick up each pie and, while holding in your hand, lightly brush the opposite side with oil. Place pies on an ungreased baking sheet. Sprinkle tops with cinnamon-sugar.

4. Bake pies for 18 to 20 minutes or until bread is lightly toasted. Transfer to a cooling rack. Cool at least 30 minutes before serving. Makes 6 servings.
Smashed Apples Peel, core, and slice 4 pounds of apples. Place apples and ½ cup water in a 4- or 5-quart heavy-bottom pan over medium heat. Simmer, covered, for 20 minutes or until apples are very tender. Remove from heat. Mash with a potato masher or blend with an immersion blender. Return to heat. Simmer, uncovered, for 5 minutes or until the fruit thickens and most of the liquid has evaporated, stirring frequently. Transfer to a covered container. Store in the refrigerator up to 2 weeks. Makes 4 cups.
EACH SERVING *278 cal, 11 g fat, 3 mg chol, 251 mg sodium, 40 g carb, 4 g fiber, 6 g pro.*

LOW FAT **KID-FRIENDLY**

Carrot Lemonade

Packed with vitamins A and C, this is a great summertime drink to have on hand.
PREP **15 min.** COOK **30 min.** CHILL **2 hr.**

1 lb. carrots, peeled and cut into chunks
2 cups water
3 cups pineapple juice and/or unsweetened white grape juice
¾ cup lemon juice
   Water
   Ice
   Lemon wedges

1. In a medium saucepan combine carrots and water. Bring to boiling; reduce heat and cover. Simmer for 30 minutes or until very tender. Cool slightly.* Transfer cooled mixture to a blender. Add 1 cup of the pineapple juice. Cover and blend until smooth.
2. Transfer the blended mixture to a pitcher. Stir in remaining pineapple juice and the lemon juice. Cover and refrigerate for 2 to 24 hours (mixture may thicken). If you like, stir in 1 to 2 cups water to reach desired consistency.
3. Serve Carrot Lemonade over ice with lemon wedges. Store, refrigerated, up to one week. Makes 6 servings.
***Note** To blend hot food in a blender or food processor, it's important to let the mixture cool first. Cooling prevents steam from building up, which could cause hot liquid to spurt out the top of the blender.
EACH SERVING *107 cal, 0 g fat, 0 mg chol, 58 mg sodium, 27 g carb, 3 g fiber, 1 g pro.*

Home Cooking

Summer's half over, but the red and yellow show rolls on. Three cooking methods—roasting, melting, and simmering—keep the rave reviews coming all season.

Roasted Tomato-Bread Toss

PREP 20 min.   ROAST 20 min.
OVEN 400°F

2   lb. cherry or grape tomatoes (about 6 cups)
6   cups torn baguette or Italian bread (12 oz.)
2   to 3 Tbsp. olive oil
½   cup pitted Kalamata and/or green olives
2   Tbsp. olive oil
2   Tbsp. balsamic vinegar
4   cloves garlic, minced
½   tsp. kosher salt
½   tsp. freshly ground black pepper

1. Position one oven rack in upper third of oven. Preheat oven to 400°F. Line 15×10×1-inch baking pan with parchment paper. Wash tomatoes; pat dry with paper towels. Arrange tomatoes in single layer in prepared pan. Place bread in large bowl; drizzle 2 to 3 tablespoons oil over pieces. Toss to coat. Arrange bread in single layer on second large baking pan.
2. Roast tomatoes on upper rack and bread on lower rack for 20 to 25 minutes. Roast tomatoes just until skins begin to split and wrinkle, gently stirring once. Roast bread until lightly toasted, stirring once.
3. Transfer bread and olives to tomato pan. Combine remaining 2 tablespoons olive oil, balsamic vinegar, garlic, salt, and pepper; drizzle over tomatoes, olives, and bread. Toss gently; transfer to serving bowl. Makes 8 side-dish servings.
EACH SERVING 215 cal, 10 g fat, 0 mg chol, 494 mg sodium, 28 g carb, 3 g fiber, 5 g pro.

Melted Tomatoes

PREP 15 min. BAKE 1 hr. 30 min.
COOL 15 min. OVEN 300°F

2   lb. medium tomatoes, cut up
    (about 7 cups)
3   Tbsp. olive oil
¼   cup snipped fresh basil
¼   tsp. salt
¼   tsp. ground black pepper
1   recipe Green Onion Chicken, right
    Lemon wedges and fresh basil

1. Preheat oven to 300°F. Place tomatoes in an even layer in a 3-quart baking dish. Drizzle with olive oil, then sprinkle with basil, salt, and pepper. Bake, uncovered, for 1½ to 2 hours or until tomatoes are slightly dried and soft. Cool 15 minutes.
2. To serve, transfer tomatoes to serving platter. Add Green Onion Chicken, lemon wedges, and fresh basil. Makes 4 servings.
EACH SERVING *134 cal, 11 g fat, 0 mg chol, 157 mg sodium, 11 g carb, 3 g fiber, 2 g pro.*

KID-FRIENDLY
Green Onion Chicken

PREP 15 min. CHILL 8 hr.
GRILL 55 min.

4   whole chicken legs (drumstick and
    thigh)
½   cup chopped green onions, white and
    green portions (about 4)
¼   cup olive oil
    Salt and ground black pepper

1. Skin chicken, if desired. In plastic bag set in shallow dish place chicken, green onions, and olive oil. Sprinkle with salt and pepper. Turn chicken to coat in green onions. Cover and refrigerate at least 8 hours.
2. For charcoal grill, arrange medium-hot coals around drip pan. Test for medium heat above pan. Place chicken, bone side down, on grill rack over drip pan. Cover and grill 30 minutes. Turn, then grill 25 to 30 minutes more or until chicken is no longer pink (180°F). (For gas grill, preheat grill. Reduce heat to medium; adjust for indirect cooking. Grill as above.) Makes 4 to 6 servings.
EACH SERVING *436 cal, 34 g fat, 139 mg chol, 280 mg sodium, 1 g carb, 0 g fiber, 31 g pro.*

Melted Slow, low-temp baking intensifies the flavor of tomatoes. Use this method to rescue tomatoes that come off the vine a little under- or over-ripe.

FAST **KID-FRIENDLY**

Quick Paprika Steaks with Tomato Gravy

START TO FINISH 25 min.

For steaks

1	Tbsp. olive oil
¼	cup all-purpose flour
1	tsp. paprika
½	tsp. salt
¼	to ½ tsp. ground black pepper
4	4-oz. beef breakfast or skillet steaks, about ½ inch thick
2	oz. queso fresco or Monterey Jack cheese, thinly sliced
	Arugula

For Tomato Gravy

6	medium tomatoes, seeded and cut up
6	cloves garlic, chopped
2	Tbsp. olive oil
1	to 2 Tbsp. snipped fresh sage
¼	tsp. salt
½	tsp. ground black pepper

1. For steaks, in a 12-inch skillet heat oil over medium-high heat. Reduce heat to medium. In a shallow dish combine flour, paprika, salt, and pepper. Dredge steaks in flour mixture (reserve any remaining flour mixture). Cook steaks, uncovered, in hot oil 4 to 5 minutes per side or until medium doneness (160°F); top with cheese the last 2 minutes of cooking. Set aside; keep warm.
2. While steaks are cooking, for Tomato Gravy, place tomatoes in food processor. Cover and pulse, with several on-off turns, until tomatoes are coarsely chopped.
3. In the same skillet cook and stir garlic in the 2 tablespoons oil over medium heat about 1 minute or until garlic is golden. Stir in tomatoes, snipped sage, reserved flour mixture, salt, and pepper. Bring mixture to boiling, reduce heat and simmer, uncovered, about 5 minutes or until desired consistency. To serve, place a small handful of arugula leaves on each plate, top with a steak, then ladle over some of the Tomato Gravy; pass any remaining gravy. Makes 4 servings.

EACH SERVING *310 cal, 16 g fat, 67 mg chol, 551 mg sodium, 16 g carb, 3 g fiber, 26 g pro.*

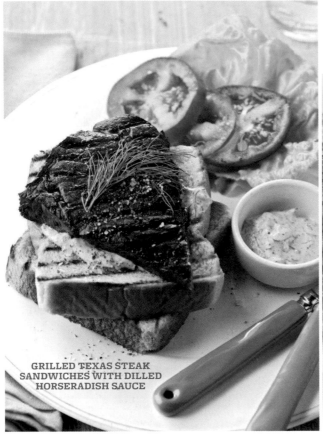

GRILLED TEXAS STEAK
SANDWICHES WITH DILLED
HORSERADISH SAUCE

CORN AND BEAN
FRITTERS WITH
TOMATOES

FAST

Grilled Texas Steak Sandwiches with Dilled Horseradish Sauce

START TO FINISH 20 minutes
BUDGET $2.87 per serving

2   10-oz. top round steaks
    Olive oil
    Salt and freshly ground black pepper
¼   cup sour cream
2   to 3 Tbsp. horseradish mustard
1   Tbsp. snipped fresh dill
4   to 8 thick slices of bread (for Texas toast)
    Fresh dill sprigs

1. Preheat grill. Trim any fat from steaks; halve steaks crosswise. Lightly brush steaks with oil and sprinkle with salt and pepper. Grill directly over medium heat for 3 to 4 minutes per side or until desired doneness.
2. Meanwhile, for horseradish sauce, in a small bowl combine the sour cream, horseradish mustard, and dill; set aside.

3. Remove steaks to platter. Lightly brush each side of the bread with olive oil. Grill bread 1 minute per side. Serve steaks on grilled toast with horseradish sauce. Top with dill and additional salt and pepper. Makes 4 servings.
EACH SERVING *434 cal, 25 g fat, 71 mg chol, 485 mg sodium, 21 g carb, 1 g fiber, 33 g pro.*

FAST   **LOW FAT**

Corn and Bean Fritters with Tomatoes

START TO FINISH 30 minutes
BUDGET $1.85 per serving

4   ears fresh sweet corn or 2 cups frozen whole kernel corn, thawed
1   lb. grape or cherry tomatoes
1   Tbsp. vinegar
1   15.5-oz. can butter beans, rinsed and drained
1   6-oz. pkg. Southern-style corn bread mix
1   egg
1   tsp. ground ancho chili or chili powder

    Olive oil
    Fresh Italian (flat-leaf) parsley or cilantro leaves (optional)

1. If using fresh corn, cut kernels from cobs; set aside.
2. Meanwhile, coarsely chop, halve, and/or slice tomatoes. In a small saucepan combine tomatoes, vinegar, ½ teaspoon *salt*, and ¼ cup *water*. Cook, covered, over medium-low heat, stirring occasionally. For fritter batter, in a large bowl mash beans with a fork. Add corn, corn bread mix, egg, ground chili, ½ teaspoon *salt*, and ½ cup *water*; stir to combine.
3. Heat a large griddle or 12-inch skillet over medium heat. Add 1 teaspoon oil. Drop four ½-cup scoops of batter on griddle at a time. Cook 4 minutes per side. Serve fritters with warm tomatoes and parsley and/or cilantro. Makes 4 servings.
EACH SERVING *384 cal, 11 g fat, 75 mg chol, 1,574 mg sodium, 65 g carb, 10 g fiber, 14 g pro.*

Delicious on a Dollar

A cool, colorful dessert doesn't have to be expensive or hard to make.

Fat-Free Watermelon Sherbet

PREP **25 min.** FREEZE **8 hr.**

5   cups cubed, seeded watermelon
½   cup sugar
1   envelope unflavored gelatin
⅓   cup cranberry juice

1. Place watermelon cubes in a blender or food processor. Cover and blend or process until smooth. (You should have about 3 cups) Stir in sugar.

2. In a small saucepan combine the gelatin and cranberry juice. Let mixture stand for 5 minutes. Stir mixture over low heat until gelatin is dissolved.

3. Stir the gelatin mixture into the pureed melon. Pour into an 8×8×2-inch baking pan. Cover and freeze about 2 hours or until firm.

4. Break up frozen sherbet and place in a chilled mixer bowl. Beat with a mixer on medium to high speed until sherbet is fluffy. Return to pan. Cover and freeze about 6 hours or until firm.

5. To serve, let stand at room temperature for 5 minutes before scooping. Makes 8 (½-cup) servings.

EACH SERVING *83 cal, 0 g fat, 0 mg chol, 3 mg sodium, 20 g carb, 0 g fiber, 1 g pro.*

FAT-FREE WATERMELON SHERBET

food life

IDEAS AND INSPIRATION FOR SHARING TIME AROUND THE TABLE

The White House Garden

Even before moving into the White House, Michelle Obama envisioned a garden to demonstrate how fresh food can play a stronger role in Americans' lives. But there was a good precedent: Eleanor Roosevelt's Vistory Garden.

On the lush green lawn of the White House, Michelle Obama grins at the exuberant fifth-graders from Harriet Tubman Elementary—all members of the school's garden club—and asks, "Do you like vegetables?" "Yes!" they reply in unison. "What's your favorite food on the picnic table?" The response is comically predictable. "The fries have it," the First Lady says with a laugh. Then she seizes the teachable moment. "They're not even fried. They're baked," she says. "I love fries. But do you know how much sugar there is in ketchup?"

It's not easy to change the way children eat—

even this group of veggie-savvy kids who joined her this day for a tasting party of garden-fresh recipes. Mrs. Obama has made it her mission to champion healthy living through her Let's Move exercise campaign and, in the backyard of the White House, the vegetable garden that inspired this summer picnic. This two-year effort has had laudable successes and unanticipated side effects. The First Lady faced vocal opposition at home (daughter Malia "was not happy about the fact that we were going to have a beehive—she's terrified of bees"). She also discovered just how influential she can be (convincing Walmart to

A few steps from the White House vegetable garden, fifth-graders from the garden club at Harriet Tubman Elementary School in Washington, D.C., join Michelle Obama for a "tasting picnic," *above.* **The lunch,** *opposite,* **is lined up for the kids' inspection: Recipes created by** *Better Homes and Gardens* **play off perennial favorites—spaghetti, lemonade, sub sandwiches—yet are packed with vegetables. The hands-down favorite? Sweet potato fries, with carrot lemonade coming in second.**

"You can't say to kids, 'you can never have a cookie —you can never have anything fun'," Michelle Obama says. "There's a way to [promote a healthy life] and to do it in a way that is tasty and fun."

offer healthier items, the Treasury Department to use tax incentives to entice grocery stories to inner cities, and cooking professionals to partner with local schools as part of the Chefs Move to Schools program).

Federal policy and corporate good citizenship matter; still, Michelle Obama knows that what happens on the home front is key to shaping children's attitudes and appetites. She sympathizes with working parents who do not spend much time analyzing their children's eating habits, because until recently, she was one of them. "I had two little kids; I was busy," she says. "We had take-out at least three times a week. I didn't realize that these habits were affecting my kids' health. It was just what I felt I had to do to survive and keep the household going."

Then a pediatrician noticed her daughters were gaining a bit more weight than was healthy. So she eliminated juice boxes and served lighter dishes such as baked chicken. "Children don't have control over their diet—we do," says Mrs. Obama.

A toast to tomatoes—and carrots, lettuce, and zucchini. The Tubman fifth-graders are already veggie-savvy; Maria De La Rosa (*lower left, in blue*) has remade a corner of her grandmother's yard into a garden plot. (Maria's favorite dish? The Chopped Green Salad.)

TAMALE PIES

COCONUT-POACHED MAHI MAHI

Tamale Pies

START TO FINISH 30 minutes
BUDGET $2.35 per serving

1 lb. ground beef
1 lb. tomatoes, chopped
½ cup pitted olives (such as green, ripe, Kalamata, and/or Niçoise), coarsely chopped
½ tsp. each salt and ground black pepper
1 8½-oz. pkg. corn muffin mix
½ cup shredded cheddar cheese (2 oz.)
   Pitted olives, coarsely chopped tomatoes, and cilantro leaves (optional)

1. Preheat oven to 425°F. In 12-inch skillet cook beef until browned. Drain off fat. Add chopped tomatoes, olives, ¼ cup *water*, salt, and pepper. Cook, stirring occasionally, until heated through.
2. Prepare corn muffin mix according to package directions. Divide hot ground beef among four 12- to 16-oz. casserole dishes.

Top with muffin mix; sprinkle with cheddar cheese.
3. Bake 15 to 17 minutes or until topping is lightly golden and cooked through. Top with olives, tomatoes, and cilantro. Makes 4 servings.

EACH SERVING *384 cal, 11 g fat, 75 mg chol, 1,574 mg sodium, 65 g carb, 10 g fiber, 14 g pro.*

Coconut-Poached Mahi Mahi

START TO FINISH 20 minutes
BUDGET $2.56 per serving

1 small lime
1 15-oz. can light coconut milk
1 Thai green chile, thinly sliced
1 Tbsp. sugar
1 lb. skinless, boneless mahi mahi or other firm whitefish fillets
1 tsp. salt
1 small head bok choy, torn (about 3 cups)
   Crystallized ginger, green chiles (optional)

1. Finely shred peel from lime, then juice the lime. Set aside peel. In a large saucepan over medium heat combine lime juice, coconut milk, green chile, and sugar.
2. Cut fish in 8 portions; rinse and pat dry with paper towels. Rub salt onto fish portions, then place in coconut milk mixture. Cook fish, covered, for 5 minutes. Uncover; gently stir in bok choy. Cook for 3 to 5 minutes more or until fish flakes easily when tested with a fork. Ladle fish with cooking liquid into bowls. Top with lime peel and, if desired, ginger and green chiles. Makes 4 servings.

EACH SERVING *189 cal, 7 g fat, 83 mg chol, 744 mg sodium, 10 g carb, 1 g fiber, 22 g pro.*

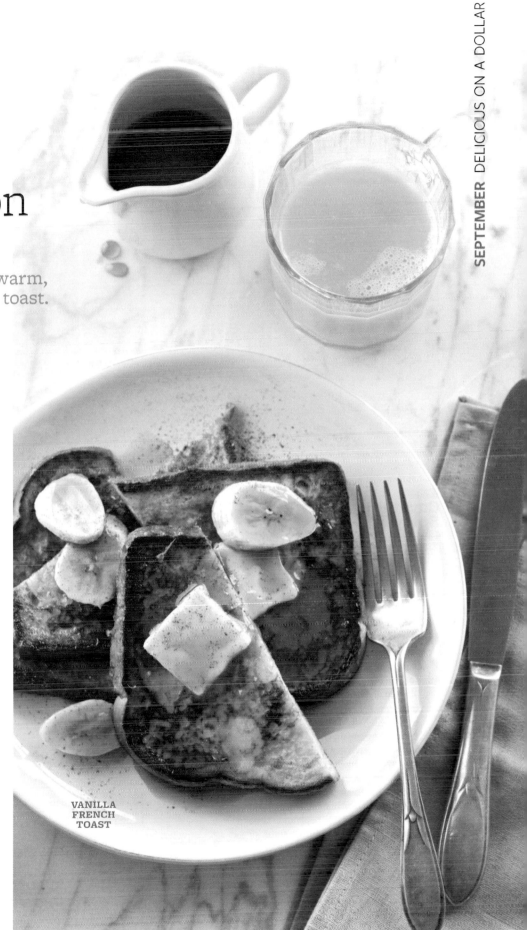

Delicious on a Dollar

Turn leftover bread into warm, sweet, and crispy French toast.

FAST   **LOW FAT**   **KID-FRIENDLY**

Vanilla French Toast

PREP 10 min.   COOK 4 min. per slice

- 4 eggs, lightly beaten
- 1 cup half-and-half or milk
- 2 Tbsp. sugar
- 2 tsp. vanilla
- 1 tsp. cinnamon
- ¼ tsp. nutmeg
- 8 slices dry white or whole wheat bread
- 2 Tbsp. butter or vegetable oil
- Butter
- Maple syrup
- Banana slices
- Ground cinnamon

1. In a shallow bowl beat together eggs, milk, sugar, vanilla, cinnamon, and nutmeg. Dip bread slices into egg mixture, coating both sides.

2. Preheat oven to 200°F. Place a plate or serving platter in the oven. In a 12-inch skillet or on a griddle melt 1 tablespoon of the butter over medium heat and spread over cooking surface. Add half the bread slices and cook for 4 to 6 minutes or until golden, turning once. Transfer slices to oven to keep warm. Repeat with remaining butter and bread. Serve with additional butter, maple syrup, and banana slices. Sprinkle with cinnamon. Makes 4 (2-slice) servings.

EACH SERVING 472 cal, 20 g fat, 249 mg chol, 421 mg sodium, 62 g carb, 2 g fiber, 14 g pro.

VANILLA
FRENCH
TOAST

Chili Season

The snap in the air means it's time for tailgating, apple-picking, or an evening in front of a fire—all made cozier with a bowl of chili. We simmer up flavorful recipes to suit any autumn occasion.

FAST **KID-FRIENDLY**
Beef and Bean Chili

Jalapeños vary in heat, depending on season and locale. Adjust the amount used to suit your taste.

PREP 30 min. **COOK** 20 min.

2 lb. lean ground beef
2 large onions, chopped (2 cups)
6 cloves garlic, minced
2 to 4 jalapeño peppers, seeded and finely chopped (see note, page 11)
2 Tbsp. chili powder
2 tsp. ground cumin
1 15-oz. can tomato sauce
3 15- to 16-oz. cans kidney beans, rinsed and drained
1 oz. semisweet chocolate, chopped
¼ cup chopped fresh cilantro
   Corn chips

1. In Dutch oven brown beef over medium heat; drain off fat. Add onions, garlic, and peppers; cook about 5 minutes, until almost tender. Add chili powder and cumin; cook 1 minute, until fragrant. Add tomato sauce and 2 cups *water*; bring to boiling. Reduce heat to medium-low. Simmer, covered, for 10 minutes.
2. Mash one of the cans of beans. Stir all beans into chili. Return to simmer; cook about 5 minutes. Remove from heat. Stir in chocolate until melted. Stir in ½ tsp. *salt* and the cilantro. Top with corn chips. Makes 8 servings.

EACH SERVING *389 cal, 22 g fat, 85 mg chol, 370 mg sodium, 20 g carb, 6 g fiber, 28 g pro.*

BEEF AND BEAN CHILI

TWO TOMATO
STEW CHILI

TEXAS RED
CHILI

Two-Tomato Stew Chili

Dried tomatoes add rich tomato taste. A little of the oil from the tomatoes is used while browning the beef for another layer of flavor.
PREP **30 min.** COOK **1 hr.**

1   8- to 8.5-oz. jar oil-packed dried tomatoes
2   lb. beef chuck, cut in 1-inch cubes
3   cups chopped onions
6   cloves garlic, minced
2   red sweet peppers, chopped
2   green sweet peppers, chopped
2   medium carrots, coarsely chopped
½   cup golden raisins
4   tsp. ground cumin
½   to 1 tsp. crushed red pepper
1   4.5-oz. can diced green chiles
1   28-oz. can crushed tomatoes
8   oz. smoked mozzarella, shredded
    Sliced dried tomatoes (optional)
    Toasted baguette slices (optional)

1. Drain tomatoes, reserving 2 tablespoons oil. Chop tomatoes; set aside. In a Dutch oven heat the reserved oil over medium-high. Brown half the beef at a time in the hot oil.
2. Return all meat to pan. Add onions, garlic, sweet peppers, and carrots; cook 2 minutes. Stir in chopped dried tomatoes, raisins, cumin, and crushed red pepper; cook 2 minutes. Stir in undrained green

chiles; cook 1 minute. Add crushed tomatoes and 2 cups water; bring to boiling. Reduce heat to medium. Simmer, covered, 1 to 1¼ hours, stirring occasionally, until meat is tender. Remove from heat. Add ¼ teaspoon each salt and pepper. Top with mozzarella and sliced dried tomatoes, if desired. Serve with baguette slices. Makes 8 servings.
EACH SERVING *429 cal, 18 g fat, 82 mg chol, 676 mg sodium, 36 g carb, 7 g fiber, 34 g pro.*

Texas Red Chili

Meat lovers will get their fix with this chili made with beef and bacon. And in traditional Texas fashion—no beans allowed.
PREP **40 min.** COOK **30 min.**

3   dried guajillo or pasilla chiles (see note, page 11)
2   dried ancho chiles
2   lb. 85% lean ground beef
6   slices thick-cut smoked bacon, cut in ½-inch pieces (8 oz.)
3   large Vidalia or other sweet onions, chopped
2   green sweet peppers, chopped
2   serrano peppers, finely chopped
8   cloves garlic, minced
2   Tbsp. chili powder
2   tsp. ground cumin
1   28-oz. can diced tomatoes
1   Tbsp. lime juice or cider vinegar
    Cheddar cheese wedges and sliced green onions (optional)

1. In a large skillet over medium heat cook guajillo and ancho chiles 3 to 4 minutes, turning occasionally, until toasted. Cool; remove and discard stems and seeds. Transfer to bowl; cover with boiling water. Let stand 20 minutes. Drain, reserving ⅓ cup soaking liquid. In a blender puree chiles and liquid; set aside.
2. In a 5- to 6-quart Dutch oven over medium-high heat cook beef about 8 minutes, until beginning to brown. Drain off fat; transfer beef to a bowl.
3. In the same pan cook bacon 5 to 6 minutes, stirring occasionally, until browned. Stir in onions, sweet and serrano peppers, and garlic. Cook 7 minutes, stirring occasionally. Add pureed chiles; cook and stir 3 minutes. Add chili powder and cumin; cook and stir 1 minute. Add reserved beef, undrained tomatoes, and 1 cup *water.* Bring to boiling; reduce heat to medium-low. Simmer, covered, 30 minutes.
4. Remove from heat; stir in lime juice and ¼ teaspoon *salt.* Top with cheese and onions. Makes 8 servings.
EACH SERVING *573 cal, 27 g fat, 77 mg chol, 961 mg sodium, 55 g carb, 13 g fiber, 36 g pro.*

FAST

Cajun Snapper with Red Beans and Rice

START TO FINISH 25 minutes
BUDGET $3.55 per serving

2   frankfurters, chopped
1   8.8-oz. pkg. fully cooked rice
1   Tbsp. salt-free Cajun seasoning
1   15- to 16-oz. can red beans, rinsed and drained
    Bottled hot pepper sauce (optional)
1   lb. red snapper fillet, cut in 4 pieces
2   Tbsp. butter
2   Tbsp. all-purpose flour
    Fresh Italian (flat-leaf) parsley (optional)

1. In a medium saucepan cook frankfurters over medium heat for 2 to 3 minutes. Stir in rice, ½ cup *water*, and 1 teaspoon of the Cajun seasoning. Stir in beans and a dash of bottled hot pepper sauce. Cover; cook over medium-low heat for 15 minutes.
2. Meanwhile, rinse fish; pat dry. In a 12-inch skillet, melt butter over medium heat. In a shallow dish combine flour and remaining Cajun seasoning. Press top side of fish into flour mixture, then place fish, skin side down, in hot butter. Cook 3 to 5 minutes or until skin is crisp. Carefully turn using a spatula; cook fish 3 to 5 minutes more or until it flakes easily with a fork.
3. Serve fish over rice and beans. Snip fresh parsley over top. Makes 4 servings.
EACH SERVING *438 cal, 16 g fat, 69 mg chol, 544 mg sodium, 41 g carb, 6 g fiber, 36 g pro.*

FAST

Smoky Chicken Pizzas

START TO FINISH 30 minutes
BUDGET $3.50 per serving

1   large red onion, thinly sliced
¼   cup olive oil
½   tsp. crushed red pepper
4   individual-size packaged baked pizza crusts or flatbreads
12 oz. fully cooked chicken, shredded
4   oz. smoked mozzarella, shredded
1   cup arugula
    Crushed red pepper

1. Preheat oven to 425°F. In a large skillet cook onion in 1 tablespoon hot oil over medium heat for 10 minutes, stirring occasionally. Set aside.
2. Combine remaining oil and crushed red pepper; drizzle some on pizza crusts. Place on very large baking sheet(s). Top crusts with chicken, onions and cheese. Bake for 10 minutes or until cheese is melted and pizzas are heated through. Top with greens; drizzle any remaining oil and sprinkle additional crushed red pepper. Makes 4 servings.
EACH SERVING *783 cal, 36 g fat, 98 mg chol, 1,074 mg sodium, 69 g carb, 3 g fiber, 46 g pro.*

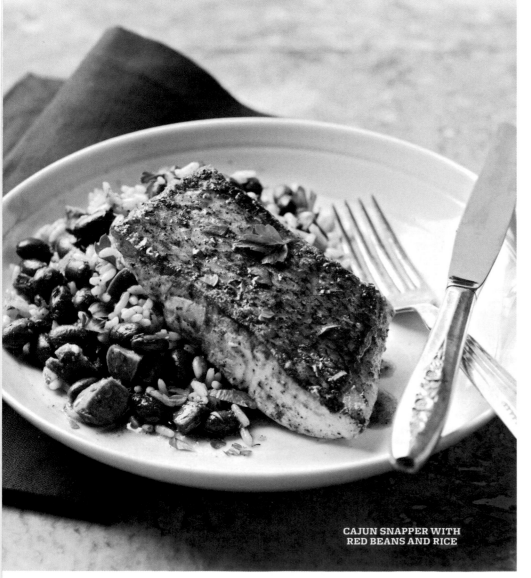

CAJUN SNAPPER WITH RED BEANS AND RICE

SMOKY CHICKEN
PIZZAS

Home Cooking

Any way you cook them, sweet potatoes deliver a wealth of nutrition, flavor, and color.

ROASTED SWEETS AND GREENS

ROASTED SWEETS and Greens

PREP 10 min. ROAST 35 min. OVEN 400°F

1½ to 2 lb. sweet potatoes, scrubbed
1 Tbsp. olive oil
½ tsp. salt
¼ tsp. ground black pepper
2 garlic cloves, sliced or minced
¼ cup chopped hazelnuts
2 cups arugula
¼ cup cider vinegar

1. Preheat oven to 400°F. Cut sweet potatoes in half lengthwise, then cut in wedges. Place on a large rimmed baking sheet. Toss with oil and season with salt and pepper.
2. Roast in oven for 15 minutes, toss, then roast 15 minutes more or until tender. Sprinkle with chopped garlic and hazelnuts. Return to oven for 5 minutes more or until nuts are toasted and garlic is softened. Remove from oven and sprinkle with arugula and vinegar.

EACH SERVING *236 cal, 9 g fat, 0 mg chol, 387 mg sodium, 37 g carb, 6 g fiber, 4 g pro.*

Sweet potato or yam?

The terms may be used interchangeably, but a true yam is quite different from a sweet potato. Yams have brownish barklike skin and off-white or white flesh. They're also sweeter and can grow to be much larger than sweet potatoes. The sweet potato (sometimes labeled as "yam") found in most supermarkets has orange to reddish skin with orange sweet flesh and a moist texture. Varieties with thin, pale yellow skin and yellow flesh tend to be less sweet and have a crumbly texture.

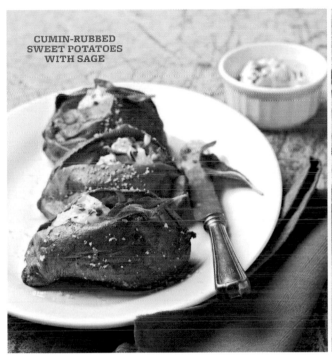

CUMIN-RUBBED
SWEET POTATOES
WITH SAGE

CANDIED SWEET
POTATO PIE

Cumin-Rubbed Sweet Potatoes with Sage

The spiced butter makes enough for leftovers and is a zesty topper for pork or rice. To store, place the log in a freezer bag and freeze up to 6 months. Cut off slices as needed.

PREP 25 min. ROAST 1 hr.
COOL 5 min. OVEN 375°F

4   medium sweet potatoes
2   Tbsp. coarse salt
1   Tbsp. cumin seeds, crushed
1   stick butter, softened
1   Tbsp. maple syrup or honey
1   tsp. crushed red pepper flakes
    Canola or peanut oil for frying
    Fresh sage leaves (about a dozen)

1. Preheat oven to 375°F. Wash and scrub potatoes. Mix together salt and cumin seeds. While skins are still damp, rub all over with salt mixture (reserve any remaining salt mixture for another use). Bake directly on oven rack 1 hour, turning once to crisp evenly on all sides.
2. Meanwhile, for spiced butter, in a bowl stir together softened butter, maple syrup, and crushed red pepper. Roll into a log using waxed paper; chill.
3. Heat 3 inches of oil in a medium saucepan over medium heat. Fry sage leaves 2 minutes or until crisp. Drain on paper towels.

4. Cool potatoes 5 minutes. If desired brush off some of the salt from the skins. With a sharp knife, slice open lengthwise. Push the ends toward the center to open each potato. Top with about 1 tablespoon of spiced butter and a few sage leaves.
EACH SERVING 278 cal, 19 g fat, 31 mg chol, 527 mg sodium, 26 g carb, 4 g fiber, 3 g pro.

Candied Sweet Potato Pie

Cooking the sweet potatoes in a skillet before adding to the pie shell helps them caramelize.

PREP 45 min. BAKE 15 min.
OVEN 450°F/425°F

1   recipe Pecan Piecrust, or 1 rolled
    refrigerated unbaked piecrust
1   small lemon
¼   cup butter
2   lb. sweet potatoes, peeled and
    sliced ¼ inch thick
½   cup sugar
½   cup pecan halves
⅛   tsp. ground nutmeg
    Whipped cream (optional)

1. Prepare Pecan Piecrust; chill. Finely shred peel from lemon. Set aside. Meanwhile, prepare candied sweet potatoes. In a straight-sided 12-inch skillet melt butter. Add sweet potatoes and stir to coat in butter. Cook 1 minute over medium heat.

2. Sprinkle with sugar and lift and fold potatoes to coat and dissolve sugar. Cook 5 to 8 minutes more or until caramelized and syrupy, stirring occasionally (take care not to stir too often so sweet potato slices can brown and caramelize). Stir in pecans, lemon peel, and nutmeg. Turn off heat; cool.
3. Meanwhile, preheat oven to 450°F. Roll Pecan Piecrust to 12-inch circle. Fit into a 9-inch pie plate. Trim crust and crimp as desired. Layer with a double thickness of foil; bake 8 minutes. Remove foil; bake 5 minutes more or until golden. Reduce oven to 425°F.
4. Carefully layer potatoes in piecrust (reserve syrup left in skillet). Bake 15 to 20 minutes or until crust is golden and sweet potatoes are tender. Cool about 15 minutes.
5. Brush top of pie with reserved syrup. Serve with whipped cream sprinkled with additional nutmeg. Makes 8 servings.
Pecan Piecrust In a large bowl combine 1 cup all-purpose flour, ¼ cup ground pecans, and ½ teaspoon salt. Cut in ¼ cup butter or shortening until peasize. Add ¼ to ⅓ cup cold water, 1 tablespoon at a time, mixing with a fork until all is moistened. Chill 30 minutes.
EACH SERVING 340 cal, 18 g fat, 23 mg chol, 232 mg sodium, 42 g carb, 4 g fiber, 4 g pro.

Sweet Potato Salad with Ham

PREP 30 min. COOK 10 min.

2   lb. sweet potatoes, peeled and sliced
8   tender young carrots with tops, scrubbed or peeled and halved lengthwise
½   small red onion, sliced and separated into half rings
¼   cup olive oil
2   Tbsp. white wine vinegar
1   Tbsp. stone ground Dijon-style mustard or Dijon-style mustard
1   tsp. snipped fresh thyme
6   oz. ham, coarsely chopped
2   oz. blue cheese, crumbled
    Fresh thyme sprig (optional)

1. Place sweet potatoes and carrots in a steamer basket. Cover and steam vegetables over simmering water for 10 minutes or until tender, adding the onion during the last 1 minute of steaming. Cool.
2. Meanwhile, for dressing, in a screw-top jar with a tight-fitting lid combine olive oil, vinegar, mustard, ⅛ each teaspoon *salt* and *ground black pepper*. Replace the lid, then shake well to combine.
3. Place cooled potatoes, carrots, and onion in a salad bowl. Gently fold in snipped fresh thyme. Top with ham and cheese. Drizzle with dressing; top with thyme sprig. Makes 6 main-dish servings.
EACH SERVING *278 cal, 13 g fat, 20 mg chol, 657 mg sodium, 31 g carb, 6 g fiber, 10 g pro.*

KID-FRIENDLY

Shoestring Sweet Potatoes and Beets

PREP 30 min. COOK 2 min. per batch

2   small sweet potatoes
1   medium beet
1   tsp. coarse salt
    Vegetable oil for deep-frying
    Thyme sprigs with tender stems* (optional)
    Coarse salt (optional)

1. Peel sweet potatoes and beets. Cut lengthwise into long narrow strips. Place each vegetable in separate bowls; toss each with ½ teaspoon coarse salt.

2. In a 4-quart Dutch oven or deep-fryer heat 2 to 3 inches of oil to 365°F. To prevent splattering, spread beet strips on a paper towel and pat dry. Carefully add beet strips and potatoes, about one-fourth at a time, to the hot oil. Fry about 2 minutes per batch or until crisp and golden brown, stirring gently once or twice. Using a slotted spoon, carefully remove fries from hot oil to paper towels to drain. If desired, add thyme sprigs to hot oil with the vegetables (CAUTION: thyme sprigs will spatter briefly when added to the oil.) Transfer to platter; sprinkle with additional coarse salt, if desired. Makes 8 rounded ½ cup servings.
EACH SERVING *203 cal, 20 g fat, 0 mg chol, 261 mg sodium, 5 g carb, 1 g fiber, 0 g pro.*

SWEET POTATO SALAD
WITH HAM

> ## "This is the kind of cake that will have you sneaking back to the kitchen for more."
>
> Scott Peacock

Caramel Glaze

8. In a medium skillet melt 6 tablespoons unsalted butter. Add ⅓ cup packed dark brown sugar, ⅓ cup packed light brown sugar, ½ cup whipping cream, and a pinch of salt (photo 6).

9. Cook and stir over medium-low heat for 2 minutes, until blended. Increase heat and boil for 2 minutes or until dime-size bubbles cover the surface of glaze (photo 7).

10. Remove from heat and cool until glaze begins to thicken, about 5 minutes (photo 8).

11. Spoon glaze over cake (photo 9). Makes 16 servings.

EACH SERVING *568 cal, 35 g fat, 61 mg chol, 256 mg sodium, 62 g carb, 2 g fiber, 5 g pro.*

Delicious on a Dollar

Combining the best of two Mexican-restaurant favorites, this appetizer makes it easy to entertain on a budget.

FAST **KID-FRIENDLY**

Fajita-Style Quesadillas

Find out which ingredients for this recipe are on sale at your local markets.

PREP 20 min.   COOK 11 min.

½   medium red or green sweet pepper, seeded and cut in bite-size strips
½   medium onion, halved and thinly sliced
1   fresh serrano pepper, halved, seeded, and cut in thin strips (see note, page 11)
2   tsp. vegetable oil
4   6-inch white corn tortillas
    Nonstick cooking spray
½   cup shredded Monterey Jack cheese (2 oz.)
2   thin slices tomato, halved crosswise
1   Tbsp. snipped fresh cilantro
    Light sour cream (optional)
    Cilantro and lime wedges (optional)

1. In a 12-inch skillet cook sweet pepper, onion, and serrano pepper in hot oil over medium-high heat for 3 to 5 minutes or just until vegetables are tender. Remove from heat.
2. Lightly coat 1 side of each tortilla with cooking spray. On uncoated side of 2 tortillas, divide half the cheese. Top each with half the sweet pepper mixture, tomato slices, cilantro, remaining cheese, then remaining tortillas, coated sides up.
3. Cook quesadillas, in same skillet, over medium heat for 4 to 5 minutes per side, until cheese is melted and tortillas are lightly browned. Cut each quesadilla in 4 wedges. Serve warm and, if desired, with sour cream, additional cilantro, and lime wedges. Makes 8 servings.

EACH SERVING *61 cal, 4 g fat, 6 mg chol, 41 mg sodium, 5 g carb, 1 g fiber, 2 g pro.*

SARA'S SILKY
PUMPKIN PIE

MOLASSES-BOURBON
PECAN PIE

Simply Thanksgiving

A Southern cookbook author brings an effortless brilliance to a beloved holiday, adding colorful, light, modern touches that stay true to tradition.

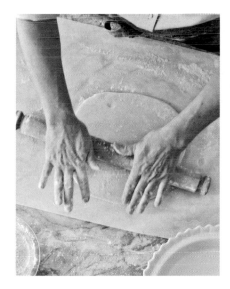

KID-FRIENDLY

Sara's Silky Pumpkin Pie

Prebaking the pie shell ensures a perfect crisp and flaky contrast to the smooth filling. Check the pie 10 minutes or so before the end of baking time and cover the edges with foil if becoming too brown.

PREP **35 min.** BAKE **50 min.** COOL **1 hr.** OVEN **325°F**

3	large eggs
⅓	cup sugar
1	14-oz. can sweetened condensed milk
1½	cups cooked Pumpkin Puree, or one 15-oz. can pumpkin
3	Tbsp. unsalted butter, melted and cooled
1	Tbsp. all-purpose flour
½	tsp. nutmeg
½	tsp. ground cinnamon
½	tsp. ground ginger
¼	tsp. ground cloves
1	prebaked 9-inch Everyday Piecrust, page 213

1. Preheat oven to 325°F. In a large bowl whisk together eggs, sugar, condensed milk, Pumpkin Puree, and butter to thoroughly combine.
2. In a bowl mix together flour, nutmeg, cinnamon, ginger, cloves, and a pinch of salt; stir into pumpkin mixture.
3. Pour filling into pie shell. Place filled pie tin on rimmed baking sheet. Bake 30 to 60 minutes, until filling is set around edges and slightly loose in center. Cool on wire rack for 1 hour. Cover and chill within 2 hours. Makes 10 servings.
Pumpkin Puree Cut 1 small pie pumpkin in half; scoop out seeds. Place pumpkin, cut side down, on rimmed baking sheet. Bake at 400°F for 45 minutes to 1 hour, until soft. Scoop flesh from pumpkin into bowl. Mash with potato masher.

EACH SERVING *364 cal, 16 g fat, 109 mg chol, 190 mg sodium, 48 g carb, 2 g fiber, 8 g pro.*
Make Ahead Prepare pie up to 2 days ahead and store in the refrigerator. Up to 1 month ahead, make and freeze Pumpkin Puree.

Molasses-Bourbon Pecan Pie

"I substitute molasses for corn syrup in this version of classic pecan pie. The filling is every bit as sticky as you'd expect, and the molasses and bourbon add a deep, almost smoky flavor," Sara says. If you prefer a milder molasses flavor, swap in light corn syrup for half the molasses.

PREP **20 min.** BAKE **55 min.**
COOL **several hours** OVEN **350°F**

1	cup molasses
1	cup sugar
4	large eggs, beaten
3	Tbsp. bourbon (optional)
2	Tbsp. unsalted butter, melted
1	Tbsp. pure vanilla extract
	Pinch of kosher salt
2	cups pecan halves
1	9-inch Everyday Piecrust

1. Preheat oven to 350°F. For filling, in a large bowl stir together molasses, sugar, eggs, bourbon, butter, vanilla, and salt. Evenly spread pecans in unbaked pie shell. Pour filling over pecans.
2. Place pie on center rack of oven, with a foil-lined baking sheet on the rack below to catch any filling that bubbles over. Bake for 55 minutes to 1 hour, until firm around the edges and slightly loose in the center. Cool pie on wire rack several hours. Makes 10 servings.
EACH SERVING *514 cal, 27 g fat, 113 mg chol, 153 mg sodium, 63 g carb, 3 g fiber, 7 g pro.*
Make Ahead Prepare pie up to 2 days ahead. Store, covered, in the refrigerator.

HERB-ROASTED TURKEY

HERB GRAVY

Herb-Roasted Turkey

This recipe has the make-ahead step built right in. "The first Thanksgiving that my mom spent in my home, she was surprised how moist and juicy the turkey was—a fresh free-range bird—and that I did not have to get up early to put it in the oven. From then on, I've cooked the holiday turkey," Sara says.

PREP **30 min.** STAND **1½ hr.**
ROAST **3 hr.** OVEN **350°F**

1 15- to 17-lb. whole fresh free-range turkey
4 Tbsp. unsalted butter
15 fresh sage leaves
   Sea salt and freshly ground black pepper
4 sprigs fresh rosemary
2 onions, quartered
1 apple, quartered
2 cups dry white wine
2 cups unfiltered apple juice

1. Rinse turkey inside and out; remove giblets and neck from body and neck cavities.
2. Loosen skin of turkey breast. Place 2 tablespoons butter and 4 sage leaves under skin of each breast. Season turkey cavity and skin with salt and pepper. Place 2 rosemary sprigs, 1 onion, half the apple, and 4 sage leaves in large cavity. Pour the wine and apple juice in roasting pan; add remaining onion, apple, sage, and rosemary. Place turkey breast side down in pan. Cover; refrigerate overnight.
3. Remove turkey from refrigerator; let stand 1 hour at room temperature. Preheat oven to 350°F. Skewer neck skin to back. Tie drumsticks to tail using kitchen string.
4. Roast turkey, breast side down, for 1½ hours, spooning pan drippings over the turkey every 30 to 45 minutes. Turn turkey breast side up.* Cut string between drumsticks. Roast 1½ to 2 hours longer, spooning over pan drippings every 30 to 45 minutes or until turkey juices run clear when a small knife is inserted in thickest part of thigh (180°F in thigh and 165°F in breast). Lightly tent turkey with foil if becoming too brown.

5. Remove turkey from oven; spoon pan drippings over it. Move turkey to a cutting board (reserve pan drippings for Herb Gravy, below). Let stand 30 to 45 minutes. Makes 8 (7-oz.) servings, plus leftovers.
EACH SERVING *331 cal, 10 g fat, 177 mg chol, 162 mg sodium, 5 g carb, 0 g fiber, 48 g pro.*
* To turn the turkey, insert large tongs into the center cavity and wear rubber gloves or use a piece of foil to hold it as you rotate it.

Herb Gravy

Just a palm full of a few fresh herbs that are already on hand for other Thanksgiving dishes makes this quick gravy a standout.
START TO FINISH **20 min.**

4 Tbsp. unsalted butter
4 Tbsp. all-purpose flour
2 tsp. fresh thyme
1 tsp. chopped fresh sage
1 cup reserved pan juices from cooked turkey
2 cups reduced-sodium chicken broth
   Sea salt and freshly ground pepper

1. Melt butter in a skillet over medium-high heat until sizzling hot. Slowly stir in flour, reduce heat to medium, then cook, stirring constantly until flour is light brown, about 2 minutes. Stir in thyme and sage. Slowly whisk in pan liquids from the turkey and the chicken broth; season with salt and pepper to taste. Cook and stir for 2 to 3 minutes, until liquid comes to boiling and begins to thicken. Makes 12 (¼-cup) servings.
EACH SERVING *54 cal, 4 g fat, 11 mg chol, 154 mg sodium, 3 g carb, 0 g fiber, 1 g pro.*

Buttermilk Mashed Creamers

"For perfect mashed potatoes—classic creamy, fluffy comfort food—use the right spuds," Sara says. "Starchy potatoes absorb moisture, which means they whip up beautifully." She recommends using potatoes such as Yukon golds, russets, or round purple-skin Caribes.
PREP **15 min.** COOK **30 min.**
STAND **5 min.**

2 lb. Yukon gold or russet potatoes
6 Tbsp. unsalted butter (¾ stick)
½ cup well-shaken buttermilk
   Sea salt and freshly ground black pepper

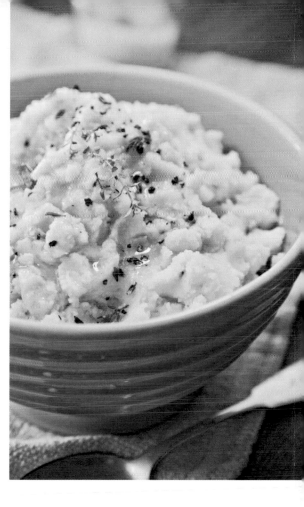

1. Peel potatoes. Cut any large potatoes in half so potatoes are uniform size. Place potatoes in a large saucepan and cover with 2 inches of cold water. Bring to low boiling over medium-high heat. Cover, reduce heat, and simmer about 30 minutes, until potatoes are tender when pierced with a small knife tip; remove from heat.
2. Drain potatoes, then return to saucepan. Add unsalted butter; cover, and let stand until butter is melted. Add buttermilk; mash with potato masher or whip with electric beaters until creamy and butter and buttermilk are incorporated. Season to taste with salt and pepper. Serve warm. Makes 8 servings.
EACH SERVING *175 cal, 9 g fat, 24 mg chol, 68 mg sodium, 22 g carb, 2 g fiber, 3 g pro.*
Make Ahead Cook potatoes up to 1 day ahead and refrigerate. Drain off most of the water. Reheat, covered, over medium heat. Drain and proceed as directed in recipe.

Beet, Carrot, and Apple Salad

This mix of crisp vegetables is super fresh and colorful. For each color to stand out, layer ingredients in a serving bowl. Right before serving, drizzle with dressing and toss.

START TO FINISH 45 min.

Zest and juice of 1 orange
Zest and juice of 1 lime
2   Tbsp. sherry vinegar
¾   cup extra virgin olive oil
Sea salt and freshly ground black pepper
1   lb. beets, peeled and cut in matchsticks*
2   large carrots, peeled and cut in matchsticks*
1   Granny Smith apple, cored, peeled, and cut in matchsticks*
1   turnip, peeled and cut in matchsticks*
1   bunch flat leaf parsley, stems removed (optional)

1. In a large bowl combine orange zest and juice, lime zest and juice, and vinegar. Slowly whisk in the olive oil and season with salt and pepper to taste.
2. Layer beets, carrots, apple, and turnip in bowl. Season with additional salt and pepper to taste. Toss salad just before serving If desired, sprinkle with parsley. Makes 8 (½-cup) servings, plus leftovers.
EACH SERVING 118 cal, 10 g fat, 0 mg chol, 87 mg sodium, 7 g carb, 2 g fiber, 1 g pro.
*To cut matchsticks, use a mandoline or food processor fitted with a julienne blade or large shredding blade.
Make Ahead Prepare dressing up to 3 days ahead. Cut vegetables and store separately in the refrigerator up to 1 day ahead.

BEET, CARROT, AND APPLE SALAD

Sweet Potato Spoon Bread

"For perfect consistency, gently fold in egg whites, leaving visible swirls," Sara says. "Spoon bread is a cross between grits and corn bread, with a lovely dense pudding-like texture. I never need an excuse to bring sweet potatoes into the mix—I add them to just about everything. In this case, they reinforce the silky texture while adding color and sweetness."

PREP 25 min.   BAKE 45 min. + 35 min.
STAND 10 min.   OVEN 400°F/350°F

4   Tbsp. unsalted butter (½ stick), melted
2   medium sweet potatoes (about 1 lb.)
2½ cups milk
1   Tbsp. fresh thyme
1   Tbsp. light brown sugar
2   tsp. coarse sea salt
½   tsp. freshly ground black pepper
1   cup finely ground white or yellow cornmeal
4   large eggs, separated
2   tsp. baking powder

1. Preheat oven to 400°F. Generously grease a 2-quart soufflé or casserole with 1 tablespoon of the butter.
2. Wrap potatoes in foil. Bake for 45 to 55 minutes, until soft to touch. Remove from oven. Discard foil; cool. When cool enough to handle, remove and discard peels. In a large bowl mash potatoes.
3. Reduce oven to 350°F. In a large saucepan bring milk, thyme, sugar, salt, and pepper to a low boil over medium heat. In a slow steady stream whisk cornmeal into milk mixture. Cook, whisking constantly, 4 to 5 minutes, until mixture is thick and pulls away from bottom of pan. Remove from heat; cool slightly. Add potatoes, egg yolks, remaining 3 tablespoons butter, and baking powder to milk mixture; stir to thoroughly mix.
4. In a large mixing bowl beat egg whites with electric mixer until soft peaks form. Gently fold whites into the potato mixture.
5. Spoon batter into prepared dish. Bake 35 to 40 minutes, until internal temperature reaches 165°F. Edges will be firm, and the center a little soft. Remove from oven. Let stand 10 minutes. Serve warm. Makes 8 servings.
EACH SERVING 234 cal, 10 g fat, 127 mg chol, 576 mg sodium, 28 g carb, 1 g fiber, 8 g pro.
Make Ahead Bake and mash potatoes up to 3 days ahead. Store, covered, in refrigerator.

SWEET POTATO
SPOON BREAD

AUNT JUNE'S
BOILED CUSTARD

APRICOT-SWEET
POTATO
HAND PIES

Aunt June's Boiled Custard

"From Thanksgiving to Christmas, my Aunt June often made this boiled vanilla custard (a beverage similar to eggnog) to keep a steady supply for entertaining at her house or to take to friends' get-togethers," Sara says.

PREP 10 min. COOK 25 min. COOL 1 hr. CHILL 4 hr.

5½ cups milk
2   cups heavy cream
1   vanilla bean, split lengthwise, seeds scraped and reserved
1½ cups sugar
1   tsp. kosher salt
6   large egg yolks

1. In a large heavy-bottom saucepan heat the milk, cream, vanilla bean, and reserved seeds over medium heat just until scalded (just before the boiling point). Remove from heat, add sugar and salt, then whisk until sugar is dissolved. Discard the vanilla bean.
2. In a medium bowl whisk the egg yolks. To temper the eggs, slowly whisk about 2 cups of the warm milk mixture into the eggs. Whisk the milk-egg mixture into remaining milk mixture in pan.
3. Place saucepan over very low heat. Cook, whisking constantly, 10 to 15 minutes, until mixture is thickened (coats back of metal spoon). Remove from heat. Strain custard to remove any lumps. Cool for 1 hour. Cover and refrigerate at least 4 hours. Serve chilled. Makes 16 (½-cup) servings.
EACH SERVING 240 cal, 14 g fat, 126 mg chol, 169 mg sodium, 24 g carb, 0 g fiber, 4 g pro.
Make Ahead Prepare up to 3 days ahead. Refrigerate, covered, until ready to serve.

Hand Pie Dough

PREP 30 min.

4   cups all-purpose flour
6   Tbsp. sugar
½   tsp. kosher salt
1   lb. (4 sticks) cold unsalted butter, cubed
2   large egg yolks
6   Tbsp. ice water, plus more if needed

1. In a very large mixing bowl combine flour, sugar, and salt. With a pastry blender or two knives, and working quickly so butter remains cool, cut butter into flour until mixture resembles coarse meal
2. Combine egg yolks and the ice water; stir to mix. Add to flour mixture and stir with fork just until dough clumps together and is moist enough to pat together; do not overmix. If dough is dry and crumbly, add more water, 1 tablespoon at a time, just until dough comes together; dough should not be wet or sticky.
3. Turn dough onto lightly floured work surface and, with lightly floured hands, form in a ball. Divide dough in 4 portions; form each in a flat disk. Wrap each disk in plastic; refrigerate at least 1 hour or up to 3 days.

Apricot-Sweet Potato Hand Pies

These little pies travel well and are just as good warm as they are at room temperature.

PREP 1 hr. BAKE 45 min. + 18 min. OVEN 400°F/375°F

1   recipe Hand Pie Dough
1   cup dried apricots, chopped
¼   cup bourbon
2   medium sweet potatoes (1 lb.)
½   cup sugar + 2 tsp. for topping
2   Tbsp. unsalted butter
½   tsp. ground cinnamon
½   tsp. freshly grated nutmeg
½   tsp. cardamom
½   tsp. kosher salt
2   Tbsp. heavy cream
1   large egg, lightly beaten

1. Prepare Hand Pie Dough.
2. In a small bowl combine apricots and bourbon; soak 1 hour, until fruit is softened and most liquid is absorbed. Meanwhile, preheat oven to 400°F.
3. Wrap sweet potatoes in foil. Bake 45 to 55 minutes, until soft. Remove from oven. Discard foil; cool potatoes. When cool enough to handle, remove and discard peels.
4. Reduce oven to 375°F. For filling, in a bowl combine potatoes, apricots and bourbon, sugar, butter, cinnamon, nutmeg, cardamom, and salt. Mash to consistency of mashed potatoes.

5. Lightly grease two rimmed baking sheets; set aside. On lightly floured surface roll Hand Pie Dough slightly less than ¼-inch thickness. With 4- to 5-inch round cookie cutter or small knife, cut 16 to 20 rounds (reroll dough as necessary). Place about 2 tablespoons filling on one side of each round, leaving ½-inch unfilled border.
6. For egg wash, in a small bowl mix cream and egg. Brush edges of rounds with egg wash; fold unfilled side over filling. Crimp edges with fork to seal. With paring knife, cut small vents in each pie.
7. Place pies on prepared baking sheets. Brush tops with remaining egg wash; sprinkle with sugar. Bake 18 to 20 minutes, rotating sheets halfway through baking, until golden brown.
8. Remove from oven; cool slightly. Serve warm or at room temperature. Makes 16 hand pies.
EACH PIE 434 cal, 26 g fat, 107 mg chol, 141 mg sodium, 44 g carb, 2 g fiber, 5 g pro.

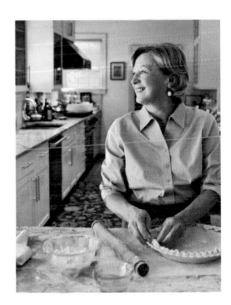

Sara Foster, *above*, likes to get Thanksgiving started early, so she bakes her pies first thing in the morning. Sweetened condensed milk makes her pumpkin pie super smooth; molasses gives the pecan pie a deep, almost smoky flavor.

LOW FAT | **KID-FRIENDLY**

Buttermilk-Sage Dinner Rolls

PREP 45 min. RISE 1 hr. BAKE 15 min.
OVEN 375°F

8   Tbsp. (1 stick) unsalted butter, cut in cubes
10 fresh sage leaves, chopped
3   Tbsp. sugar
1½ cups well-shaken buttermilk
1   Tbsp. plus 1 tsp. active dry yeast (from two ¼-oz. envelopes)
½   cup warm water (105°F to 115°F)
4½ cups all-purpose flour
2   tsp. kosher salt
½   tsp. baking soda
2   Tbsp. unsalted butter, melted

1. Lightly grease 24 muffin tins; set aside.
2. In a saucepan over medium-high heat combine butter, sage, and 2 tablespoons of the sugar, stirring just until butter is melted. Stir in buttermilk and heat just until warmed; do not let mixture come to a boil. Remove from heat; cool to room temperature.
3. In a bowl combine the yeast and remaining 1 tablespoon sugar. Stir in the warm water; set aside in a warm place for about 5 minutes, until the yeast froths and doubles in size. Add the yeast mixture to the buttermilk mixture and stir to combine.
4. In a separate large bowl stir together the flour, salt, and baking soda. Add the buttermilk-yeast mixture and stir to combine, forming a sticky dough. Loosely cover the bowl with a clean cloth; let stand in a warm place about 30 minutes, until dough has risen slightly. (At this point, the dough can be refrigerated in an airtight container up to 1 day. Before proceeding with recipe, remove from refrigerator and let rest for 15 to 20 minutes.)
5. Preheat oven to 375°F. Turn dough out onto a lightly floured surface. Knead several times, until dough is easy to work with. Pinch off pieces of dough and form into 1-inch balls. To shape clover leaf rolls, nestle three 1-inch balls in each muffin cup. Loosely cover with a clean cloth and let rise in a warm place for 30 to 45 minutes, until doubled in size.
6. Uncover rolls, brush lightly with melted butter, then bake about 15 minutes, until golden brown. Serve warm. Makes 24 rolls.
EACH SERVING *142 cal, 5 g fat, 13 mg chol, 205 mg sodium, 20 g carb, 1 g fiber, 3 g pro.*

FAST | **LOW FAT** | **KID-FRIENDLY**

Cranberry-Orange Relish

START TO FINISH 20 min.

2   (12-oz.) bags cranberries, rinsed and drained
    Shredded zest and juice of 1 orange
1   cup sugar
1   orange, peeled and quartered
    Pinch of sea salt

1. In a small saucepan combine 1 bag of cranberries, orange zest, orange juice, and sugar. Bring to boiling, then reduce heat to low. Simmer, about 3 minutes, stirring occasionally, just until some of the cranberries pop and all of the sugar is dissolved. Remove from heat; cool.
2. In a food processor combine the remaining bag of cranberries, quartered orange, and salt; pulse 6 or 7 times until coarsely chopped. Stir chopped cranberry mixture into the cooked cranberries. Cover and refrigerate relish up to 3 days. Makes 16 servings.
EACH SERVING *75 cal, 0 g fat, 0 mg chol, 7 mg sodium, 19 g carb, 2 g fiber, 0 g pro.*

Everyday Piecrust

PREP 30 min. OVEN 425°F

3 cups all-purpose flour
2 Tbsp. sugar
1 tsp. kosher salt
8 Tbsp. cold unsalted butter (1 stick)
¼ cup vegetable shortening
3 Tbsp. ice water
1 egg, lightly beaten
2 tsp. white distilled vinegar

1. In a large bowl combine flour, sugar, and salt. Using a pastry blender and working quickly to prevent butter from melting into flour, cut in butter and shortening until mixture resembles coarse crumbs.
2. In a small bowl combine the ice water, beaten egg, and vinegar; stir to mix. With a fork, mix egg mixture into flour mixture just until dough clumps together and is moist enough to pat together; do not overmix. If dough is dry and crumbly, add more ice water, 1 tablespoon at a time, just until dough comes together. Dough should not be wet or sticky.
3. Turn out dough onto lightly floured surface. With lightly floured hands, form dough in a ball. Divide dough in half; shape each half in a flat disk. Wrap each disk in plastic wrap; refrigerate at least 1 hour or up to 3 days.
4. For a basic pie shell, let dough stand at room temperature for 10 minutes. On a lightly floured surface roll dough with dusted rolling pin to ½- to ¼-inch thickness. Fold dough in half or gently roll onto rolling pin; lift and transfer to pie tin. Lightly press dough onto bottom and sides of tin. Trim dough to 1½ inches beyond edges of tin. Roll dough under to form a rim; crimp with fingers or tines of fork. Prick bottom crust two or three times with a fork. Wrap with plastic wrap; refrigerate at least 1 hour or up to 3 days.
5. To prebake shell, preheat oven to 425°F. Line chilled pastry with a double-thickness of foil. Bake 8 minutes. Remove foil and bake 6 to 8 minutes more or until golden. Cool.
Make Ahead Prepare and refrigerate up to 3 days, or freeze pastry up to 3 months. Shells can be baked up to 3 days ahead, then stored, covered, at room temperature.

KID-FRIENDLY

Sweet and Spicy Pecans

PREP 5 min. BAKE 13 min.
COOL 20 min. OVEN 400°F

4	cups pecan halves
⅓	cup natural cane sugar
2	Tbsp. fresh rosemary
1	Tbsp. sea salt, plus more to taste
½	tsp. freshly ground black pepper
½	tsp. ground cayenne pepper
4	Tbsp. (½ stick) unsalted butter, melted
1	Tbsp. pure vanilla extract

1. Preheat oven to 400°F.
2. Spread pecans on a rimmed baking sheet. Lightly toast in hot oven 5 to 7 minutes.
3. Meanwhile, in a small bowl combine sugar, rosemary, salt, black pepper, and cayenne; stir to mix. In a large bowl combine the melted butter and vanilla.
4. Remove pecans from oven; toss them in the butter-vanilla mixture to coat. Add the spice mixture; toss again to coat evenly. Evenly spread coated pecans on the same baking sheet. Bake for 8 to 10 minutes, until toasted and fragrant, stirring halfway through baking time. Sprinkle with additional salt, if desired. Cool completely; the pecans will crisp after cooling.
5. Store cooled pecans in airtight container(s) up to 1 week. Makes about 4 cups (sixteen ¼-cup servings).
EACH SERVING *240 cal, 24 g fat, 8 mg chol, 293 mg sodium, 8 g carb, 3 g fiber, 3 g pro.*

KID-FRIENDLY

Holiday Corn Bread Dressing

PREP 20 min. BAKE 45 min. OVEN 350°F

½	lb. unsalted butter (2 sticks)
1	onion, chopped
6	celery stalks, chopped (¼ cup chopped celery leaves reserved)
1	loaf challah, brioche, or other soft egg bread, cut in 1-inch cubes (about 12 cups)
1	recipe Salt & Pepper Skillet Corn Bread
2	Tbsp. chopped fresh sage
2	Tbsp. chopped fresh marjoram
1	to 1½ tsp. sea salt
1	tsp. dried crumbled sage
½	tsp. freshly ground black pepper
2	cups low-sodium chicken broth
4	large eggs

1. Preheat oven to 350°F. In a very large deep ovenproof skillet, melt butter over medium heat*. Cook onion and celery in hot butter about 5 minutes, stirring occasionally, until onion is soft and golden.
2. Remove heat. Add bread cubes, corn bread, reserved celery leaves, fresh sage, marjoram, salt, dried sage, and pepper to skillet; stir to combine. Add broth and eggs; stir to combine and moisten bread.
3. Bake, uncovered, 45 minutes to 1 hour, until golden brown on top. If dressing browns too quickly, cover with foil. Serve warm. Makes 20 servings.

Salt and Pepper Skillet Corn Bread
Preheat oven to 425°F. Coat a 9- or 10-inch cast-iron skillet with 2 tablespoons bacon grease or olive oil; heat in oven while mixing batter. In a large bowl combine 1½ cups yellow cornmeal, ½ cup all-purpose flour, ¼ cup sugar, 2 teaspoons baking powder, 1 to 2 teaspoons sea salt, 1 teaspoon freshly ground black pepper, and ½ teaspoon baking soda; stir to mix. To flour mixture add 2 cups well-shaken buttermilk, 2 large eggs (lightly beaten), and 2 tablespoons unsalted butter (melted). Stir just until combined (do not overmix; batter should be lumpy). Pour batter into hot skillet. Bake about 25 minutes, until top is golden brown and a wooden skewer inserted in center comes out clean. Remove from oven, turn out of skillet. Use to make Holiday Corn Bread Dressing or slice in wedges and serve warm.
EACH SERVING *275 cal, 15 g fat, 109 mg chol, 373 mg sodium, 28 g carb, 2 g fiber, 6 g pro.*

*Note If the skillet is not large enough to hold all the ingredients, after cooking the onion and celery, mix ingredients in a large bowl or roasting pan. Bake the dressing in the roasting pan or two 3-quart baking dishes (if baking in two dishes, cut baking time in half). Centers of dressing should read 165°F when tested with an instant-read thermometer.

Creamy Green Beans with Crispy Shallots

PREP 30 min. BAKE 45 min.
COOK 15 min. OVEN 350°F

- 2   lb. green beans, trimmed, cut in 3-inch pieces
- 6   Tbsp. unsalted butter (¾ stick)
- 1   onion, diced
- 1   lb. button mushrooms, cleaned and sliced
- ¼   cup all-purpose flour
- 2½ cups milk
- 2   tsp. sea salt
- ½   tsp. freshly ground black pepper
- 2   gratings of fresh nutmeg
     Canola oil, for frying
- 9   shallots, sliced crosswise in ¼-inch rings
- ½   cup cornstarch, sifted

1. Preheat oven to 350°F. Lightly grease a 2-quart baking dish.
2. Bring a large saucepan of salted water to boiling. Prepare and set aside a large bowl of ice water. Cook green beans in boiling water about 2 minutes, until bright green; drain and place in ice water to cool. Drain.
3. Meanwhile, in a very large skillet melt 2 tablespoons of the butter over medium heat. Cook and stir onion in hot butter about 3 minutes, until soft and translucent. Add 1 tablespoon butter; turn heat to medium-high. Sauté mushrooms about 4 minutes, until golden. Transfer onions, mushrooms, and beans to large bowl.
4. For sauce, in the same skillet melt remaining butter over medium heat; add flour. Stir constantly, about 2 minutes, until flour turns light brown. Slowly pour in milk; cook and stir about 4 minutes, until thickened. Stir in salt, pepper, and nutmeg. Remove from heat; cool completely. Pour cooled sauce over bean mixture; stir to coat evenly. Spoon into prepared baking dish. Bake about 40 minutes, until sauce bubbles around edges.
5. Meanwhile, for topping, pour 3 to 4 inches of oil into deep saucepan. Heat over medium-high heat until sizzling. Working in batches, separate shallots into rings; toss with cornstarch to coat, shaking off excess. Carefully add to hot oil. Fry 2 minutes, until golden and crisp. Remove with slotted spoon; drain on paper towels.
6. Remove casserole from oven, sprinkle with shallots. Bake 5 minutes more, until top is crisp and golden. Serve warm. Makes 8 servings.
EACH SERVING 126 cal, 8 g fat, 13 mg chol, 200 mg sodium, 12 g carb, 2 g fiber, 3 g pro.

CREAMY GREEN BEANS
WITH CRISPY
SHALLOTS

Make Ahead Bake and refrigerate untopped green bean mixture 1 day ahead. Fry shallots up to 2 days ahead; store in airtight container at room temperature. Reheat green beans, covered, at 350°F for 30 minutes, until heated through. Top with crispy shallots the last 5 minutes.

Home Cooking

Four easy versions—layer, cup, sheet, and loaf—help you sweeten every occasion from now to New Year's Day. Holiday baking expert David Bonom shows you how.

TOASTED COCONUT
CAKE WITH WALNUTS
AND CRANBERRIES

Toasted Coconut Cake with Walnuts and Cranberries

PREP 35 min. STAND 20 min.
BAKE 20 min. OVEN 350°F

Cake

2   cups cranberry juice
1½   cups dried cranberries
2⅔   cups all-purpose flour
2¼   tsp. baking powder
¼   tsp. baking soda
¼   tsp. salt
¾   cup unsalted butter, softened
1⅓   cups granulated sugar
6   large egg whites
1½   tsp. vanilla
½   tsp. coconut extract
¾   cup buttermilk

Frosting

¾   cup unsalted butter, softened
2   pounds powdered sugar
⅓   cup unsweetened coconut milk
1   tsp. coconut extract
     Milk
1   cup chopped walnuts, toasted
1½   cups flaked coconut, toasted

1. Position two racks in center of oven. Preheat oven to 350°F. Grease and flour three 9-inch round cake pans.

2. In a medium saucepan bring cranberry juice to boiling. Add dried cranberries and return to boiling. Reduce heat and simmer 1 minute. Remove from heat. Let stand, covered, 20 minutes. Drain.

3. In a medium bowl combine the flour, baking powder, baking soda, and salt. In a large mixing bowl combine ¾ cup butter and granulated sugar; beat with electric mixer on medium speed until light and fluffy. With mixer on low, beat in egg whites, vanilla, and ½ teaspoon coconut extract. On low speed, and in three additions, beat the flour mixture into the sugar mixture, alternating with buttermilk until combined. Divide batter evenly among the three pans.

4. Bake cake layers on two racks for 18 to 20 minutes or until a toothpick inserted in center of each cake comes out clean. Cool in pans on wire racks 10 minutes. Remove from pans; cool completely.

5. For frosting, in a large mixing bowl beat ¾ cup butter with electric mixer on medium speed until smooth. Gradually add 2 cups of the powdered sugar, beating well. Slowly beat in coconut milk and coconut extract. Gradually beat in remaining powdered sugar until fluffy (beat in milk, 1 teaspoon at a time, if frosting is too dry).

6. Place layer on cake plate. Spread with one-third of the frosting. Spread with cranberries. Place second cake layer on filling. Spread with one-third of the frosting. Top with ⅔ cup of the walnuts and ½ cup of the coconut. Top with remaining cake layer. Spread with remaining frosting. Top with remaining coconut and walnuts. Makes 16 servings.

EACH SERVING *608 cal, 28 g fat, 46 mg chol, 174 mg sodium, 88 g carb, 3 g fiber, 6 g pro.*

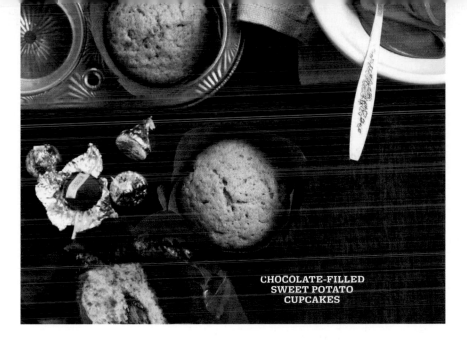

CHOCOLATE-FILLED
SWEET POTATO
CUPCAKES

KID-FRIENDLY

Chocolate-Filled Sweet Potato Cupcakes

PREP 25 min. BAKE 19 min.
STAND 10 min. OVEN 350°F

2   cups all-purpose flour
2   tsp. pumpkin pie spice
1½   tsp. baking powder
½   tsp. baking soda
¼   tsp. salt
1   cup unsalted butter, softened
1¼   cups granulated sugar
3   large eggs
1   lb. sweet potatoes, roasted*, peeled, and mashed
¼   cup milk
1   tsp. vanilla
24   milk chocolate or dark chocolate kisses, unwrapped

Frosting

8   oz. milk chocolate, chopped
4   oz. semisweet chocolate, chopped
1   cup minus 2 Tbsp. unsalted butter, softened
½   cup powdered sugar

1. Preheat oven to 350°F. Line twenty-four 2½-inch muffin cups with 5×4-inch rectangles of parchment paper or paper bake cups.

2. In medium bowl combine flour, pumpkin pie spice, baking powder, baking soda, and salt; set aside. In a large mixing bowl beat butter with an electric mixer on medium for 30 seconds. Add granulated sugar; beat until light and fluffy, about 2 minutes. With mixer on low, beat in eggs, one at a time, stopping to scrape down sides of bowl between additions. Add sweet potatoes, milk, and vanilla. Beat on low until combined. Add flour mixture; beat on low just until combined.

3. Fill prepared muffin cups about two-thirds full with batter. Bake 5 minutes. Remove from oven. Gently press kisses, tips up, about halfway into each cup. Bake 14 minutes more or until tops spring back when touched and chocolate disappears. Cool in pan 10 minutes, remove and cool completely on wire rack.

4. For frosting, in a medium saucepan over low heat bring 1 inch of water to simmering. Place chopped milk and semisweet chocolate in medium mixing bowl; set bowl over saucepan. With rubber spatula, stir until chocolate is melted. Remove from heat; cool 15 minutes. With electric mixer on low beat chocolate 30 seconds. Beat in butter 1 to 2 tablespoons at a time. Add sugar; beat until smooth. Spread on tops of cupcakes. Makes 24 cupcakes.

*To roast sweet potatoes, preheat oven to 425°F. Prick unpeeled potatoes all over with fork. Place in roasting pan. Roast 50 minutes or until tender. When cool, peel away skin.

Make Ahead Sweet potatoes can be roasted, peeled, mashed, covered, and refrigerated up to 3 days.

EACH SERVING *341 cal, 21 g fat, 68 mg chol, 110 mg sodium, 36 g carb, 1 g fiber, 4 g pro.*

Milk Chocolate Marble Loaf Cake

PREP 30 min.   STAND 1 hr. 20 min.
BAKE 65 min.   COOL 40 min.
OVEN 350°F

Cake
4   large eggs
1½   cups sugar
6   Tbsp. unsalted butter, melted
½   cup whole milk
2   tsp. vanilla
1¾   cups all-purpose flour
1   tsp. baking powder
¼   tsp. salt
3   oz. milk chocolate, chopped

Citrus Compote
¼   cup sugar
¼   cup orange juice
4   oranges, segmented
1   small pink grapefruit, segmented
10   kumquats, halved (optional)

1. Let eggs stand at room temperature 30 minutes. Butter and flour a 9×5×3-inch loaf pan; set aside.
2. Preheat oven to 350°F. In medium bowl whisk together the eggs, sugar, butter, milk, and vanilla. In a separate bowl combine the flour, baking powder, and salt.

3. In a small saucepan bring 1 inch of water to simmering over low heat. Place small bowl over water. Add chocolate. Stir with rubber spatula until chocolate is melted. Remove from heat.
4. Stir flour mixture into the egg mixture just until combined. Transfer about one-third of the batter (a generous cup) to separate bowl. Stir the melted chocolate into the small amount of batter, mixing well. Drop ¼ cup of plain batter into the prepared pan; top with 2 tablespoons of chocolate batter. Repeat with remaining batter. Do not stir.
5. Bake in center of the oven for 65 minutes, until toothpick inserted into center of a loaf comes out clean.
6. Meanwhile, prepare Citrus Compote. In a saucepan combine sugar and orange juice. Cook and stir over medium heat until hot and sugar has dissolved. Transfer to a bowl and stir in orange and grapefruit segments and kumquats. Set aside to cool. (Can be made up to 2 days ahead.)
7. Cool cake in pan on wire rack 10 minutes. Remove from pan, return to the wire rack, and cool at least 40 minutes before slicing. Serve slices topped with Citrus Compote. Makes 12 servings.
EACH SERVING *330 cal, 10 g fat, 88 mg chol, 123 mg sodium, 55 g carb., 2 g fiber, 5 g pro.*

KID-FRIENDLY

Triple-Ginger Squares

PREP 20 min. BAKE 33 to 35 min.
STAND 4 hr. OVEN 350°F

2½ cups all-purpose flour
1 Tbsp. baking powder
1 Tbsp. ground ginger
2 tsp. freshly grated ginger
1 tsp. ground black pepper
1 tsp. salt
1 cup unsalted butter, at room temperature
1½ cups granulated sugar
¼ cup honey
¼ cup mild-flavor molasses
2 large eggs
1 cup milk

Glaze
3½ cups confectioners' sugar
5 Tbsp. whipping cream
6 Tbsp. unsalted butter
1 Tbsp. mild-flavor molasses
10 pieces crystallized ginger, cut into 48 strips (buy ginger in strips or slices rather than nuggets)

1. Preheat oven to 350°F. Butter and line bottom of 13×9×2-inch baking pan with parchment or waxed paper. Butter paper; set aside.

2. In a medium bowl combine flour, baking powder, ground ginger, fresh ginger, black pepper, and salt. In large mixing bowl combine butter and granulated sugar. Beat with electric mixer on medium speed until light and fluffy, about 2 minutes. With mixer on low, beat in honey and molasses until well incorporated. Beat in eggs. On low speed beat flour mixture into sugar mixture and in three additions, alternating with milk until combined. Transfer batter to prepared baking pan. Bake in center of oven 33 to 35 minutes until toothpick inserted into center of cake comes out clean. Remove from oven; cool 5 minutes. Invert cake and turn out on wire rack; remove paper. Invert again onto another rack set over waxed paper.

3. Meanwhile, prepare glaze. Sift confectioners' sugar into medium bowl. In small saucepan over medium heat combine cream, butter, and molasses. Cook and stir until butter is melted. Pour cream mixture into sugar and stir until smooth. Pour glaze over hot cake and, working quickly, spread evenly with spatula to cover top. Let stand at least 4 hours.

4. With serrated knife dipped in hot water and wiped dry, cut into 24 squares, about 2×2 inches. Top each square with 2 ginger strips. Makes 24 servings.

EACH SERVING 308 cal, 12 g, 51 mg chol, 158 mg sodium, 48 g carb, 2 g pro.

Glazed Buttery Rum Fruit Cake

PREP 30 min. STAND 30 min. + 20 min.
COOL 10 min. + 45 min. FREEZE 15 min.
BAKE 65 min. OVEN 325°F

1   cup dried apricots, chopped
1   cup dried peaches, chopped
¾   cup dark rum or orange juice
1¾   cups unsalted butter
3⅓   cups all-purpose flour
1   tsp. baking powder
½   tsp. salt
¼   tsp. ground nutmeg
6   eggs, lightly beaten
2   cups granulated sugar
½   cup buttermilk
1   Tbsp. vanilla
2   cups powdered sugar

1. In a small saucepan combine apricots, peaches, and rum. Cook and stir over medium heat just until warm (do not boil). Remove from heat. Let stand for 30 minutes, stirring occasionally. Reserving soaking liquid to make glaze, drain the fruit well. Transfer fruit to a bowl.
2. Meanwhile, in a medium saucepan melt butter over medium heat. Cook for 10 to 16 minutes, until milk solids brown and butter smells nutty. Remove from heat, transfer to a bowl. Cool for 10 minutes. Transfer to freezer for 15 to 20 minutes, until butter congeals but is not solid.
3. Preheat oven to 325°F. Butter a 10-inch fluted tube pan, then lightly dust with flour; set aside.
4. In a large bowl combine 3 cups of the flour, the baking powder, salt, and nutmeg. In a very large mixing bowl combine congealed butter, eggs, granulated sugar, buttermilk, and vanilla; beat with electric mixer on medium speed until well combined. Add flour mixture; beat on low speed just until combined. Toss remaining ⅓ cup flour with drained fruits; gently fold fruit into cake batter. Pour batter into prepared pan.
5. Bake in center of oven for 65 to 75 minutes, until a wooden pick inserted in center of cake comes out clean. Cool in pan for 25 minutes. Remove from pan; cool completely on wire rack.
6. Place the cake on a serving platter. For the glaze, in a small bowl combine the powdered sugar, 2 tablespoons reserved soaking liquid, and 1 tablespoon water until smooth. Add 1 to 2 teaspoons water, if needed, to thin to drizzling consistency. Drizzle glaze over the cake, spreading slightly to reach the edges and allowing some to run down the sides. Let stand 20 minutes before slicing. Makes 16 servings.
EACH SERVING *530 cal, 23 g fat, 133 mg chol, 141 mg sodium, 72 g carb, 2 g fiber, 6 g pro.*

Delicious on a Dollar

Roasting brings out the sweetness and boosts the flavor of fall vegetables in this hearty side dish.

Roasted Vegetables and Chickpeas

PREP 30 min.   ROAST 45 min.
OVEN 425°F

1   lb. carrots, peeled and cut into 2-inch pieces
1   lb. sweet potatoes, peeled and cut into chunks
1   large red onion, peeled, halved, and cut into 1-inch wedges
1   lb. red or russet potatoes, cut into cubes
6   cloves garlic, minced
1   16-oz. can chickpeas (garbanzos), rinsed and drained
2   to 3 Tbsp. vegetable oil or olive oil
1   tsp. dried rosemary, crushed
1   tsp. packed brown sugar or granulated sugar
¼   tsp. kosher salt
½   tsp. freshly ground black pepper

1. Position oven rack in center of oven. Preheat oven to 425°F. Place all vegetables, garlic, and chickpeas in a large shallow roasting pan. In a small bowl combine oil, rosemary, brown sugar, salt, and pepper. Drizzle over vegetables; toss well to coat.
2. Roast, uncovered, about 45 minutes or until vegetables are lightly browned and tender, stirring twice. Makes 8 side-dish servings.

EACH SERVING 223 cal, 4 g fat, 301 mg sodium, 42 g carb, 7 g fiber, 6 g pro.

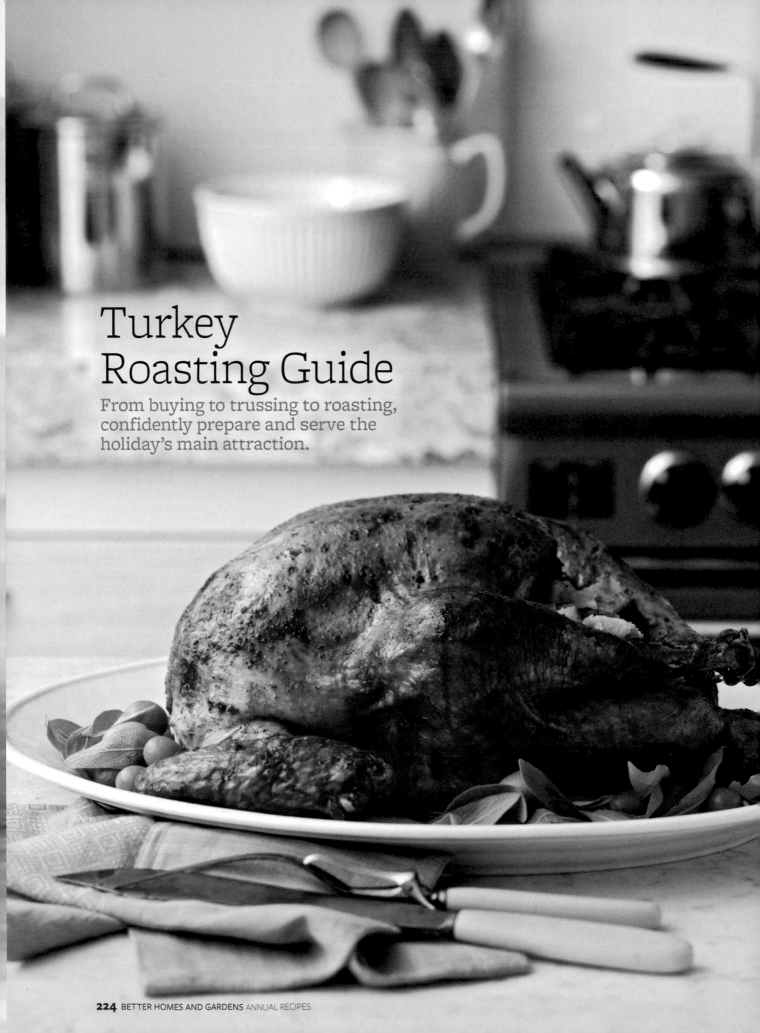

Turkey Roasting Guide

From buying to trussing to roasting, confidently prepare and serve the holiday's main attraction.

Buying and thawing

Estimate 1 to 1½ pounds of turkey for each person, which allows for leftovers. Buy a fresh turkey no more than 2 days before you plan to prepare it. Keep it wrapped and refrigerated until ready to marinate and/or prepare for roasting. Buy a frozen turkey well enough in advance to allow for thawing. To thaw a turkey, place it in a large pan, set it in the refrigerator, and allow 24 hours for each 4 pounds. For example, a frozen 12 pound turkey requires 3 days of thawing.

Step 1

Determine the roasting time for unstuffed turkey. For an 8- to 12-pound turkey roast in a 325°F oven 2 to 3 hours; 12- to 14-pounds for 3 to 3¾ hours; 14- to 18-pounds for 3¾ to 4¼ hours; 18- to 20-pounds for 4¼ to 4½ hours; 20- to 24-pounds for 4½ to 5 hours. For a stuffed turkey increase the total roasting time by 15 minutes.

Prepare the oven by positioning an oven rack low in the oven (not on the oven floor). Preheat the oven to 325°F. Unwrap the turkey and remove the giblets from neck and body cavities. Discard the giblets or cook them, while the turkey is roasting, to make stuffing or gravy.

Have ready a roasting rack and shallow roasting pan (no higher than 2 inches to ensure that thighs roast evenly) that is large enough to accommodate the turkey, allowing space to lift the bird in and out and room to spoon juices during roasting.

Step 2

Blot the turkey inside and out with paper towels. It is not necessary to rinse the turkey under running water.

Step 3

To ensure that both the turkey and stuffing are cooked to a safe temperature bake stuffing separately in a baking dish rather than in the bird. However, if you stuff the cavities, loosely fill one or both with about ¾ cup of stuffing per pound of turkey (11 cups total for a 15 pound turkey). Packed stuffing will not cook to a safe temperature.

Step 4

Pull the neck skin over the stuffing or empty cavity and secure it to the back with a bamboo or wooden skewer.

Step 5

Loosely fill the body cavity with stuffing or with other flavorings (fruit, onion, herbs, butter) or leave unfilled. Fill a baking dish with any remaining stuffing, cover it with

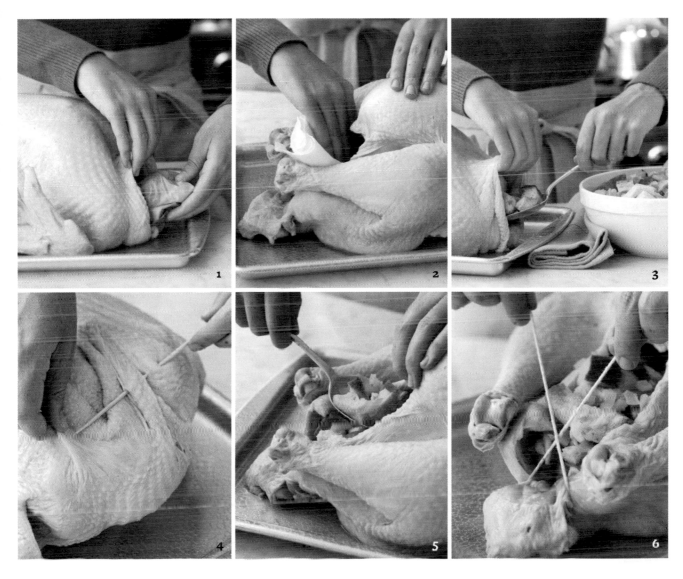

GINGERBREAD
TRIFLE

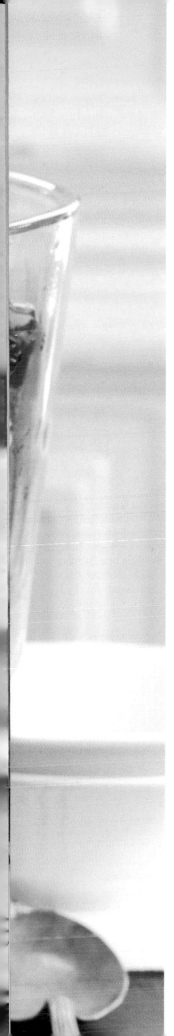

KID FRIENDLY

Gingerbread Trifle

The gingerbread in this trifle has dense texture and peppery ginger flavor. About two-thirds of the cake is used for the trifle. Save the rest for snacking or cut it in cubes to toast and serve with ice cream.

PREP **50 min.** BAKE **25 min.**
CHILL **2 hr.** OVEN **350°F**

Homemade Gingerbread

2	cups flour
1½	tsp. baking soda
1	Tbsp. ground ginger
1	tsp. ground cinnamon
½	tsp. salt
½	cup unsalted butter
1	cup molasses
¼	cup firmly packed brown sugar
¾	cup very hot water
2	eggs

Lemon-White Chocolate Cream

4	egg yolks
2	eggs
½	cup sugar
½	cup lemon juice
2	oz. white chocolate, chopped
1	cup whipping cream

Cranberry Compote

1	12-oz. bag cranberries
½	cup water
⅓	to ½ cup sugar
1½	cups sliced strawberries
2	Tbsp. slivered candied ginger

Homemade Gingerbread

1. Preheat oven to 350° F. Grease a 9×9×2-inch square pan then line bottom with parchment paper. In a medium bowl sift together flour, baking soda, ginger, cinnamon, and salt; set aside.

2. In a small saucepan heat butter, molasses, brown sugar, and water until hot, stirring, until butter and brown sugar are melted. In a large bowl whisk the 2 eggs until blended. Slowly whisk in molasses mixture. Stir in dry ingredients. Pour batter into prepared pan. Bake for 25 minutes, until a skewer inserted near center comes out clean. Cool gingerbread in pan. Remove from pan. Tear two-thirds of the cake into pieces (about 7 cups). Set aside until ready to assemble trifle.

Lemon-White Chocolate Cream

1. In a bowl whisk together egg yolks, whole eggs, sugar, and lemon juice. Transfer to a heavy medium-size saucepan. Cook over medium-low heat, stirring constantly with a wooden spoon until thick. If mixture becomes lumpy, whisk until smooth. Remove from heat. Whisk in white chocolate until smooth. Strain into bowl. Cover with plastic wrap directly on surface. Refrigerate until cold.

2. Meanwhile, whip cream until soft peaks form (remove, cover, and chill ½ cup whipped cream for topper). Fold remaining whipped cream into Lemon-White Chocolate Cream. Refrigerate until ready to assemble trifle.

Cranberry Compote

In a medium saucepan combine cranberries, water, and sugar. Cook over medium heat, stirring occasionally, until cranberries are soft, about 10 minutes. Cool completely. Stir in strawberries.

Trifle Assembly

Layer 1: In a 7- to 9-inch trifle bowl or container, spoon in half the Lemon-White Chocolate Cream.
Layer 2: Evenly top with gingerbread pieces.
Layer 3: Spoon remaining Lemon-White Chocolate Cream on gingerbread.
Layer 4: Top with Cranberry Compote.
Layer 5: Top with reserved whipped cream and slivered candied ginger. Makes 10 to 12 servings.

EACH SERVING *452 cal, 21 g fat, 205 mg chol, 257 mg sodium, 63 g carb, 3 g fiber, 6 g pro.*

RED WINE-
POACHED PEAR
AND HAZELNUT
CREAM TRIFLE

Red Wine-Poached Pear and Hazelnut Cream Trifle

The crisp streusel topping may remind you of hazelnut shortbread cookies. Save leftover topping for snacking.

PREP 1 r. BAKE 40 min.
COOK 1 hr. 5 min. COOL 10 min.
OVEN 350°F /325°F

Poached Pears

10 medium Bartlett or Comice Pears
2 750 ml bottles light bodied red wine, such as Pinot Noir, or 6¼ cups cranberry juice
1¼ cups sugar
⅓ cup fresh cranberries

Vanilla Cake

2 eggs
¾ cup sugar
1 Tbsp. vanilla
½ cup milk
1 Tbsp. unsalted butter
1 cup all-purpose flour
1 tsp. baking powder
½ tsp. salt

Hazelnut Cream

8 oz. mascarpone cheese
1 cup whipping cream
2 Tbsp. sugar
½ tsp. vanilla
½ cup chopped hazelnuts, toasted

Streusel Topping

⅓ cup flour
¼ cup sugar
3 Tbsp. unsalted butter, softened
¼ cup chopped hazelnuts, toasted

A traditional trifle layers fruit, cake, and whipped cream. It's about contrasting flavors and textures. Have fun and break from tradition to create your own dazzling dessert.

Poached Pears

1. Peel, halve, and core pears. In 6- to 8-quart Dutch oven combine wine and sugar. Bring to boiling over medium heat, stirring to dissolve sugar. Add pears. Place parchment paper or a plate on top of pears to keep submerged. Simmer 20 to 30 minutes, until pears are soft (knife inserted goes in easily). With slotted spoon, remove pears from liquid. Cool pears to room temperature. Slice pears, if desired. Bring poaching liquid to a gentle boil, uncovered, for 30 minutes, until liquid is syrupy and reduced to 2 cups. Stir in cranberries. Set aside to cool.

Vanilla Cake

1. Preheat oven to 350°F. Grease two 8×1½-inch round cake pans (or a size close to the diameter of trifle dish). Line bottoms of pans with waxed paper. Grease and flour pans. In medium mixing bowl beat eggs, sugar, and vanilla with mixer on medium to high speed until thick.
2. In small saucepan heat milk over medium heat until hot. Stir in butter until melted. Slowly stir hot milk into egg mixture. Stir in flour, baking powder, and salt until smooth. Divide batter between pans; spread evenly.
3. Bake 20 minutes or until a toothpick inserted near center comes out clean. Cool on rack 10 minutes. Remove from pans; cool completely on rack.

Hazelnut Cream

In a medium mixing bowl beat mascarpone, whipping cream, sugar, and vanilla with mixer on medium to high speed until thick. Stir in ½ cup hazelnuts. Cover; chill until ready to assemble trifle.

Streusel Topping

Preheat oven to 325°F. In a medium bowl combine flour, sugar, butter, and a pinch of salt until crumbly. Spread in single layer in a 15×10×1-inch baking pan. Bake 20 minutes or until golden brown, stirring once or twice. Cool. Place streusel in a large self-sealing plastic bag. Crush with a rolling pin, leaving some large pieces. Stir in ½ cup hazelnuts.

Trifle Assembly

Layer 1: In 9-inch diameter straight-side trifle dish layer pears, cranberries, and reduced poaching liquid, reserving some pear slices and cranberries for the top.
Layer 2: Place one cake layer on pears.
Layer 3: Spoon three-fourths the Hazelnut Cream on cake.
Layer 4: Top with second cake layer.
Layer 5: Top with remaining Hazelnut Cream, some of the streusel, and pears.
Makes 16 servings.

EACH SERVING 482 cal, 19 g fat, 71 mg chol, 139 mg sodium, 59 g carb, 4 g fiber, 7 g pro.

Home Cooking

Follow this step-by-step plan to make a dinner in about 3 hours. Then serve an herb-crusted roast, cheddary biscuits, creamy scalloped potatoes, and Brussels sprouts—all in Scott's stress-free style.

Double-Cheddar Holiday Biscuits

PREP 20 min. BAKE 15 min.
OVEN 425°F

5   cups unbleached all-purpose
     flour, sifted before measuring
1   Tbsp. plus 1 tsp. baking powder
2½   tsp. kosher salt
1   tsp. granulated sugar
⅛   tsp. cayenne pepper
4   oz. shredded extra-sharp white
     cheddar cheese, at room
     temperature (about 1 cup)
4   oz. shredded sharp orange
     cheddar cheese, at room
     temperature (about 1 cup)
6   Tbsp. cold unsalted butter,
     cut in ½-inch pieces
2   cups heavy cream
¼   cup buttermilk

1. Preheat oven to 425°F. Line a baking sheet with foil. In a large mixing bowl whisk together flour, baking powder, salt, sugar, and cayenne. With your fingers add grated cheeses and work in well. Add the cold butter. Quickly rub butter into flour mixture with fingers until mixture resembles the texture of oatmeal with some large marble-size pieces.

2. Stir in cream; add buttermilk and stir just until absorbed. Dough will look chunky and dry at this point. Turn out onto a lightly floured board and use your hands, press and knead to a cohesive dough.

3. Roll to a thickness of ½ inch, stamp out 2½-inch rounds, and place on prepared baking sheet ½ inch apart. Gather scraps, re-roll, cut out, and add to baking sheet. (Biscuits may be refrigerated, lightly covered, for 1 hour before baking.) With a fork dipped in flour, prick three sets of evenly spaced holes on tops of biscuits.

4. Bake on center rack of preheated oven for 15 to 17 minutes until well browned, rotating pans if needed to ensure even browning. Allow to cool slightly before serving. Makes 24 to 28 biscuits.

EACH BISCUIT *197 cal, 12 g fat, 39 mg chol, 259 mg sodium, 18 g carb, 1 g fiber, 5 g pro.*

Biscuit tips
• This is a sturdy, forgiving dough, so don't be afraid to knead firmly.
• Piercing the tops of the biscuits lets steam escape and helps them rise tall.

"There are so many wonderful sharp American cheddars— use two! The white cheddar gives the biscuits their edge; the orange adds creamy texture."

Scalloped Russet and Sweet Potatoes

PREP 45 min. BAKE 1 hr. STAND 10 min.
OVEN 350°F/425°F

1   clove garlic
     Butter, softened
5   medium russet potatoes
1   medium sweet potato
     Freshly grated nutmeg
1   medium onion, peeled
2   Tbsp. olive oil
½   tsp. fresh thyme leaves
2½   cups milk
½   cup whipping cream
3   Tbsp. butter
3   Tbsp. all-purpose flour

1. Preheat oven to 350°F. Rub inside of 2½- to 3-quart gratin dish aggressively with garlic clove; butter generously; set aside.

2. Peel russet and sweet potatoes. With mandoline or very sharp knife slice all potatoes about 1/16 inch thick. Layer half the russet and sweet potato slices in prepared dish. Season with *salt, ground pepper*, and *fresh nutmeg*.

3. With a mandoline or very sharp knife slice onion about 1/16 inch thick. In skillet over low heat cook onions in olive oil until tender, sprinkling well with *salt* and *pepper*. Remove from heat, stir in thyme leaves. Spoon half the cooked onions on potatoes. Add remaining potato slices, sprinkle with additional salt, pepper, and fresh nutmeg.

4. In a small saucepan heat milk and cream just until simmering. In a medium saucepan over medium heat melt butter. Whisk in flour until combined. Remove from heat and whisk in hot milk and cream a little at a time until incorporated. Return to heat; bring to a gentle boil and cook 8 to 10 minutes until thickened. Spread cream mixture on potatoes.

5. Bake, uncovered, for 45 minutes. Increase oven temperature to 425°F. Bake about 15 minutes more or until until bubbly, golden crusty brown, and potatoes are tender when pierced with a wooden pick. Remove from oven; let stand 10 minutes. Makes 10 servings.

EACH SERVING *273 cal, 16 g fat, 42 mg chol, 341 mg sodium, 27 g carb, 3 g fiber, 5 g pro.*

SCALLOPED RUSSET AND SWEET POTATOES

FAST

Caramelized Brussels Sprouts with Lemon

PREP 15 min. COOK 6 min.

¼ cup extra-virgin olive oil
2 cups Brussels sprouts, trimmed and halved lengthwise
2 Tbsp. water
Juice of lemon half, about 1 Tbsp.

1. In a 12-inch nonstick skillet heat 3 tablespoons of the olive oil over medium heat. Arrange Brussels sprouts in a single layer, cut sides down. Drizzle with remaining olive oil and sprinkle generously with *salt* and a grind or two of *black pepper*. Cover and cook 3 minutes. Remove lid and sprinkle sprouts with water. Cover and cook 2 minutes more. Sprouts should be just tender when pierced with a fork, and beginning to caramelize.

2. Remove cover and increase heat slightly. When cut sides are well-carmelized, toss sprouts in pan, drizzle with lemon juice, and sprinkle with more *salt* and *pepper* to taste.

EACH SERVING *106 cal, 9 g fat, 0 mg chol, 209 mg sodium, 6 g carb, 2 g fiber, 2 g pro.*

CARAMELIZED BRUSSELS SPROUTS WITH LEMON

"The caramelized sprouts and delicious jolt of lemon are the perfect complement to the other dishes on the menu."

Herb-and-Garlic-Crusted Pork Roast

Look for natural pork that has not been enhanced with flavoring solutions. If not available, omit the brining step.

PREP **25 min.** MARINATE **overnight**
ROAST **1 hr.** STAND **15 min.**
OVEN **425°F/350°F**

½ cup kosher salt
¼ cup brown sugar
8 cups cold water
3 Tbsp. peanut oil or vegetable oil
1 center cut, boneless pork loin, approximately 3 to 3½ lbs.
4 slices Black Forest bacon or other bacon, cut in 1-inch pieces (uncooked)
1 Tbsp. apricot preserves
2 tsp. finely chopped fresh garlic
1 Tbsp. fresh rosemary, chopped
1½ cups fresh bread crumbs
3 Tbsp. fresh parsley, chopped
3 Tbsp. melted butter

1. For brine, in large bowl dissolve salt and sugar in the cold water. Transfer pork to brine, cover and refrigerate overnight, or up to 2 days, turning occasionally if roast isn't fully submerged.

2. Remove loin from brine and blot dry with paper towels. Heat oil in a nonstick skillet then brown roast on all sides, about 10 minutes. Set aside to cool slightly.

3. In a food processor puree bacon to a smooth paste. Transfer half the bacon to a mixing bowl.* Stir in apricot preserves, garlic, and 2 teaspoons of the chopped rosemary.

4. Place cooled pork loin on waxed paper. Spread with a thin coat of pureed bacon. In separate bowl mix bread crumbs, remaining rosemary, parsley, melted butter, and ½ teaspoon each *kosher salt,* and *ground black pepper.* Toss well to mix. Press crumb mixture on roast, except ends, applying pressure for crumbs to stick well.

5. Position oven rack in lowest position; preheat oven to 425°F. Transfer roast to wire rack in foil-lined baking dish or roasting pan. Roast 15 minutes. Reduce temperature to 350°F. and Roast 45 minutes or until an instant read thermometer registers 145° F. (If crust begins to brown too deeply, tent with foil.) Remove from oven and allow roast to rest for 15 minutes, tented with foil in warm place. Makes 6 servings plus leftovers.

*Note This amount of bacon is required to process well. Serve remaining pureeed bacon, spread on baguette slices and broiled until golden, as an appetizer.

EACH SERVING *412 cal, 23 g fat, 118 mg chol, 621 mg sodium, 13 g carb, 1 g fiber, 36 g pro.*

CURRIED
CHICKEN STEW

Everyday Easy

Assemble ingredients in less than 30 minutes.
Set your slow cooker. Then sit down to a hot,
hearty meal when it suits your schedule.

FAST

Curried Chicken Stew

PREP **20 min.** SLOW COOKER **3 hr. 30 min.**
on **HIGH; 7 hr. on LOW** BUDGET **$2.08**

8   bone-in chicken thighs (2½ to 3 lb.)
2   tsp. olive oil
6   carrots, cut in 2-inch chunks
1   medium sweet onion, cut in narrow
     wedges
1   cup unsweetened coconut milk
¼   cup mild (or hot) curry paste
     Chopped pistachios, golden raisins,
     cilantro, and/or crushed red pepper
     (optional)

1. Trim excess skin and fat from chicken.
In 12-inch skillet cook chicken, skin side
down, in hot olive oil for 8 minutes, or
until browned. (Do not turn thighs.)
Remove from heat; drain and discard fat.
2. In a 3½- or 4-quart slow cooker combine
carrots and onion. In a bowl whisk
together half the coconut milk and the
curry paste; pour over carrots and onion
(refrigerate remaining coconut milk).
Place chicken, skin side up, on vegetables.
Cover. Cook on HIGH for 3½ to 4 hours or
on LOW for 7 to 8 hours. Remove chicken.
Skim off excess fat, then stir in remaining

coconut milk. Ladle stew into bowls. Top
with chicken. Top servings with pistachios,
raisins, cilantro, and crushed red pepper.
Makes 4 servings.
EACH SERVING *850 cal, 63 g fat, 238 mg
chol, 1,314 mg sodium, 221 g carb, 5 g fiber,
52 g pro.*

WINTER
GARDEN
POLENTA

SAUSAGE
JAMBALAYA

FAST LOW FAT

Winter Garden Polenta

PREP 15 min. SLOW COOKER 1 hr. 30 min.
on HIGH; 3 hr. on LOW BUDGET $2.43

½   cup oil-packed dried tomatoes
5   cups boiling water
1½ cups coarse polenta or cornmeal
½   cup finely shredded Parmesan cheese
1   tsp. dried basil, crushed
¼   tsp. crushed red pepper
1   8-oz. pkg. sliced fresh mushrooms
4   cups packaged fresh baby spinach
    Crumbled Parmesan cheese
    (optional)

1. Drain tomatoes, reserving 1 tablespoon
oil. Snip tomatoes. In 3½ or 4 quart slow
cooker combine tomatoes, boiling water,
polenta, the ½ cup Parmesan, 1 teaspoon
salt, the basil, and crushed red pepper;
stir to combine. Cover and cook on HIGH
for 1½ hours or on LOW for 3 hours, until
polenta is tender.

2. About 15 minutes before serving, in
a large skillet heat reserved oil from
tomatoes. Add mushrooms. Cook and
stir for 5 minutes until tender. Add
spinach. Cook and stir just until wilted.
Season to taste with *salt*. Stir polenta,
then spoon into bowls. Top with spinach
and mushroom mixture and crumbled
Parmesan. Makes 4 servings.
EACH SERVING 293 cal, 10 g fat, 7 mg chol,
859 mg sodium, 43 g carb, 6 g fiber, 11 g pro.

FAST KID FRIENDLY

Sausage Jambalaya

PREP 15 min. SLOW COOKER 2 hr. on
HIGH; 4 hr. on LOW BUDGET $2.12

12 oz. cooked andouille sausage or
    cooked kielbasa (Polska kielbasa)
1   pint miniature sweet peppers or
    2 large yellow and/or orange sweet
    peppers
1   15- to 16-oz. can red kidney beans,
    rinsed and drained
1   14.5-oz. can fire-roasted diced
    tomatoes
1   cup chopped celery (2 stalks)

1. Slice sausage in 1-inch chunks. Halve,
stem, and seed the miniature peppers.
If using large peppers, stem, seed, and
coarsely chop.

2. In a 3½ or 4 quart slow cooker combine
the sausage, sweet peppers, drained beans,
undrained tomatoes, and celery. Cover
and cook on HIGH for 2 hours or on LOW
for 4 hours. Stir before serving. Makes
4 servings.
EACH SERVING 409 cal, 24 g fat, 56 mg chol,
1,295 mg sodium, 32 g carb, 8 g fiber, 18 g pro.

Pork Loin with Butternut Squash

PREP 20 min.
SLOW COOKER 2 hr. on HIGH;
4 hr. on LOW BUDGET $2.33

1   small butternut squash
½   tsp. each salt, pepper, pumpkin pie
     spice, and onion or garlic powder
1-   to 1½-lb. boneless pork loin roast
1   Tbsp. olive oil
1   18.8-oz. can caramelized French
     onion soup
½   cup chunky-style applesauce

1. Halve and peel squash, discard seeds, then cut squash in large chunks. Place squash in a 3- or 3½-quart slow cooker.
2. In a small bowl combine salt, pepper, spice, and onion or garlic powder; rub seasoning on all sides of pork. Heat oil in a large skillet; brown pork on all sides in the hot oil. Place pork on the squash in slow cooker. Pour soup and applesauce over all. Cover and cook on HIGH for 2 hours or on LOW for 4 hours.
3. Slice pork on cutting board. To serve, drizzle sauce over pork and squash. Makes 4 servings.

EACH SERVING *322 cal, 14 g fat, 76 mg chol, 732 mg sodium, 22 g carb, 3 g fiber, 26 g pro.*

Beef and Carrot Ragu

PREP 25 min.
SLOW COOKER 3 hr. on HIGH; 6 hr. on LOW BUDGET $2.55

1-   to 1½-lb. boneless beef short ribs
     Salt and ground black pepper
10   cloves garlic
1   8-oz. pkg. peeled fresh baby carrots,
     chopped
1   lb. Roma tomatoes, chopped
½   6-oz. can tomato paste with basil,
     garlic, and oregano
½   cup water or red wine
     Fresh basil leaves (optional)

1. Trim excess fat from rib meat. Cut beef in chunks, then sprinkle lightly with salt and pepper. Place beef in a 3½- or 4-quart slow cooker.
2. Smash garlic cloves with the flat side of a chef's knife or meat mallet. Separate and discard skins from garlic. Place smashed garlic on beef. Add carrots and tomatoes to slow cooker.
3. In a medium bowl, whisk together tomato paste and water or wine. Pour over meat and vegetables. Cover and cook on HIGH for 3 to 4 hours or on LOW for 6 to 8 hours.
3. Stir well before serving. Top with fresh basil leaves. Makes 4 servings.

EACH SERVING *509 cal, 42 g fat, 86 mg chol, 568 mg sodium, 15 g carb, 4 g fiber, 19 g pro.*

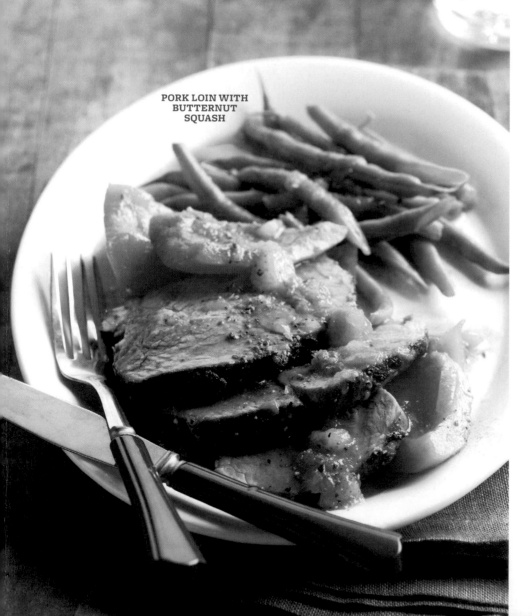

PORK LOIN WITH
BUTTERNUT
SQUASH

BEEF AND
CARROT RAGU

Night Before Christmas Cookies

No time to bake? No problem! These fast and fun cookies from cookbook author and baking guru Dorie Greenspan go together in minutes.

QUICK JAM DROPS

FROZEN COCO-COFFEE BITES

TANGY SPICE SQUARES

NO-BAKE CHOCOLATE CRUNCHERS

NO-BAKE CHOCOLATE CRUNCHERS (S'MORES VARIATION)

VANILLA-ALLSPICE THUMBPRINTS

Frozen Coco-Coffee Bites

PREP 30 min. FREEZE 1 hr.

1½ tsp. instant espresso powder
  (or 2 tsp. instant coffee granules)
2½ Tbsp. boiling water
½ stick (2 oz.) unsalted butter
1 cup sweetened shredded coconut
2 Tbsp. graham cracker or
  shortbread-type cookie crumbs
5 oz. cream cheese, softened
5 Tbsp. sugar
½ tsp. ground cinnamon
  Pinch salt
½ tsp. pure vanilla extract

1. Line 24 (1¾-inch) mini muffins tins with paper bake cups; set aside. Dissolve espresso powder in boiling water; set aside.
2. For crust, in a medium-size nonstick skillet melt butter over medium-low heat. When bubbling, add coconut. Cook and stir until coconut is toasted and golden brown. Stir in graham cracker crumbs; remove pan from heat.
3. Spoon 1 tsp. crust mixture into each muffin cup; press firmly to pack. Place muffin tins in freezer. Keep remaining crust mixture at room temperature.
4. Meanwhile, for filling, in a medium mixing bowl beat cream cheese with a sturdy spatula until soft, smooth, and creamy. Beat in the sugar, cinnamon, and salt until smooth and blended. Beat in vanilla and espresso.
5. Evenly spoon filling into crust in each muffin cup. Top with a pinch of remaining reserved crust mixture. With a fingertip, gently press topping into filling. Freeze about 1 hour, until firm. Makes 24 cookies.
EACH COOKIE *62 cal, 5 g fat, 12 mg chol, 30 mg sodium, 4 g carb, 0 g fiber, 1 g pro.*

No-Bake Chocolate Crunchers

START TO FINISH 40 min.

½ cup walnuts, pecans, or peanuts, finely chopped
½ cup dried cranberries or raisins, finely chopped
1 cup corn flakes, hand crushed coarsely
1⅓ cups semisweet chocolate pieces
48 vanilla wafers

1. In a large bowl combine nuts, cranberries, and crushed cereal.
2. In a small microwave-safe bowl, microcook 1 cup of the chocolate pieces on 100% power (high) for 1½ to 2 minutes, stirring once midway. Stir until melted and smooth. Using a rubber spatula scrape melted chocolate over cereal mixture. Mix to evenly coat with chocolate.
3. In a small microwave-safe bowl, microcook remaining ⅓ cup chocolate for 30 seconds; stir until smooth.
4. To assemble, cover flat side of one vanilla wafer with small amount of melted chocolate, then top with about 1 tsp. chocolate-cereal mixture. Brush flat side of a second wafer with chocolate; press against chocolate cereal mixture to make sandwich. Repeat with remaining wafers, chocolate, and chocolate cereal mixture. Let cookies stand at room temperature to firm. Store at room temperature. Makes 24.
EACH COOKIE *125 cal, 6 g fat, 4 mg chol, 95 mg sodium, 17 g carb, 1 g fiber, 1 g pro.*

Cruncher S'mores Position oven rack about 8 inches below broiler. Preheat broiler. Line baking sheet with foil; set aside. Cut 12 large marshmallows in half; set aside. Break each of 12 whole graham cracker planks in quarters. Spread half the quarters with warm chocolate, place on prepared sheet; top with a marshmallow half. Top remaining quarters with chocolate crunch; place on baking sheet. Broil about 2 minutes, until marshmallows are soft and melted, watching to prevent burning. While warm, sandwich two layers together. Cool. Makes 24 cookies.

Tangy Spice Squares

START TO FINISH 40 min. OVEN 350°F

Crust
1 cup all-purpose flour
1 tsp. cinnamon
½ tsp. ginger
⅛ tsp. ground cloves
  Pinch of salt
3 Tbsp. sugar
3 Tbsp. brown sugar
1 stick (4 oz.) cold unsalted butter, cut in 8 pieces

Custard
½ cup sugar
3 Tbsp. all-purpose flour
¼ tsp. baking powder
¼ cup orange juice (such as Tropicana No Pulp)
¼ cup freshly squeezed lemon juice
  Powdered sugar (optional)

1. Position an oven rack in center of oven. Preheat oven to 350° F. Line an 8×8-inch baking pan with foil. Grease foil; set aside.
2. For crust, in a food processor combine flour, spices, salt, and sugars. Pulse just until mixed. Add cold butter; pulse several times to break up pieces. Process for 1 minute, just until dough forms moist popcorn-like clumps that hold together when pressed between fingers. Turn dough into prepared pan; pressing evenly.
3. Bake crust for 17 to 20 minutes, or until firm and bubbly. Cool on wire rack.
4. Meanwhile, for custard, in a large mixing bowl beat sugar, flour, baking powder, orange juice, and lemon juice with electric mixer for 1 minute, scraping down side of bowl as needed. Remove bowl from machine. With a spatula, swirl custard a couple of times in bowl; lightly tap bowl against counter to remove any air bubbles. Pour custard into crust, tilting pan to smooth evenly.
5. Bake about 20 minutes or until golden and set. Cool completely on wire rack. Dust with powdered sugar. Cut in 2-inch squares. Makes 16 squares.
EACH SQUARE *131 cal, 6 g fat, 15 mg chol, 17 mg sodium, 19 g carb, 0 g fiber, 1 g pro.*

FROZEN COCO-COFFEE BITES

QUICK JAM DROPS

FAST | KID FRIENDLY

Quick Jam Drops

START TO FINISH **25 min.**
OVEN **375°F**

1½ sticks (6 oz.) unsalted butter (room temperature)
1 egg (room temperature)
2 cups all-purpose flour
1 tsp. baking powder
¼ tsp. salt
¾ cup sugar
2 Tbsp. milk
1½ tsp. pure vanilla extract
½ cup cranberry relish or orange marmalade
1 cup powdered sugar, sifted
2 Tbsp. milk
3 Tbsp. dried cranberries, snipped
Food coloring (optional)

1. Line two cookie sheets with parchment paper; set aside.
2. Preheat oven to 375°F. In a large bowl whisk together flour, baking powder, and salt; set aside.
3. In a large mixing bowl beat butter with electric mixer at medium-low speed until smooth and creamy. Add granulated sugar. Beat for 2 minutes or until well blended. Reduce speed to low. Add egg. Beat for 1 minute. Add milk and vanilla extract. Beat for 1 minute more.
4. With mixer at lowest speed, steadily add flour mixture, beating a few seconds after flour is incorporated and soft dough forms. Beat in relish until evenly incorporated.
5. Using a small (2-teaspoon) cookie scoop, drop dough onto prepared baking sheets, spacing 2 inches between mounds. Bake for 10 to 12 minutes or just until slightly firm and golden on bottoms. (If cookies seem to bake unevenly, rotate baking sheets top to bottom and front to back after 5 minutes.) Transfer to cooling racks. Cool completely.
6. For icing, in a medium bowl combine the powdered sugar and milk. Using a small spatula, stir until smooth for an icing the consistency of heavy cream. If needed, add milk in droplets to reach desired consistency. Stir in snipped cranberries and, if desired, food coloring. Line a baking sheet with parchment or waxed paper. Top each cookie with about ½ teaspoon of icing. Let stand until set. Makes 45 drops.
EACH DROP *79 cal, 3 g fat, 13 mg chol, 24 mg sodium, 12 g carb, 0 g fiber, 1 g pro.*

"You CAN don your cookie-making cap, even at the last minute. No one—even Santa—can resist these treats."
—Dorie Greenspan

KID FRIENDLY

Vanilla-Allspice Thumbprints

START TO FINISH **39 min.** OVEN **350°F**

½ cup (1 stick) unsalted butter (room temperature)
1 egg yolk (room temperature)
1¼ cups all-purpose flour
½ tsp. ground allspice
¼ tsp. baking powder
¼ tsp. salt
¼ cup sugar
¾ tsp. pure vanilla extract
½ cup white baking pieces or semisweet chocolate pieces
¼ tsp. ground allspice (optional)

1. Line two baking sheets with parchment paper; set aside.
2. Preheat oven to 350°F. In a small bowl whisk together flour, the ½ tsp. allspice, baking powder, and salt. Set aside.
3. In a large mixing bowl beat butter with electric mixer on medium speed for 30 seconds. Add the sugar and beat for 2 minutes or until well blended. Reduce mixer speed to low. Add the egg yolk and beat for 1 minute. Beat in vanilla.

4. With mixer at lowest speed, steadily beat in flour mixture, beating only a few seconds after flour is incorporated in the soft dough. Make sure all dry ingredients are well incorporated.
5. Using a rounded teaspoonful of dough, shape dough in a ball between palms of hands. Place balls about 2 inches apart on prepared baking sheets. With the handle end of a wooden spoon or thumb, make indentations in the center of each ball. Bake for 9 to 10 minutes or until cookies are dry and firm to the touch. If the oven has hot spots, rotate baking sheets top to bottom and front to back after 4 minutes of baking time. Let cookies stand on baking sheets on wire racks while preparing filling.
6. Place chocolate pieces in a small microwave-safe bowl. Microcook on 100% power (high) for 45 to 60 seconds, stirring until melted. Use a small spoon to fill each indentation with chocolate.
7. Refrigerate cookies for 15 minutes to set chocolate. Serve cookies at room temperature. Makes 36 cookies.
EACH COOKIE *63 cal, 4 g fat, 13 mg chol, 24 mg sodium, 7 g carb, 0 g fiber, 1 g pro.*

Dorie Greenspan is the James Beard award-winning author of 10 cookbooks. She just launched an app, *Baking with Dorie,* that includes recipes and step-by-step videos. "Each recipe is like a private baking lesson," Dorie says.

Delicious on a Dollar

This smooth potato soup with crunchy topping is a savory budget dish that has colorful flair.

LOW FAT

Rosemary Potato Soup with Crispy Carrots

PREP 10 min. COOK 35 min.

- 1 Tbsp. butter
- 1 medium white or yellow onion, chopped
- ½ tsp. salt
- ¼ tsp. pepper
- 4 medium russet or white potatoes (1 to 1½ lb.), peeled and cut in 2-inch chunks
- 4 cups water
- 1 tsp. dried rosemary, crushed
- ⅓ cup vegetable oil
- 2 medium carrots, peeled, then cut in ribbons with a vegetable peeler
  Kosher salt or salt
  Coarse ground black pepper

1. In a 4- or 5-quart Dutch oven melt butter over medium heat. Add onion, salt, and pepper. Cook, stirring occasionally, until onions are translucent but not brown. Add potatoes, 2 cups of the water, and rosemary. Bring to boiling; reduce heat. Simmer, covered, for 20 minutes or until potatoes are tender and can be pierced with a fork. Remove from heat.

2. With a potato masher, mash potatoes until no lumps remain. Or, for a smoother soup, transfer soup, a portion at a time, to a blender or food processor. Cover and blend or process until nearly smooth. Return all to Dutch oven. Add remaining 2 cups of water. Bring to boiling; reduce heat. Simmer, uncovered, about 10 minutes or until thickened and desired consistency, stirring frequently to prevent soup from sticking to pan.

3. While soup is simmering, in a 10-inch skillet heat oil over medium-high heat. Add carrot ribbons, a few at a time, to hot oil. Cook for 1 to 2 minutes or until crisp. Transfer to a cooling rack or paper towels; immediately sprinkle with kosher salt.

4. Spoon soup into serving bowls; top with crispy carrots and sprinkle with coarse pepper. Makes 6 to 8 side-dish servings.

EACH SERVING 236 cal, 5 g fat, 5 mg chol, 313 mg sodium, 26 g carbo, 3 g fiber, 2 g pro.

Categories

prize tested recipes

Each month home cooks share their creative recipes for specific two categories—plus several of our favorites!

259

269

291

CHOCOLATE-BANANA
DOUGHNUTS

Weeknight Vegetarian

**FETTUCCINE ALFREDO
WITH SUN-DRIED
TOMATOES AND VEGGIES**

FAST

Fettuccine Alfredo with Sun-Dried Tomatoes and Veggies

START TO FINISH 30 min.

8   oz. dried fettuccine
½   cup dried tomatoes (not oil-packed), chopped
4   Tbsp. butter
1   Tbsp. olive oil
4   oz. fresh asparagus spears, trimmed
4   oz. fresh Brussels sprouts, trimmed and quartered
1½   cups fresh broccoli florets
8   fresh mushrooms, sliced
2   Tbsp. all-purpose flour
1¼   cups milk
½   cup finely shredded Parmesan cheese
2   tsp. finely shredded lemon peel

1. Cook pasta according to package directions, adding dried tomatoes the last 2 minutes of cooking. Drain and return to saucepan; keep warm.
2. Meanwhile, in a large skillet heat 1 tablespoon of the butter and the oil over medium heat. Add asparagus, Brussels sprouts, broccoli, and mushrooms. Cook over medium heat for 8 minutes or until vegetables are tender. Remove vegetables from skillet; set aside.
3. In same skillet melt remaining butter over medium heat. Stir in flour. Cook and stir 1 minute. Stir in milk. Cook and stir until thickened and bubbly. Stir in Parmesan cheese. Gently stir in pasta and vegetables. Stir in additional *milk* to reach desired consistency. Sprinkle with lemon peel and additional shredded *Parmesan cheese*. Makes 4 servings.
EACH SERVING 500 cal, 21 g fat, 46 mg chol, 491 mg sodium, 60 g carb, 5 g fiber, 20 g pro.

Gnocchi with Mushroom Sauce

PREP 30 min.   STAND 15 min.
COOK 16 min.

2   oz. dried porcini mushrooms
     Boiling water
⅓   cup thinly sliced leek (1 medium)
3   cloves garlic, minced
2   Tbsp. butter
2   Tbsp. olive oil
1½   lb. fresh portobello* and/or button mushrooms, sliced
1   lb. fresh cremini mushrooms, sliced
¾   cup Chardonnay or other dry white wine
¾   tsp. salt
¼   tsp. ground black pepper
⅔   cup whipping cream
2   Tbsp. all-purpose flour
1   Tbsp. snipped fresh Italian (flat-leaf) parsley
2   16- or 17-oz. pkgs. shelf-stable potato gnocchi

1. Soak dried mushrooms in enough boiling water to cover about 15 minutes or until soft. Drain, discarding liquid. Squeeze mushrooms to remove additional liquid.
2. Meanwhile, for mushroom sauce, in a 4- to 5-quart Dutch oven cook and stir leek and garlic in hot butter over medium heat for 2 minutes. Using a slotted spoon, remove leek mixture. Add oil to Dutch oven; heat over medium-high heat. Add porcini mushrooms, portobello and/or button mushrooms, and cremini mushrooms. Cook about 15 minutes or until mushrooms are lightly browned and liquid is evaporated, stirring occasionally. Stir in wine, salt, and pepper.
3. In a small bowl whisk together cream and flour; stir into mushroom mixture. Cook and stir until thickened. Cook and stir for 1 minute more. Stir in leek mixture and the parsley.
4. Meanwhile, cook gnocchi according to package directions; serve with mushroom sauce. Makes 6 servings.
EACH SERVING 543 cal, 20 g fat, 47 mg chol, 878 mg sodium, 78 g carb, 7 g fiber, 13 g pro.
*For a lighter color sauce, use a knife or a teaspoon to gently scrape away the gills (the black portions underneath the caps) from the portobello mushrooms before slicing.

FAST   LOW FAT

Cheesy Eggplant Burgers

PREP 15 min.   GRILL 6 min.

1   tsp. garlic powder
½   tsp. black pepper
⅛   tsp. salt
½   cup chopped, seeded tomato (1 medium)
2   Tbsp. olive oil
1   Tbsp. snipped fresh oregano
2   tsp. snipped fresh thyme
2   tsp. cider vinegar
6   ½-inch slices eggplant
6   ¾-oz. slices smoked gouda cheese
6   ½-inch slices whole grain baguette-style French bread, toasted

1. In a small bowl combine garlic powder, pepper, and salt. In another small bowl combine half the garlic powder mixture, the tomato, 1 tablespoon of the oil, the oregano, thyme, and vinegar. Set aside.
2. Brush both sides of eggplant slices with the remaining 1 tablespoon oil. Sprinkle with the remaining garlic powder mixture.
3. For a charcoal grill, grill eggplant on the rack of an uncovered grill directly over medium coals for 6 to 8 minutes or just until tender and golden brown, turning once halfway through grilling and topping with cheese during the last 2 minutes of grilling. (For a gas grill, preheat grill. Reduce heat to medium. Place eggplant on grill rack over heat. Cover and grill as above.)
4. Serve eggplant on toasted bread slices with tomato mixture. Makes 6 servings.
EACH SERVING 201 cal, 11 g fat, 17 mg chol, 506 mg sodium, 19 g carb, 4 g fiber, 7 g pro.

Take-a-Bag-of-Spinach

PRIZE TESTED RECIPES® $500 WINNER
Vikki Boyle, WHITEHOUSE STATION, NJ

GREEK SPINACH-
PASTA SALAD WITH
FETA AND BEANS

FAST **LOW FAT**

Greek Spinach-Pasta Salad with Feta and Beans

START TO FINISH 30 min.

1   5- to 6-oz. pkg. fresh baby spinach
1   15-oz. can Great Northern beans, rinsed and drained
4   oz. crumbled feta cheese
¼   cup dried tomatoes (not oil-packed), snipped
2   green onions, chopped
2   cloves garlic, minced
1   tsp. finely shredded lemon peel
2   Tbsp. lemon juice
2   Tbsp. extra virgin olive oil
1   Tbsp. snipped fresh oregano
1   Tbsp. snipped fresh lemon thyme or thyme
½   tsp. kosher salt or sea salt
½   tsp. freshly ground black pepper
12 oz. dried cavatappi or farfalle pasta
    Shaved Parmesan or Pecorino Romano cheese

1. In a large serving bowl combine spinach, beans, cheese, tomatoes, onions, garlic, lemon peel and juice, oil, oregano, thyme, salt, and pepper. Cover; let stand at room temperature while cooking pasta or up to 2 hours; stir occasionally.
2. Shortly before serving, cook pasta according to package directions. Drain pasta, reserving ¼ cup of the cooking water. Toss cooked pasta and pasta water with spinach salad mixture. Serve warm or at room temperature. Top with shaved Parmesan cheese. Makes 6 (2-cup) main dish servings.
EACH SERVING *408 cal, 10 g fat, 19 mg chol, 487 mg sodium, 62 g carb, 6 g fiber, 17 g pro.*

FAST **LOW FAT** **KID FRIENDLY**

Spinach Panini

PREP 20 min.   COOK 2 min. per batch

    Nonstick olive oil cooking spray
4   6-inch whole wheat hoagie rolls, split, or 8 slices whole wheat bread or 2 whole wheat pita bread rounds, halved crosswise and split horizontally
4   cups fresh baby spinach leaves
8   thin tomato slices (1 medium tomato)
¼   tsp. kosher salt
⅛   tsp. freshly ground black pepper
¼   cup thinly sliced red onion
2   Tbsp. shredded fresh basil leaves
½   cup crumbled feta cheese (2 oz.)

1. Lightly coat an unheated panini griddle, covered indoor electric grill, or large nonstick skillet with nonstick cooking spray; set aside.
2. Place hoagie roll bottoms or 4 of the bread slices or 4 pita pieces on a work surface; divide half the spinach leaves among rolls, bread, or pita pieces. Top spinach with tomato and sprinkle lightly with kosher salt and pepper. Add red onion slices and basil. Top with feta and remaining spinach. Top with roll tops, bread slices, or pita. Press down firmly.
3. Preheat griddle, grill, or skillet over medium heat or according to manufacturer's directions. Cook sandwiches, in batches if necessary. If using griddle or grill, close lid and grill for 2 to 3 minutes or until bread is toasted. (If using skillet, place a heavy plate on top of sandwiches. Cook for 1 to 2 minutes or until bottoms are toasted. Carefully remove plate, which may be hot. Turn sandwiches and top with the plate. Cook for 1 to 2 minutes more or until bread is toasted.) Makes 4 panini.
EACH PANINI *299 cal, 7 g fat, 13 mg chol, 826 mg sodium, 50 g carb, 8 g fiber, 13 g pro.*

Ground Lamb, Spinach, and Cauliflower

PREP 25 min.   BAKE 20 min.
OVEN 350°F

1   lb. lean ground lamb or ground beef
1   cup chopped onion (1 large)
½   a 2-lb. head cauliflower, cut in small florets (3 cups)
1   Tbsp. garam masala
½   tsp. salt
1   10-oz. pkg. frozen chopped spinach, thawed and well drained
1   8-oz. pkg. cream cheese, cut up
    Chopped peanuts (optional)
    Pita bread wedges or naan bread

1. Preheat oven to 350°F. In a large skillet cook ground meat and onion until meat is browned and onion is tender. Drain off fat. Return meat mixture to skillet; add cauliflower. Cook and stir for 1 minute. Stir in garam masala and salt. Add spinach and cream cheese. Heat and stir just until cream cheese is melted. Spoon into an ungreased 2-quart square baking dish.
2. Bake, covered, for 20 to 25 minutes or until bubbly. If desired, sprinkle with peanuts. Serve with pita bread wedges. Makes 4 to 6 servings.
EACH SERVING *746 cal, 48 g fat, 47 mg chol, 944 mg sodium, 47 g carb, 6 g fiber, 33 g pro.*

Nut Desserts

PRIZE TESTED RECIPES® $500 WINNER
Tamara Cadle, LEON, WV

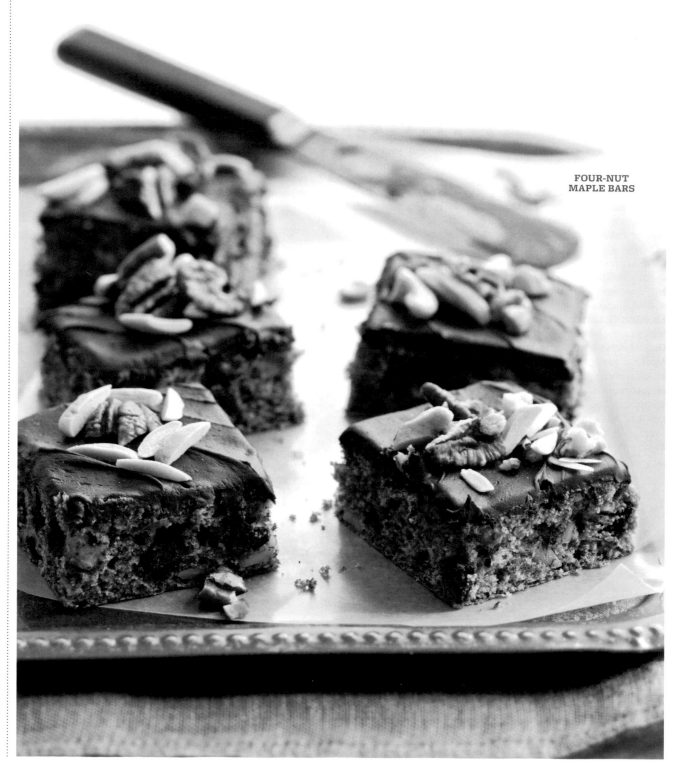

**FOUR-NUT
MAPLE BARS**

KID FRIENDLY

Four-Nut Maple Bars

PREP 20 min. BAKE 25 min.
OVEN 350°F

2 cups whole wheat flour
1 tsp. baking powder
1 tsp. baking soda
2 egg whites
¾ cup pure maple syrup
½ cup canola oil
½ cup fat-free milk
1½ cups toasted chopped cashews, almonds, walnuts, and/or pecans
1 cup semisweet chocolate pieces
1 recipe Chocolate-Hazelnut Frosting
⅔ cup toasted pecan halves, chopped cashews, slivered almonds, and/or chopped walnuts

1. Preheat oven to 350°F. Grease and lightly flour a 13×9×2-inch baking pan. In a large bowl combine flour, baking powder, and soda. In a medium bowl whisk together egg whites, maple syrup, oil, and milk; add to flour mixture. Stir to combine. Stir in the 1½ cups nuts and the chocolate. Spread in prepared pan.
2. Bake for 25 to 30 minutes or until a toothpick inserted near center comes out clean. Cool on rack. Spread with Chocolate-Hazelnut Frosting; sprinkle with the ⅔ cup nuts. Cut into bars. Makes 24 bars.
Chocolate-Hazelnut Frosting In a medium mixing bowl combine ¼ cup chocolate-hazelnut spread, 3 tablespoons fat-free milk, and 1 tablespoon pure maple syrup. Stir in ½ cup unsweetened cocoa powder. Stir in 1 to 1¼ cups powdered sugar until spreading consistency.
EACH BAR *174 cal, 11 g fat, 3 mg chol, 253 mg sodium, 18 g carb, 4 g fiber, 2 g pro.*

Coffee Nut Torte

PREP 30 min. STAND 30 min.
BAKE 20 min. COOL 10 min.
OVEN 350°F

6 eggs
2 cups all-purpose flour
1 Tbsp. baking powder
1½ cups sugar
½ cup strong brewed coffee or espresso, room temperature
1 cup ground walnuts or pecans
1 recipe Creamy Butter Frosting
Coarsely chopped nuts (optional)

1. Preheat oven to 350°F. Separate eggs. Allow egg yolks and egg whites to stand at room temperature for 30 minutes. Grease the bottoms of three 9×1½-inch round cake pans. Line pans with waxed paper; grease waxed paper. Set pans aside. In a medium bowl stir together flour and baking powder; set aside.
2. In a large mixing bowl beat egg yolks, sugar, and coffee with an electric mixer on low speed until combined. Beat on high about 5 minutes or until satin smooth. Add flour mixture and beat until combined; stir in nuts. Set aside.
3. Thoroughly wash beaters. In a very large mixing bowl beat egg whites on medium until stiff peaks form (tips stand straight). Gradually fold batter into beaten egg whites until combined. Pour into prepared baking pans.
4. Bake for 20 to 25 minutes or until cake tops spring back when lightly touched (centers may dip slightly). Cool cake layers on wire racks for 10 minutes. Remove cake layers from pans; remove waxed paper. Cool thoroughly on wire racks. Spread ½ cup Creamy Butter Frosting on each layer; stack layers. Frost sides of cake with remaining frosting. If desired, garnish with chopped nuts. Loosely cover and chill cake. Makes 12 to 14 servings.
Creamy Butter Frosting In a saucepan whisk ½ cup milk into 2 teaspoons cornstarch. Cook and stir over medium heat until thickened and bubbly. Reduce heat; cook and stir for 2 minutes more. Stir in 1 tablespoon rum or ½ teaspoon rum extract. Cover surface with plastic wrap.

Cool to room temperature (do not stir). In a large mixing bowl beat ¾ cup softened butter for 30 seconds. Add 2 cups powdered sugar; 2 tablespoons unsweetened cocoa powder, if using; and 1 teaspoon vanilla. Beat with electric mixer on medium until light and fluffy. Add cooled milk mixture to butter mixture, half at a time, beating on low after each addition until smooth. Beat in 5 to 6 cups additional powdered sugar until spreading consistency. Makes about 3¼ cups.
EACH SERVING *655 cal, 21 g fat, 137 mg chol, 183 mg sodium, 113 g carb, 1 g fiber, 7 g pro.*

KID FRIENDLY

German Chocolate Wonder Bars

PREP 25 min. BAKE 35 min.
OVEN 350°F

½ cup butter, softened
½ cup packed brown sugar
1 cup all-purpose flour
½ cup chocolate-hazelnut spread
¼ cup peanut butter
2 eggs, slightly beaten
¾ cup packed brown sugar
2 Tbsp. all-purpose flour
½ tsp. baking powder
1 tsp. vanilla
1½ cups shredded coconut
1 cup walnut halves or pieces

1. Preheat oven to 350°F. In a medium bowl combine butter, ½ cup brown sugar, and 1 cup flour. Press mixture into a 9×9×2-inch baking pan. Bake for 10 minutes or until light brown.
2. Meanwhile, in another medium bowl combine chocolate spread and peanut butter; set aside. In a large bowl combine eggs, ¾ cup sugar, 2 tablespoons flour, baking powder, and vanilla. Stir in coconut and walnuts.
3. Spread chocolate mixture over partially baked crust. Spread coconut mixture over chocolate layer. Bake for 25 to 30 minutes or until set in the center. Makes 24 bars.
EACH BAR *182 cal, 12 g fat, 28 mg chol, 61 mg sodium, 17 g carb, 1 g fiber, 3 g pro.*

Jams, Jellies, and Preserves

STRAWBERRY-
KIWI JAM

FAST LOW FAT KID FRIENDLY

Strawberry-Kiwi Jam

START TO FINISH 30 min.

3 cups fresh strawberries, hulled and quartered
3 medium fresh kiwifruit, peeled and finely chopped
1 1.75-oz. pkg. powdered fruit pectin
1 Tbsp. finely chopped crystallized ginger
1 Tbsp. butter
1 Tbsp. lemon juice
1 tsp. finely shredded orange peel
   Dash salt
5 cups sugar

1. In a bowl slightly mash strawberries. In a Dutch oven combine strawberries, kiwifruit, pectin, crystallized ginger, butter, lemon juice, orange peel, and salt. Heat on medium-high, stirring constantly, until mixture comes to a full rolling boil.
2. Add sugar. Return to boiling; boil 1 minute, stirring constantly. Remove from heat; skim off foam with a metal spoon.
3. Ladle jam into hot, sterilized half-pint canning jars, leaving ¼-inch headspace. Wipe rims of jars; adjust lids. Process in a boiling-water canner for 5 minutes (start timing when water returns to boiling). Remove jars; cool on racks. Makes about 6 half-pint jars.

EACH 1-TABLESPOON SERVING *45 cal, 0 fat, 0 mg chol, 3 mg sodium, 11 g carb, 0 g fiber, 0 g pro.*

LOW FAT KID FRIENDLY

Carrot Cake Jam

PREP 25 min. COOK 21 min.
PROCESS 10 min.

2 cups finely shredded carrots (4 medium)
1 cup finely chopped, peeled pears (1 medium)
1 15-oz. can crushed pineapple (juice pack), undrained
2 Tbsp. lemon juice
1 tsp. ground cinnamon
½ tsp. ground nutmeg
1 1.75-oz. pkg. regular powdered fruit pectin
4 cups granulated sugar
2 cups packed brown sugar
¼ cup flaked coconut or raisins (optional)
1 tsp. vanilla

1. In a 4- to 6-quart heavy pot combine carrots, pears, pineapple with the juice, lemon juice, cinnamon, and nutmeg. Bring to boiling, stirring constantly; reduce heat. Simmer, covered, for 20 minutes, stirring frequently. Remove from heat. Sprinkle mixture with pectin; stir until pectin dissolves.
2. Bring carrot mixture to boiling, stirring constantly. Add granulated sugar and brown sugar. Return to a full rolling boil; boil for 1 minute, stirring constantly. Remove from heat. Quickly skim off foam with a metal spoon. Stir in coconut or raisins (if desired) and vanilla.
3. Ladle hot jam into hot, sterilized half-pint canning jars, leaving ¼-inch headspace. Wipe jar rims; adjust lids.
4. Process filled jars in a boiling-water canner for 10 minutes (start timing when water returns to boiling). Remove jars from canner; cool on wire racks. Makes 7 half-pint jars.

EACH 1-TABLESPOON SERVING *48 cal, 0 g fat, 0 mg chol, 3 mg sodium, 13 g carb, 0 g fiber, 0 g pro.*

LOW FAT

Peach-Lavender Preserves

PREP 45 min. PROCESS 5 min.

7 cups sugar
4 cups coarsely chopped, peeled peaches* (about 3 lb.)
¼ cup lemon juice
½ a 6-oz. pkg. (1 foil pouch) liquid fruit pectin
2 Tbsp. fresh or dried lavender buds

1. In a 6- to 8-quart heavy pot combine sugar, peaches, and lemon juice. Bring to boiling over medium-high heat, stirring constantly until sugar dissolves. Quickly stir in liquid pectin. Bring to a full rolling boil, stirring constantly. Boil hard for 1 minute, stirring constantly. Remove from heat. Quickly skim off foam with a metal spoon. Stir in lavender buds.
2. Ladle hot preserves into hot, sterilized half-pint canning jars, leaving ¼-inch headspace. Wipe jar rims; adjust lids.
3. Process filled jars in a boiling-water canner for 5 minutes (start timing when water returns to boiling). Remove jars from canner; cool on wire racks. Makes 7 half-pint jars.

EACH 1-TABLESPOON SERVING *51 cal, 0 g fat, 0 mg chol, 0 mg sodium, 13 g carb, 0 g fiber, 0 g pro.*

* Tip To peel peaches, immerse them in boiling water for 30 to 60 seconds or until the skins start to split; remove fruit and plunge into cold water. Using a paring knife, carefully peel off and discard skins. Halve and pit peaches.

Tacos with a Twist

PRIZE TESTED RECIPES **$500 WINNER**
Barbara Boltjes, COLORADO SPRINGS, CO

THAI CHICKEN
TACOS

FAST **LOW FAT**
Thai Chicken Tacos
START TO FINISH **30 min.**

1   lime, halved
1   lb. skinless, boneless chicken breasts
    or tenders, cut in ½- to ¾-inch pieces
¼   cup chopped fresh cilantro
1   large shallot, finely chopped
3   cloves garlic, minced
1   Tbsp. fish sauce
2   tsp. reduced-sodium soy sauce
½   to 1 tsp. crushed red pepper
⅓   to 1 tsp. hot chili sauce (such
    as Sriracha)
2   Tbsp. vegetable oil
16 corn tortillas, heated
1   recipe Cabbage Slaw

1. Juice 1 lime half (about 1 tablespoon);
cut remaining half in wedges. In a bowl stir
together chicken, cilantro, shallot, garlic,
the 1 tablespoon lime juice, fish sauce,
soy sauce, pepper, and chili sauce. Cover;
refrigerate 1 hour.
2. In a large skillet cook chicken mixture
in hot oil over medium-high heat 5 minutes
or until chicken is cooked throughly,
stirring occasionally.
3. To serve, layer 2 tortillas. Top with
chicken and Cabbage Slaw. Serve with
remaining slaw and lime wedges. Makes
4 servings.
Cabbage Slaw In a bowl toss 2 cups
shredded napa cabbage, ½ cup shredded
carrot, ½ cup sliced green onions, ⅓ cup
sliced radishes, ¼ cup chopped fresh
cilantro, and ¼ cup coarsely chopped
peanuts (optional). Add ¼ cup rice
vinegar; toss.
EACH SERVING *454 cal, 11 g fat, 66 mg chol,
596 mg sodium, 55 g carb, 9 g fiber, 34 g pro.*

Margarita Fish Tacos with Mango Salsa
START TO FINISH **35 min.**

1   lb. fresh or frozen swordfish, halibut,
    or mahi mahi steaks, cut 1 inch thick
½   cup margarita drink mix (contains
    no alcohol)
1   tsp. Jamaican jerk seasoning
1   15-oz. can black beans, rinsed
    and drained
1   large mango, seeded, peeled and
    chopped
1   large tomato, seeded and chopped
2   to 4 Tbsp. snipped fresh cilantro
2   Tbsp. thinly sliced green onion (1)
1   fresh jalapeño pepper, seeded and
    chopped (see note, page 11)
1   Tbsp. lime juice
½   tsp. ancho chili powder
¼   tsp. salt
1   Tbsp. cooking oil
8   6-inch flour or corn tortillas
2   cups shredded fresh spinach
    or leaf lettuce

1. Thaw fish, if frozen. Cut fish in ¾-inch
strips. In a shallow dish combine margarita
mix and jerk seasoning. Add fish strips,
turning to coat. Cover and marinate in the
refrigerator for 15 minutes, turning fish
once or twice.
2. Meanwhile, for salsa, in a large bowl
stir together the beans, mango, tomato,
cilantro, green onion, jalapeño pepper,
lime juice, chili powder, and salt. Set aside.
3. Drain fish, discarding marinade. Heat
oil in a large skillet over medium heat.
Add fish. Cook for 2 to 4 minutes or until
fish flakes easily with a fork, turning fish
occasionally to brown evenly. Meanwhile,
heat tortillas according to package
directions. Fill tortillas with spinach,
fish strips, and salsa. Serve immediately.
Makes 4 servings.
EACH SERVING *522 cal, 16 g fat, 43 mg chol,
580 mg sodium, 58 g carb, 7 g fiber, 36 g pro.*

FAST
Salmon Tacos
START TO FINISH **20 min.**

14 to 16 oz. cooked salmon, flaked
1   Tbsp. lime juice
8   6-inch corn tortillas, warmed
1   cup pkg. shredded cabbage with
    carrot (coleslaw mix)
½   cup thinly sliced red sweet pepper
1   recipe Sour Cream Drizzle
    Snipped fresh cilantro (optional)
    Lime wedges (optional)

1. In a small bowl toss together salmon and
lime juice until combined.
2. Place 2 tortillas on each of four serving
plates. Top each tortilla with cabbage,
sweet pepper, and salmon mixture. Fold
tortillas in half. Top each taco with Sour
Cream Drizzle. If desired, sprinkle with
snipped cilantro and serve with lime
wedges.
Sour Cream Drizzle In a small bowl stir
together ⅓ cup light sour cream,
1 tablespoon snipped fresh cilantro,
1 tablespoon lime juice, ⅛ teaspoon salt,
and ⅛ teaspoon ground chipotle chile
pepper or chili powder. Makes 4 servings.
EACH SERVING *354 cal, 15 g fat, 72 mg chol,
229 mg sodium, 27 g carb, 4 g fiber, 7 g pro.*

Smoothies and Shakes

PRIZE TESTED RECIPES® $500 WINNER
Jennifer Knight, RUCKERSVILLE, VA

BLUEBERRY SUNRISE
SMOOTHIE

FAST | KID FRIENDLY

Blueberry Sunrise Smoothie

START TO FINISH 15 min.

Nonstick cooking spray
1 egg, beaten
1 banana, peeled, cut up, and frozen
1 6-oz. carton plain low-fat yogurt
⅓ cup halved seedless grapes, frozen
⅓ cup frozen blueberries
2 Tbsp. frozen orange juice concentrate, thawed
Blueberries and halved seedless grapes (optional)

1. Lightly coat a small unheated nonstick skillet with cooking spray; heat over medium-low heat. Add egg. With a spatula, lift and fold the egg mixture until set. Transfer to a blender.
2. Add banana, yogurt, grapes, blueberries, and orange juice concentrate. Cover and blend until smooth. Serve immediately. If desired, top with blueberries and halved grapes. Makes 2 servings.
EACH SERVING 206 cal, 4 g fat, 111 mg chol, 96 mg sodium, 36 g carb, 3 g fiber, 9 g pro.

FAST | KID FRIENDLY

Coconut-Almond Smoothies

START TO FINISH 10 min.

1 cup fat-free milk
2 medium bananas, peeled, sliced and frozen
3 Tbsp. shredded coconut
3 Tbsp. purchased almond butter
½ tsp. vanilla

1. In a blender combine milk, bananas, coconut, almond butter, and vanilla. Cover and blend until smooth. Makes 3 servings.
EACH SERVING 236 cal, 12 g fat, 2 mg chol, 131 mg sodium, 29 g carb, 3 g fiber, 7 g pro.

FAST | LOW FAT | KID FRIENDLY

Date and Spice Smoothie

PREP 10 min. STAND 20 min.

1 cup pitted whole dates
1 medium Bartlett pear, cored and cut up
1 medium banana, peeled and cut up
1 cup ice cubes
1 6-oz. carton maple and brown sugar low-fat yogurt
¾ to 1 cup milk
½ tsp. grated fresh ginger
¼ tsp. ground cinnamon
¼ tsp. ground nutmeg

1. Place dates in a bowl and add enough boiling water to cover. Let stand 20 minutes; drain.
2. In a blender combine drained dates, pear, banana, ice cubes, yogurt, milk, ginger, cinnamon, and nutmeg. Cover and blend until smooth. Makes 4 servings.
EACH SERVING 234 cal, 2 g fat, 6 mg chol, 51 sodium, 54 g carb, 6 g fiber, 5 g pro.

FAST | KID FRIENDLY

Chocolate-Peanut Butter Smoothies

START TO FINISH 10 min.

1 cup chocolate-flavored soy milk or chocolate-flavored lowfat milk
2 medium bananas, peeled, sliced and frozen
2 Tbsp. creamy peanut butter

1. In a blender combine soy milk, bananas, and peanut butter. Cover and blend until smooth. Makes 2 servings
EACH SERVING 271 cal, 11 g fat, 0 mg chol, 131 mg sodium, 41 g carb, 5 g fiber, 8 g pro.

FAST | KID FRIENDLY

Elvis Smoothies

START TO FINISH 5 min.

1½ cups small ice cubes or crushed ice
1½ cups milk
1 large banana, halved
¼ cup creamy peanut butter
2 Tbsp. honey
1 to 2 Tbsp. protein powder (optional)

1. In a blender combine ice cubes and milk; cover and pulse with several on/off turns until ice is finely chopped. Add banana, peanut butter, honey, and protein powder, if desired; cover and blend until smooth. Makes 2 servings.
EACH SERVING 413 cal, 20 g fat, 15 mg chol, 224 mg sodium, 50 g carb, 4 g fiber, 15 g pro.

FAST | LOW FAT | KID FRIENDLY

Cherry-Berry Smoothie

START TO FINISH 10 min.

½ cup fresh or frozen unsweetened pitted red tart cherries
½ cup lowfat milk
¼ cup plain fat-free or lowfat yogurt
2 Tbsp. fresh or frozen unsweetened blueberries or raspberries
1 Tbsp. frozen tart cherry juice or cranberry juice concentrate, thawed
1 Tbsp. honey
½ tsp. vanilla
8 ice cubes
Fresh pitted red tart cherries or chopped dried cherries (optional)

1. In a blender combine ½ cup cherries, milk, yogurt, blueberries, juice concentrate, honey, and vanilla. Cover and blend about 45 seconds or until smooth. Add ice cubes. Cover and blend about 15 seconds more or until smooth. Pour into two chilled glasses.
2. If desired top each with additional cherries or chopped dried cherries. Makes 2 servings.
EACH SERVING 117 cal, 1 g fat, 4 mg chol, 52 mg sodium, 24 g carb, 1 g fiber, 4 g pro.

Raspberry Chai Smoothies

START TO FINISH 10 min.

1   12-oz. pkg. frozen red raspberries
1   6-oz. carton vanilla fat-free yogurt
1½ cups chai tea concentrate or double-strength brewed black tea, chilled
1   ripe banana, sliced and frozen
2   Tbsp. honey (optional)

1. In a blender combine raspberries, yogurt, chai tea concentrate, banana, and honey, if desired. Cover and blend for 1 to 2 minutes or until almost smooth, stopping blender occasionally to scrape sides. Pour into glasses.Serve immediately. Makes 4 servings.

EACH SERVING 196 cal, 0 g fat, 1 mg chol, 40 mg sodium, 47 g carb, 5 g fiber, 3 g pro.

Piña Colada Chai Smoothies Prepare as above except, substitute half a 10-ounce can frozen piña colada mix concentrate (½ cup) for the red raspberries. Add 1½ cups ice cubes and omit honey.

Protein-Packed Smoothies

START TO FINISH 10 min.

2   cups plain fat-free yogurt
2   ripe medium bananas
2   cups sliced fresh strawberries or frozen unsweetened strawberries
2   Tbsp. honey
2   Tbsp. peanut butter
    Whole fresh strawberries (optional)

1. In a blender combine yogurt, bananas, sliced strawberries, honey, and peanut butter. Cover and blend until smooth. Serve immediately. If desired, top with whole strawberries. Makes 4 servings.

EACH SERVING 223 cal, 5 g fat, 2 mg chol, 133 mg sodium, 39 g carb, 3 g fiber, 10 g pro.

Peanut Butter, Banana, and Chocolate Smoothies

PREP 10 min. FREEZE 1 hr 30 min.

1   medium banana, peeled
1½ cups vanilla frozen yogurt
1   cup fat-free chocolate milk or light chocolate soy milk
2   Tbsp. creamy peanut butter

1. Cut banana into 1-inch pieces; place in a single layer on a baking sheet. Cover and freeze about 1½ hours or until frozen.
2. In a blender combine frozen banana pieces, frozen yogurt, milk, and peanut butter. Cover and blend until smooth. Serve immediately. Makes 4 servings.

EACH SERVING 188 cal, 7 g fat, 9 mg chol, 98 mg sodium, 28 g carb, 2 g fiber, 6 g pro.

Antioxidant Power Smoothies

START TO FINISH 10 min.

1   cup fresh blueberries
1   cup fresh blackberries
1   6-oz. carton blueberry fat-free yogurt
½   cup pomegranate juice
1   Tbsp. honey
    Fresh blueberries and/or blackberries (optional)

1. In a blender combine the 1 cup blueberries, the 1 cup blackberries, yogurt, pomegranate juice, and honey. Cover and blend until almost smooth. If desired, press mixture through a fine-mesh sieve to remove blackberry seeds. Serve immediately. If desired, garnish with additional berries. Makes 2 servings.

EACH SERVING 190 cal, 1 g fat, 2 mg chol, 54 mg sodium, 43 g carb, 6 g fiber, 5 g pro.

Wake-Me-Up Smoothies

START TO FINISH 10 min.

2   cups ice cubes
1   cup fat-free milk
¾   cup double-strength coffee
2   Tbsp. sugar
1   Tbsp. sugar-free caramel ice cream topping
    Fat-free frozen whipped dessert topping, thawed (optional)
    Chocolate-covered espresso beans, coarsely chopped (optional)

1. In a blender combine ice, milk, coffee, sugar, and ice cream topping. Cover and blend until smooth. Serve immediately. If desired, top with additional whipped topping and chocolate-covered espresso beans. Makes 4 servings.

EACH SERVING 57 cal, 0 g fat, 1 mg chol, 36 mg sodium, 12 g carb, 2 g pro.

Apple Berry Smoothie

START TO FINISH 15 min.

1   21-oz. can apple pie filling
1   cup sliced fresh strawberries
½   cup fresh or frozen unsweetened blueberries or blackberries
1   6-oz. carton plain fat-free yogurt
2   Tbsp. sugar
2   tsp. vanilla
1   cup ice cubes
    Fresh strawberries and blueberries (optional)

1. In a blender combine pie filling, 1 cup sliced strawberries, ½ cup blueberries, yogurt, sugar, and vanilla. Cover and blend about 45 seconds or until smooth. Add the ice cubes. Cover and blend about 15 seconds more or until smooth.
2. Serve in tall chilled glasses. Makes 4 servings.

EACH SERVING 225 cal, 0 g fat, 1 mg chol., 103 mg sodium, 54 g carb, 3 g fiber, 3 g pro.

Ginger-Peach Smoothies

FAST LOW FAT KID FRIENDLY

START TO FINISH 10 min.

2 cups frozen unsweetened peach slices
1¼ to 1 ½ cups apricot nectar
2 tsp. honey
⅛ tsp. ground ginger

1. In a blender combine peaches, apricot nectar, honey, and ginger. Cover and blend until smooth. Makes 2 servings.
EACH SERVING 182 cal, 0 g fat, 0 mg chol, 5 mg sodium, 47 g carb, 3 g fiber, 1 g pro.

Banana Split Smoothies

FAST KID FRIENDLY

START TO FINISH 10 min.

1 8-oz. carton vanilla low-fat yogurt
½ to ¾ cup fat-free milk
1 cup frozen unsweetened whole strawberries
1 medium banana, peeled, sliced and frozen
1 Tbsp. unsweetened cocoa powder
½ tsp. vanilla

1. In a blender combine yogurt, milk, strawberries, banana, cocoa powder, and vanilla. Cover and blend until smooth. Makes 2 servings.
EACH SERVING 209 cal, 3 g fat, 7 mg chol, 105 mg sodium, 40 g carb, 3 g fiber, , 9 g pro.

Vanilla-Orange Smoothies

FAST LOW FAT KID FRIENDLY

START TO FINISH 10 min.

1 8-oz. carton vanilla low-fat yogurt
½ cup orange juice, chilled
¼ tsp. vanilla
1 cup small ice cubes or crushed ice

1. In a blender combine yogurt, orange juice, and vanilla. Cover and blend until smooth.
2. Add ice cubes; cover and blend until cubes are crushed. Makes 2 servings.
EACH SERVING 126 cal, 2 g fat, 6 mg chol, 76 mg sodium, 22 g carb, 0 g fiber, , 6 g pro.

Blueberry Breakfast Shakes

FAST LOW FAT KID FRIENDLY

START TO FINISH 10 min.

3 6-oz. cartons plain low-fat yogurt
1 cup fresh or frozen blueberries
½ cup crushed ice
¼ cup sugar
¼ cup light vanilla soy milk
¼ tsp. almond extract

1. In a blender container combine yogurt, blueberries, ice, sugar, soy milk, and almond extract. Cover and blend until smooth. Serve immediately. Makes 5 servings.
EACH SERVING 126 cal, 2 g fat, 6 mg chol, 82 mg sodium, 22 g carb, 1 g fiber, 6 g pro.

Milk Shakes

FAST KID FRIENDLY

START TO FINISH 5 min.

1 pint vanilla ice cream
½ to ¾ cup milk
2 Tbsp. malted milk powder (optional)

1. Place ice cream, milk, and malted milk powder, if using, in a blender. Cover and blend until smooth. Makes 2 servings.
EACH SERVING 329 cal, 17 g fat, 68 mg chol, 140 mg sodium, 37 g carb, 1 g fiber, 7 g pro.
Peanut Butter-Banana Shakes Prepare as above, except increase milk to 1 cup and add 1 medium ripe banana, sliced, and 3 tablespoons creamy peanut butter with the milk. If desired, substitute chocolate ice cream for the vanilla ice cream. To make a malt, use chocolate malted milk powder rather than plain. Makes 3 servings.
Fruity Milk Shake Prepare as above, except add 2 cups sliced fresh or frozen fruit, such as peeled peaches, strawberries, mango, and/or whole blueberries. Omit the malted milk powder. Makes 3 servings.

Frosty Mocha-Cacao Shakes

FAST

START TO FINISH 15 min.

1 pint premium-quality coffee or chocolate ice cream (2 cups)
½ cup cold strong-brewed coffee
¼ cup light rum or 3 Tbsp. bourbon
2 Tbsp. crème de cacao or coffee liqueur
6 chocolate-covered espresso beans Whipped cream
4 chocolate-covered espresso beans (optional) Chocolate curls (optional)

1. In a blender combine ice cream, coffee, rum, crème de cacao, and 6 espresso beans. Cover and blend until almost smooth. Pour the mixture into 4 tall chilled tall glasses. If desired, garnish each serving with whipped cream, a chocolate-covered espresso bean, and chocolate curls. Serve immediately. Makes 4 servings.
EACH SERVING 357 cal, 21 g fat, 96 mg chol, 68 mg sodium, 26 g carb, 0 g fiber, 7 g pro.

Cupcake Shakes

FAST KID FRIENDLY

PREP 5 min.

1 pint vanilla or desired flavor ice cream, softened
1 frosted cupcake
2 Tbsp. milk

1. Place ice cream, cupcake, and milk in a blender. Cover and blend until combined. Pour into glasses. Makes 2 servings.
EACH SERVING 459 cal, 22 g fat, 91 mg chol, 218 mg sodium, 60 g carb, 2 g fiber, 7 g pro.

Ice Cream, Sherbet, and Sorbet

**BANANA-BUTTER PECAN
ICE CREAM**

KID FRIENDLY

Banana-Butter Pecan Ice Cream

PREP 40 min. BAKE 8 min.
COOL 30 min. CHILL 4 hr. FREEZE per
manufacturer's directions RIPEN 4 hr.
OVEN 350°F

1½ cups finely chopped pecans
2   Tbsp. butter, melted
¼   tsp. salt
1½ cups packed brown sugar
2   cups whipping cream
6   egg yolks
½   cup granulated sugar
1   tsp. vanilla
3   ripe medium bananas
4   cups whole milk
    Banana slices (optional)

1. Preheat oven to 350°F. In bowl toss pecans with butter and salt. Spread in 15×10×1-inch baking pan. Bake 8 to 10 minutes or until toasted; stir once. Set aside.
2. In medium saucepan combine brown sugar and 1½ cups of the cream; cook and stir over medium heat until sugar is melted. In bowl whisk together yolks and remaining cream; gradually whisk in ¾ cup hot brown sugar mixture. Gradually add to mixture in saucepan. Cook and stir over medium heat until bubbles begin to form (190°F). Remove from heat. Whisk in granulated sugar and vanilla. Cool 30 minutes. Cover; chill 4 to 24 hours.
3. In a small bowl mash bananas (1 cup); gradually stir in chilled mixture. Pour in a 4- to 5-quart ice cream freezer along with whole milk. Freeze according to manufacturer's directions. Stir in pecan mixture. If desired, ripen at least 4 hours.* Top with banana slices, if desired. Makes 24 servings.
EACH ½-CUP SERVING 245 cal, 16 g fat, 86 mg chol, 61 mg sodium, 25 g carb, 0 g fiber, 3 g pro.

KID FRIENDLY

Lemon Custard Ice Cream

PREP 30 min. CHILL 4 hr. FREEZE per
manufacturer's directions

1½ cups milk
6   egg yolks
¾   cup sugar
1   Tbsp. finely shredded lemon peel
½   tsp. salt
1½ cups whipping cream
⅓   cup lemon juice

1. In a small saucepan heat milk over medium heat until tiny bubbles begin to appear around the edge of the saucepan.
2. For custards, in a medium saucepan whisk together egg yolks, sugar, lemon peel, and salt. Gradually whisk in warmed milk. Cook and stir over medium heat until mixture thickens and coats the back of a spoon (do not boil).
3. Quickly place the saucepan in a large bowl of ice water. Stir constantly for 2 to 3 minutes, to quickly cool the mixture. Pour custard into a bowl. Stir in whipping cream. Cover and chill at least 4 hours or up to overnight.
4. Stir in lemon juice. Strain custard to remove lemon peel. Discard peel.
5. Freeze custard in a 2-, 3-, or 4-quart ice cream freezer according to manufacturer's directions. If desired, ripen up to 4 hours.* Makes 8 servings.
EACH ½-CUP SERVING 295 cal, 21 g fat, 223 mg chol, 187 mg sodium, 24 g carb, 0 g fiber, 5 g pro.

LOW FAT   KID FRIENDLY

Melon-Mango Ice Cream

PREP 20 min. FREEZE per
manufacturer's directions

2   cups whole milk
2   cups buttermilk
2   cups fat-free half-and-half
1   cup sugar
1   Tbsp. vanilla
1½ cups chopped cantaloupe
1½ cups chopped mango

1. In a large bowl combine milk, buttermilk, fat-free half-and-half, sugar, and vanilla. Stir to dissolve sugar.
2. In a blender or food processor, combine cantaloupe and mango. Cover and blend or process until smooth. Stir pureed fruit into milk mixture. Freeze in a 4- to 5-quart ice cream freezer according to the manufacturer's directions. If desired, ripen for 4 hours.* Makes 24 servings.
EACH ½-CUP SERVING 76 cal, 1 g fat, 4 mg chol, 60 mg sodium, 15 g carb, 0 g fiber, 2 g pro.
* **Tip** Ripening homemade ice cream improves the texture and helps to keep it from melting too quickly during eating. To ripen in a traditional-style ice cream freezer, after churning, remove the lid and dasher and cover the top of the freezer can with waxed paper or foil. Plug the hole in the lid with a small piece of cloth; replace the lid. Pack the outer freezer bucket with enough ice and rock salt to cover the top of the freezer can (use 1 cup salt for each 4 cups ice). Ripen about 4 hours.

When using an ice cream freezer with an insulated freezer bowl, transfer the ice cream to a covered freezer container and ripen by freezing it in your regular freezer about 4 hours (or check the manufacturer's recommendations).

Peach and Nectarine Desserts

CHEESECAKE-STUFFED
PEACHES

Cheesecake-Stuffed Peaches

PREP 10 min. BAKE 30 min.
OVEN 350°F

6 peaches, halved and pitted
¼ cup butter, melted
3 Tbsp. cinnamon-sugar*
½ of an 8-oz. pkg. cream cheese, softened
¼ cup sugar
1 egg yolk
1½ tsp. vanilla

1. Preheat oven to 350°F. Line a 15×10×1-inch baking pan with parchment paper; set aside. Trim a very thin slice from the round side of each peach half so halves stand flat in the baking pan. Dip peach halves in melted butter to coat. Arrange peach halves, cut sides up, in prepared pan. Sprinkle cut sides of peaches with cinnamon-sugar; set aside.
2. In a medium mixing bowl beat cream cheese with a mixer on medium speed until smooth. Add sugar, egg yolk, and vanilla. Beat until combined. Spoon cream cheese mixture into peach centers.
3. Bake, uncovered, about 30 minutes or until lightly browned and softened. Serve warm or at room temperature. Makes 6 servings.
EACH SERVING 261 cal, 15 g fat, 76 mg chol, 117 mg sodium, 30 g carb, 2 g fiber, 3 g pro.
*Note Use a purchased cinnamon-sugar mixture or combine 3 tablespoons granulated sugar with 1 teaspoon ground cinnamon.

Creamy Peaches-and-Cream Coffee Cake

PREP 30 min. STAND 30 min.
BAKE 55 min. COOL 20 min.
OVEN 325°F

½ cup butter or margarine
2 eggs
½ cup all-purpose flour
½ cup sugar
¼ cup cold butter or margarine
¼ cup sliced almonds
2 cups all-purpose flour
1 tsp. baking powder
1 tsp. baking soda
¼ tsp. salt
1 cup sugar
1 tsp. vanilla
1 8-oz. carton sour cream
1 egg yolk, slightly beaten
1 8-oz. pkg. cream cheese, softened
1 tsp. vanilla
½ cup sugar
1 cup peach preserves

1. Allow the ½ cup butter and the 2 eggs to stand at room temperature for 30 minutes. Meanwhile, grease and lightly flour a 9-inch springform pan; set aside. Preheat oven to 325°F.
2. For the topping, in a bowl combine the ½ cup flour and the ½ cup sugar. Using a pastry blender cut in the ¼ cup cold butter until mixture resembles coarse crumbs. Stir in almonds. Set side.
3. For the cake, in a medium bowl stir together the 2 cups flour, baking powder, baking soda, and salt. Set aside. In a large mixing bowl, beat the ½ cup softened butter with an electric mixer on medium to high speed for 30 seconds. Add the 1 cup sugar and 1 teaspoon vanilla; beat until well combined. Add room temperature eggs 1 at a time, beating well after each addition. Alternately add flour mixture and sour cream to butter mixture, beating on low speed after each addition just until combined. Set aside.
4. For the filling, in another mixing bowl beat the egg yolk, cream cheese, and 1 teaspoon vanilla until light and fluffy. Gradually add the ½ cup sugar, beating well. Set aside.
5. Spread half the cake batter into prepared pan. Spread filling over cake batter. Spread peach preserves over the filling. Spread the remaining cake batter over the preserves. Sprinkle with topping. Place cake pan on oven rack with a baking sheet positioned on a lower rack to catch any spills.
6. Bake for 55 to 60 minutes or until a wooden toothpick inserted near center comes out clean. Cool coffee cake on a wire rack for 20 minutes. (Center may fall slightly during cooling.) Remove sides of the pan. Serve warm. Makes 10 to 12 servings.
EACH SERVING 634 cal, 30 g fat, 134 mg chol, 411 mg sodium, 85 g carb, 2 g fiber, 8 g pro.

Tart Cherry-Nectarine Crisp

PREP 40 min. BAKE 30 min.
OVEN 375°F

4 cups fresh tart red cherries, pitted, or 3 cups frozen pitted tart red cherries, thawed (do not drain)
3 nectarines, halved, pitted, and sliced
¼ cup granulated sugar
2 Tbsp. all-purpose flour
⅛ tsp. ground nutmeg
⅔ cup all-purpose flour
½ cup rolled oats
⅓ cup packed brown sugar
1 tsp. finely shredded lemon peel
⅓ cup butter
½ cup coarsely chopped pecans
   Vanilla ice cream (optional)

1. Preheat oven to 375°F. In a shallow 1½- to 2-quart baking dish combine cherries and nectarines. In a bowl stir together granulated sugar, the 2 tablespoons flour, and the nutmeg. Add to fruit and toss to coat.
2. For toppping, in a medium bowl stir together the ⅔ cup flour, the oats, brown sugar, and lemon peel. Cut in butter until mixture resembles coarse crumbs. Stir in pecans. Sprinkle over fruit mixture.
3. Bake for 30 to 40 minutes or until bubbly in center. Serve warm. If desired, serve with vanilla ice cream. Makes 8 servings.
EACH SERVING 306 cal, 14 g fat, 20 mg chol, 58 mg sodium, 44 g carb, 4 g fiber, 5 g pro.

Roll-Ups and Wraps

PRIZE TESTED RECIPES® $500 WINNER
Royanne Kerr, FORT WORTH, TX

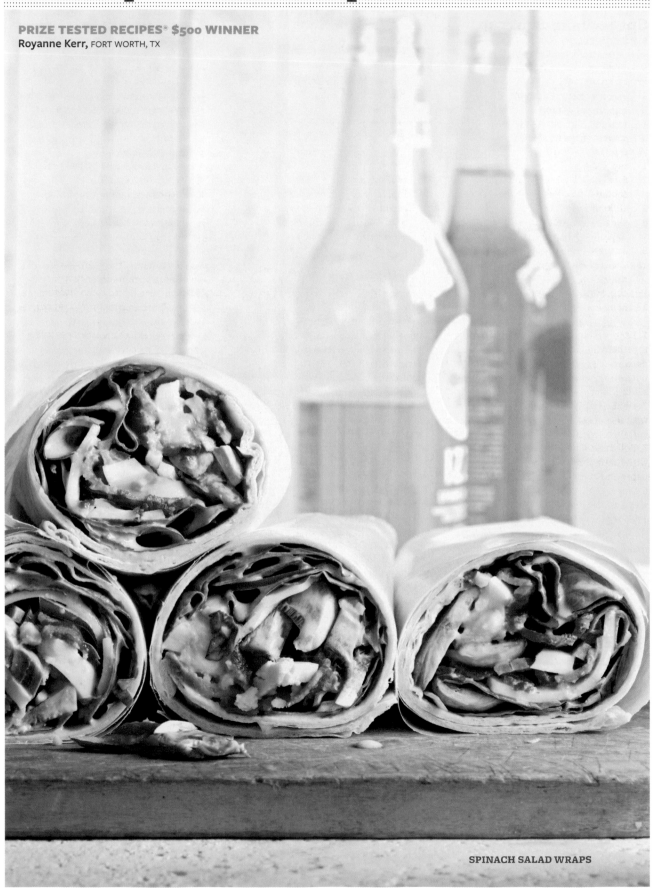

SPINACH SALAD WRAPS

FAST
Spinach Salad Wraps
START TO FINISH 30 min.

5   Tbsp. red wine vinegar
¼   cup sour cream
2   Tbsp. sugar
2   tsp. snipped fresh parsley
1   tsp. salt
2   cloves garlic, minced
½   tsp. dry mustard
1   tsp. olive oil
1   5-oz. pkg. fresh baby spinach
     (about 5 cups)
6   10-inch flour tortillas
6   slices mozzarella cheese, torn
     in half
8   oz. fresh mushrooms, sliced
12   slices bacon, crisp-cooked and
     drained
½   cup thinly sliced red onion
3   hard-cooked eggs, sliced

1. For dressing, in a small bowl whisk together vinegar, sour cream, sugar, parsley, salt, garlic, and dry mustard until combined. Whisk in the olive oil; set dressing aside.
2. Divide spinach among flour tortillas. Top with cheese, mushrooms, bacon, red onion, and sliced eggs. Drizzle with dressing.
3. Roll up tortillas. If necessary, secure with toothpicks. If desired, wrap in waxed paper and cut in half to serve. Makes 6 wraps.
EACH WRAP *481 cal, 23 g fat, 150 mg chol, 1,454 mg sodium, 45 g carb, 4 g fiber, 23 g pro.*

Salmon Wrapsody
PREP 30 min. MARINATE 1 hr.
GRILL 4 min. per ½-inch thickness
of fish

1   lb. fresh or frozen skinless salmon,
     cod, or tilapia fillets
½   cup lemon juice
¼   cup finely chopped shallots or onion
3   Tbsp. olive oil
2   Tbsp. snipped fresh dill
2   cloves garlic, minced
½   tsp. kosher salt or ¼ tsp. regular salt
¼   tsp. freshly ground black pepper
1   recipe Garlic-Lemon Mayo
4   6- to 8-inch flour tortillas
2   cups shredded lettuce
     Lemon wedges (optional)

1. Thaw fish, if frozen. Rinse fish; pat dry. Place fish in a resealable plastic bag set in a shallow dish.
2. For marinade, in a small bowl combine lemon juice, shallots, oil, dill, garlic, salt, and pepper. Pour over fish in bag. Seal bag. Marinate in the refrigerator up to 1 hour, turning the bag occasionally. Remove fish from marinade, reserving marinade.
3. For a charcoal grill fish on a well-greased grill rack of an uncovered grill directly over medium coals for 4 to 6 minutes per ½-inch thickness of fish or until fish flakes easily when tested with a fork, brushing with reserved marinade and gently turning halfway through grilling. (Discard any remaining marinade.) (For a gas grill, preheat grill. Reduce heat to medium. Place fish on grill rack over heat. Cover and grill as above.)
4. Transfer fish to a cutting board. Using a fork, flake fish into bite-size pieces. Spread Garlic-Lemon Mayo on each tortilla. Top with lettuce and fish. Roll up; secure with toothpicks, if necessary. If desired, serve with lemon wedges. Makes 4 wraps.
Garlic-Lemon Mayo In a small bowl stir together ⅓ cup mayonnaise, 2 tablespoons finely chopped celery, 2 tablespoons finely chopped green onion, 1 tablespoon snipped fresh dill, ½ teaspoon finely shredded lemon peel, and 1 clove minced garlic. Makes about ½ cup.
EACH WRAP *583 cal, 13 g fat, 60 mg chol, 619 mg sodium, 23 g carb, 2 g fiber, 27 g pro.*

FAST
Thai Pork Roll-Ups
START TO FINISH 30 min. OVEN 350°F

6   8- to 10-inch spinach, tomato, and/or
     plain flour tortillas
½   tsp. garlic salt
¼   to ½ tsp. ground black pepper
12   oz. pork tenderloin, cut in
     1-inch strips
1   Tbsp. cooking oil
4   cups packaged shredded broccoli
     (broccoli slaw mix)
1   medium red onion, cut in thin
     wedges
1   tsp. grated fresh ginger
1   recipe Peanut Sauce

1. Wrap tortillas in foil. Heat in a 350°F oven about 10 minutes or until warm. Meanwhile, in a medium bowl combine garlic salt and pepper. Add pork, tossing to coat evenly.
2. In a large skillet cook and stir seasoned pork in hot oil over medium-high heat for 4 to 6 minutes or until no longer pink. Turn down heat if pork gets too brown. Remove pork from skillet; keep warm. Add broccoli, onion, and ginger to skillet. Cook and stir for 4 to 6 minutes or until vegetables are crisp-tender. Remove from heat.
3. To assemble, spread one side of each tortilla with Peanut Sauce. Top with pork strips and vegetable mixture. Roll up each tortilla, securing with a wooden toothpick. Serve immediately. Makes 6 roll-ups.
Peanut Sauce In a small saucepan combine ¼ cup creamy peanut butter, 3 tablespoons water, 1 tablespoon sugar, 2 teaspoons soy sauce, and ½ teaspoon bottled minced garlic. Heat over medium-low heat, whisking constantly, until sauce is smooth and warm. Use immediately or keep warm over very low heat, stirring occasionally.
EACH ROLL-UP *389 cal, 13 g fat, 37 mg chol, 649 mg sodium, 44 g carb, 5 g fiber, 22 g pro.*

Slow Cooker Chicken

PRIZE TESTED RECIPES® $500 WINNER
Karen Heyse, ST. LOUIS, MO

DRIED PLUM AND
OLIVE CHICKEN

Dried Plum and Olive Chicken

PREP 25 min. COOK 5 hr. (low)

13   chicken thighs and/or drumsticks, skinned
¼   tsp. salt
¼   tsp. black pepper
1   cup pitted dried plums (prunes)
1   cup pimiento-stuffed green olives
2   Tbsp. capers
1   Tbsp. dried Italian seasoning, crushed
2   cloves garlic, minced
2   bay leaves
1   14.5-oz. can chicken broth
¼   cup honey
¼   cup cider vinegar
3   cups hot cooked rice

1. Place chicken in a 5- or 6-quart slow cooker; sprinkle with the salt and pepper. Add plums, olives, capers, Italian seasoning, garlic, and bay leaves. Pour broth, honey, and vinegar over all in the cooker.
2. Cover and cook on low heat setting for 5 to 6 hours. Skim excess fat from broth; remove and discard bay leaves. Serve with hot cooked rice. Makes 6 servings.
EACH SERVING 414 cal, 9 g fat, 115 mg chol, 907 mg sodium, 53 g carb, 4 g fiber, 31 g pro.

Chinese Red-Cooked Chicken

PREP 25 min. COOK 6 hr. (low) or 3 hr. (high)

2½   to 3 lb. chicken drumsticks and/or thighs, skinned
5   whole star anise
2   3-inch strips orange peel*
3   inches stick cinnamon, broken
1   2-inch piece fresh ginger, thinly sliced
2   cloves garlic, minced
1   tsp. whole Szechwan peppercorns
2   14-oz. cans reduced-sodium chicken broth
¾   cup soy sauce
4   green onions (white and green parts), cut in 2-inch pieces
¼   cup packed brown sugar
1   Tbsp. dry sherry
1   8-oz. pkg. dried Chinese egg noodles or fine egg noodles
1   tsp. sesame oil (not toasted)
2   Tbsp. fresh cilantro leaves

1. Arrange chicken in a 3½- or 4-quart slow cooker. For spice bag, cut an 8-inch square from a double thickness of 100%-cotton cheesecloth. Place star anise, orange peel, cinnamon, ginger, garlic, and peppercorns in the center of the cloth. Bring up corners; tie closed with 100%-cotton kitchen string. Add spice bag to the cooker.
2. In a large bowl combine broth, soy sauce, green onions, brown sugar, and sherry. Pour over chicken.
3. Cover and cook on low-heat setting for 3 to 3½ hours or 6 to 7 hours on high-heat setting.
4. Cook noodles according to package directions; drain. Remove chicken from cooker, reserving cooking juices. Strain juices, discarding spice bag and solids; skim off fat. Serve chicken over hot cooked noodles. Drizzle chicken with cooking juices and sesame oil. Garnish with cilantro. Makes 6 servings.
EACH SERVING 404 cal, 16 g fat, 85 mg chol, 2,608 mg sodium, 36 g carb, 2 g fiber, 29 g pro.

*Tip Use a vegetable peeler to remove 3-inch strips of peel from an orange, avoiding the bitter white pith.

LOW FAT   KID FRIENDLY
Barbecue-Chutney Chicken

PREP 15 min. COOK 6 hr. (low) or 3 hr. (high)

1   medium onion, cut in wedges
3   lb. meaty chicken pieces (breast halves, thighs, and drumsticks), skinned
¼   tsp. salt
⅛   tsp. ground black pepper
½   cup mango chutney
⅔   cup barbecue sauce
1   tsp. curry powder
2   to 3 cups hot cooked rice
     Finely chopped mango (optional)
     Chopped green onion (optional)

1. Place onion in a 3½- or 4-quart slow cooker. Add chicken; sprinkle with salt and pepper. Snip any large pieces of chutney. In a small bowl combine chutney, barbecue sauce, and curry powder. Pour over chicken.
2. Cover and cook on low-heat setting for 6 to 7 hours or 3 to 3½ hours on high-heat setting.
3. If desired, toss rice with chopped mango and/or green onion. Serve chicken and chutney mixture over rice. Makes 4 to 6 servings.
EACH SERVING 538 cal, 12 g fat, 138 mg chol, 647 mg sodium, 57 g carb, 2 g fiber, 48 g pro.

LOW FAT   KID FRIENDLY
Italian Braised Chicken with Fennel and Cannellini

PREP 25 min. COOK 5 hr. (low) or 2½ (high)

2   to 2½ lb. chicken drumsticks and/or thighs, skinned
¾   tsp. salt
¼   tsp. ground black pepper
1   15-oz. can cannellini (white kidney) beans, rinsed and drained
1   medium fennel bulb, cored and cut in thin wedges
1   medium yellow sweet pepper, seeded and cut in 1-inch pieces
1   medium onion, cut in thin wedges
3   cloves garlic, minced
1   tsp. snipped fresh rosemary
1   tsp. snipped fresh oregano
¼   tsp. crushed red pepper
1   14.5-oz. can diced tomatoes, undrained
½   cup dry white wine or reduced-sodium chicken broth
¼   cup tomato paste
¼   cup shaved Parmesan cheese (1 oz.)
1   Tbsp. snipped fresh parsley

1. Sprinkle chicken with ¼ teaspoon of the salt and the black pepper. Place chicken in a 3½- or 4-quart slow cooker. Top with drained beans, fennel, sweet pepper, onion, garlic, rosemary, oregano, and crushed red pepper. In a medium bowl combine undrained tomatoes, wine, tomato paste, and the remaining ½ teaspoon salt; pour over mixture in cooker.
2. Cover and cook on low-heat setting for 2½ to 3 hours or 5 to 6 hours or on high-heat setting for.
3. Sprinkle each serving with cheese and parsley. Makes 6 servings.
EACH SERVING 225 cal, 4 g fat, 68 mg chol, 777 mg sodium, 23 g carb, 7 g fiber, 25 g pro.

Sandwiches

SOUTHWESTERN
CHICKEN PANINI

FAST

Southwestern Chicken Panini

PREP 25 min.   GRILL 3 min.

- ½ cup chopped onion
- 3 Tbsp. olive oil
- ½ cup red enchilada sauce
- ¼ cup pine nuts
- 2 Tbsp. golden raisins
- 1½ tsp. finely chopped chipotle chile in adobo sauce plus 1 tsp. adobo sauce
- 1½ tsp. packed brown sugar
- 1½ tsp. white wine vinegar
- ¼ tsp. ground cinnamon
- 2 cups shredded cooked chicken
- 8 ½-inch slices Italian country-style bread
- 1 cup shredded colby and Monterey Jack cheese
- 1 recipe Mango Slaw

1. In a large skillet cook onion in 1 tablespoon hot oil for 3 to 4 minutes until softened. Stir in enchilada sauce, nuts, raisins, chipotle chile and sauce, sugar, vinegar, and cinnamon. Stir in chicken; heat through.
2. Preheat panini press or cast-iron skillet. Brush one side of 4 bread slices with some remaining oil. Turn over; place about ½ cup filling on each. Top with ¼ cup cheese and bread slices; brush with oil. Place sandwich(es) in panini press and cook for 3 to 5 minutes or until golden and cheese is melted. If using skillet, toast both sides until golden. Serve with Mango Slaw. Makes 4 sandwiches.
Mango Slaw In a small bowl whisk together 2 tablespoons olive oil and 1 tablespoon lime juice. Add 2 cups finely shredded cabbage, ½ cup chopped mango, 2 tablespoons chopped cilantro, and salt and pepper to taste. Toss together.
EACH SANDWICH 663 cal, 37 g fat, 86 mg chol, 941 mg sodium, 47 g carb, 4 g fiber, 36 g pro.

KID FRIENDLY

Applejack Turkey Sandwich

PREP 30 min.   GRILL 8 min.
COOK 6 min.

- 1 medium red sweet pepper, seeded and cut in ¼-inch rings
- 1 medium green sweet pepper, seeded and cut in ¼-inch rings
- 1 medium sweet red or yellow onion, halved and thinly sliced
- 1 Tbsp. olive oil
- 8 ½- to ¾-inch slices sourdough bread
- ¼ cup apple butter
- ¼ cup honey mustard
- 4 slices Swiss cheese (3 oz.)
- 4 slices thick-cut bacon, cooked and drained
- 4 slices American or cheddar cheese (3 oz.)
- 8 to 10 oz. sliced cooked turkey breast
- 3 Tbsp. olive oil

1. In a large bowl combine pepper rings and onion slices; drizzle with 1 tablespoon oil and toss to evenly coat. Transfer vegetables to a grill basket.
2. For a charcoal grill, place grill basket directly over medium coals. Grill for 8 to 10 minutes or until vegetables are crisp-tender, turning to brown evenly. (For a gas grill, preheat grill. Reduce heat to medium. Grill as above.) Or preheat an electric sandwich press, covered indoor grill, grill pan, or large skillet.
3. To assemble sandwiches, spread one side of 4 of the bread slices with apple butter and one side of remaining 4 bread slices with honey mustard. Layer the Swiss cheese, grilled vegetables, bacon, American cheese, and turkey on the 4 bread slices with apple butter. Top with remaining 4 bread slices, mustard side down. Brush both sides of each sandwich with the 3 tablespoons oil.
4. Place sandwiches (half at a time, if necessary) in the sandwich press or indoor grill; cover and cook about 6 minutes or until bread is toasted. (If using a grill pan or skillet, place sandwiches on grill pan. Weight sandwiches down with a heavy skillet and grill 2 to 3 minutes or until bread is toasted. Turn sandwiches over, weight down and grill until remaining side is toasted.)

5. To serve, cut sandwiches in half and serve immediately. Makes 4 sandwiches.
EACH SANDWICH 668 cal, 32 g fat 74 mg chol, 1,339 mg sodium, 66 g carb, 4 g fiber, 30 g pro.

FAST KID FRIENDLY

Pork and Apple Sandwiches with Honey-Pecan Glaze

PREP 20 min.   GRILL 7 min.

- 2 tenderized butterflied pork chops, halved, or 4 tenderized boneless pork loin slices (1¼ lb. total)
  Salt
  Black pepper
- 1 large tart apple, cored and cut crosswise in 4 rings
- 1 recipe Honey-Pecan Glaze
- 4 1-oz. slices provolone cheese
- ⅓ cup sour cream
- ⅓ cup mayonnaise
- 2 tsp. prepared horseradish
- 4 kaiser rolls, split and toasted

1. Lightly sprinkle chops with salt and pepper. For a charcoal grill, grill chops and apple rings on the rack of an uncovered grill directly over medium coals for 7 to 9 minutes or until chops are slightly pink in center (160°F) and apples are tender, turning once halfway through grilling and brushing with Honey-Pecan Glaze during the last 3 minutes of grilling. Add provolone cheese to chops the last 1 minute of grilling. (For a gas grill, preheat grill. Reduce heat to medium. Place chops and apple rings on grill rack over heat. Cover and grill as directed.)
2. Meanwhile, in a small bowl stir together sour cream, mayonnaise, and horseradish; spread on cut sides of toasted rolls. Place a chop and an apple slice on roll bottoms; add roll tops. Makes 4 sandwiches.
Honey-Pecan Glaze In a small saucepan combine ¼ cup honey; ¼ cup chopped pecans, toasted; 2 tablespoons butter or margarine; and ½ teaspoon finely shredded lemon peel. Heat and stir until butter melts.
EACH SANDWICH 822 cal, 46 g fat, 126 mg chol, 936 mg sodium, 55 g carb, 3 g fiber, 46 g pro.

Chocolate Cookies

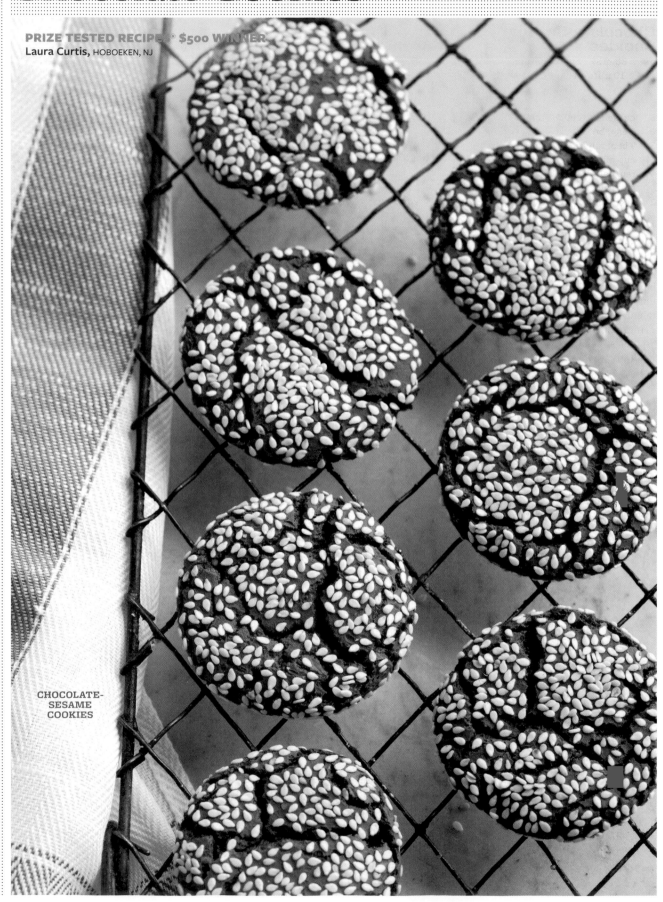

PRIZE TESTED RECIPE $500 WINNER

Laura Curtis, HOBOEKEN, NJ

CHOCOLATE-
SESAME
COOKIES

KID-FRIENDLY

Chocolate-Sesame Cookies

PREP 30 min. CHILL 30 min.
BAKE 10 min. per batch OVEN 350°F

8 oz. semisweet chocolate
2 Tbsp. butter
3 Tbsp. tahini (sesame seed paste)
⅔ cup all-purpose flour
⅓ tsp. baking powder
½ tsp. salt
2 eggs
¾ cup packed brown sugar
1 tsp. vanilla
½ cup sesame seeds, toasted

1. In a small saucepan melt chocolate and butter over low heat, stirring frequently until smooth. Remove from heat; stir in tahini. Set aside.
2. In a small bowl combine flour, baking powder, and salt; set aside. In a large mixing bowl beat eggs until frothy. Add brown sugar and vanilla; beat until combined and light. Beat in chocolate mixture. Beat in flour mixture just until combined. Cover; chill dough about 30 minutes or until easy to handle.
3. Preheat oven to 350°F. Roll dough into 1-inch balls; roll balls in sesame seeds to coat. Place on cookie sheets 2 inches apart.
4. Bake for 10 to 12 minutes or until puffed and set on the bottoms. Transfer cookies to a wire rack to cool completely. Makes about 42 cookies.

EACH COOKIE *73 cal, 4 g fat, 12 mg chol, 41 mg sodium, 9 g carb, 1 g fiber, 1 g pro.*

KID-FRIENDLY

Triple-Chocolate Cookies

PREP 40 min. STAND 30 min.
BAKE 9 min. per batch OVEN 350°F

7 oz. bittersweet chocolate, chopped
5 oz. unsweetened chocolate, chopped
½ cup butter
1 cup granulated sugar
¾ cup packed brown sugar
4 eggs
⅓ cup all-purpose flour
¼ tsp. baking powder
¼ tsp. salt
¼ cup finely chopped pecans, toasted
6 oz. semisweet chocolate pieces (1 cup)
4 tsp. shortening

1. In a medium saucepan combine bittersweet and unsweetened chocolates and butter; heat and stir over low heat until chocolate is melted and smooth. Remove from heat. Let cool for 10 minutes.
2. In a large mixing bowl combine granulated sugar, brown sugar, and eggs; beat with an electric mixer on medium to high speed for 2 to 3 minutes or until well mixed and color lightens slightly. Add cooled melted chocolate mixture; beat until combined. In a small bowl stir together flour, baking powder, and salt. Add to chocolate mixture, beating until combined. Stir in toasted pecans (the dough will look similar to brownie batter).
3. Cover surface of cookie dough with plastic wrap or waxed paper. Let stand at room temperature for 20 minutes (dough thickens as it stands).
4. Preheat oven to 350°F. Line cookie sheets with parchment paper or foil. Drop dough by rounded teaspoons 2 inches apart on prepared cookie sheets. Bake about 9 minutes or until tops are set. Let cookies stand on cookie sheet on a wire rack for 1 minute. Transfer cookies to a wire rack; let cool.
5. In a small saucepan combine semisweet chocolate pieces and shortening. Stir over low heat until chocolate is melted and smooth. Remove from heat. Line a cookie sheet with parchment paper or foil. Place cookies on lined cookie sheet and drizzle with chocolate mixture. Place cookie sheet in freezer for 4 to 5 minutes or until chocolate is firm. Makes about 5 dozen cookies.

EACH COOKIE *92 cal, 6 g fat, 18 mg chol, 29 mg sodium, 11 g carb, 1 g fiber, 1 g pro.*

KID-FRIENDLY

Mexican Chocolate Icebox Cookies with Dulce De Leche Filling

PREP 45 min. CHILL 5 hr.
BAKE 12 min. per batch OVEN 325°F

¾ cup butter, softened
1 cup sugar
¾ cup Dutch-process cocoa powder
½ tsp. ground cinnamon
¼ tsp. salt
¼ tsp. cayenne pepper
1 egg
1½ tsp. vanilla
1¼ cups all-purpose flour
½ cup jarred or canned dulce de leche

1. In a large mixing bowl, beat butter with an electric mixer on medium to high for 30 seconds. Add sugar, cocoa powder, cinnamon, salt, and cayenne pepper. Beat until combined, scraping bowl occasionally. Beat in egg and vanilla until combined. Beat in flour.
2. Divide dough in half; cover and chill 1 hour or until dough is easy to handle. Shape each portion of dough into a 6-inch-long roll about 1¾ inches in diameter. Wrap rolls in plastic wrap or waxed paper and chill about 4 hours or until dough is firm enough to slice.
3. Preheat oven to 325°F. Line a cookie sheet with parchment paper. Cut rolls in ¼-inch slices. Place slices 1 inch apart on prepared cookie sheet. Bake for 12 to 14 minutes or until edges are firm. Cool on cookie sheet for 2 minutes. Transfer cookies to a wire rack; let cool.
4. Spread a rounded tablespoon of dulce de leche on the bottom flat side of each of half the cookies. Top with remaining cookies, flat sides down, pressing together lightly. Makes 24 sandwich cookies.

EACH COOKIE *137 cal, 7 g fat, 26 mg chol, 77 mg sodium, 18 g carb, 1 g fiber, 2 g pro.*

Brunch Bests

CHEESY
POTATO BAKE
WITH EGGS

Cheesy Potato Bake with Eggs

PREP 30 min. BAKE 55 min.
OVEN 325°F

1 medium onion, finely chopped
2 Tbsp. butter
4 tsp. all-purpose flour
1½ cups milk
8 oz. sharp cheddar cheese, shredded (2 cups)
3 lb. russet potatoes, peeled and thinly sliced
1½ cups chopped fresh broccoli
1 Tbsp. vegetable oil
8 eggs
2 Tbsp. water
6 slices bacon, crisp-cooked and crumbled
1 large tomato, chopped

1. Preheat oven to 325°F. For sauce, in a saucepan cook onion in butter over medium heat until tender; stirring occasionally. Stir in flour, ½ teaspoon *salt*, and ½ teaspoon *pepper*. Add the milk. Cook and stir until slightly thickened and bubbly. Stir in cheese until melted.
2. In a 3-quart baking dish layer potatoes. Top with sauce. Bake, covered, for 55 minutes or until tender.
3. In a large skillet cook broccoli in hot oil over medium heat for 5 minutes or until nearly tender; stirring often. In a bowl beat eggs, water, ½ teaspoon salt, and ¼ teaspoon *pepper*. Pour over broccoli in skillet. Cook over medium heat, without stirring, until egg mixture begins to set. Using a spatula, lift and fold partially cooked egg so uncooked portion flows underneath. Cook 2 minutes more or until egg is cooked but still moist. Spoon over potatoes. Top with bacon and chopped tomato. Serve immediately. Makes 8 to 12 servings.

EACH SERVING *421 cal, 22 g fat, 259 mg chol, 708 mg sodium, 36 g carb, 3 g fiber, 21 g pro.*

Herbed Cheese and Bacon Biscuits

PREP 20 min. BAKE 10 min. OVEN 450°F

2 slices bacon
½ cup chopped red onion
3 cups all-purpose flour
1 Tbsp. baking powder
1 tsp. sugar
¼ tsp. salt
¼ tsp. ground black pepper
1 5.2-oz. pkg. semi-soft cheese with garlic and herbs
1 cup half-and-half or light cream

1. Preheat oven to 450°F. In a skillet cook bacon over medium heat for 8 to 10 minutes or until crisp, turning occasionally. Remove bacon from skillet and drain on paper towels; reserve drippings in skillet. Crumble bacon; set aside. Cook onion in bacon drippings over medium heat for 4 to 5 minutes or until tender and beginning to brown. Remove from heat; set aside.
2. In a large bowl stir together the flour, baking powder, sugar, salt, and pepper. Using a pastry blender, cut in cheese until mixture resembles coarse crumbs. Stir in bacon and onion. Make a well in the center of the flour mixture. Add half-and-half all at once. Using a fork, stir just until mixture is moistened.
3. Turn dough out onto a lightly floured surface. Knead dough by folding and gently pressing for four to six strokes or just until dough holds together. Pat or lightly roll dough to ¾-inch thickness. Using a floured 2½-inch biscuit cutter, cut out dough, rerolling as necessary. Place biscuits 1 inch apart on an ungreased baking sheet.
4. Bake about 10 minutes or until golden. Remove biscuits from baking sheet; serve warm. Makes 10 to 12 biscuits.

EACH BISCUIT *261 cal, 11 g fat, 28 mg chol, 262 mg sodium, 31 g carb, 1 g fiber, 7 g pro.*

Reuben Breakfast Strata

PREP 20 min. CHILL 2 hrs.
BAKE 40 min. STAND 10 min.
OVEN 350°F

8 slices rye bread, cubed (6 cups)
12 oz. sliced deli corned beef, chopped
1½ cups shredded Swiss cheese (6 oz.)
8 beaten eggs
1¼ cups milk
½ cup bottled Thousand Island salad dressing
½ tsp. caraway seeds
½ tsp. dry mustard
½ tsp. salt

1. In a bowl combine bread cubes, corned beef, and 1 cup of the cheese; spread in a greased 3-quart rectangular baking dish.
2. In a medium bowl whisk together eggs, milk, dressing, caraway seeds, dry mustard, and salt. Pour egg mixture over bread mixture in dish, pressing lightly to thoroughly moisten the bread. Cover and refrigerate for 2 to 24 hours.
3. Sprinkle with remaining ½ cup cheese. Bake, uncovered, for 40 to 45 minutes or until a knife inserted near center comes out clean. Let stand for 10 minutes before serving. Makes 6 servings.

EACH SERVING *561 cal, 35 g fat, 373 mg chol, 1,469 mg sodium, 28 g carb, 3 g fiber, 32 g pro.*

Mushroom-Olive Frittata

PREP 30 min. BROIL 2 min.
STAND 5 min.

1 Tbsp. olive oil
1 cup sliced fresh cremini mushrooms
2 cups coarsely shredded fresh Swiss chard or spinach
1 large shallot, thinly sliced
4 eggs
2 egg whites
2 tsp. snipped fresh rosemary or ½ teaspoon dried rosemary, crushed
¼ tsp. ground black pepper
⅛ tsp. salt
¼ cup thinly sliced, pitted kalamata olives
⅓ cup shredded Parmesan cheese

1. Preheat broiler. In a medium-size nonstick broilerproof skillet, heat oil over medium heat. Add mushrooms; cook 3 minutes, stirring occasionally. Add chard and shallot; cook 5 minutes, until mushrooms and chard are tender, stirring occasionally.
2. Meanwhile, in a medium bowl whisk together eggs, egg whites, rosemary, pepper, and salt. Pour egg mixture over vegetables in skillet. Cook over medium heat. As mixture sets, run a spatula around edge of skillet, lifting egg so the uncooked portion flows underneath. Continue cooking and lifting edge until egg mixture is almost set and surface is slightly moist.
3. Sprinkle with olives; top with cheese. Broil about 4 inches from heat for 2 minutes, until top is lightly browned and center is set. Let stand 5 minutes. Makes 4 servings.

EACH SERVINGS *165 cal, 11 g fat, 216 mg chol, 416 mg sodium, 4 g carb, 1 g fiber, 12 g pro.*

Turkey Leftovers

PRIZE TESTED RECIPES® $500 WINNER
Joyce Van Meter, THORTON, CO

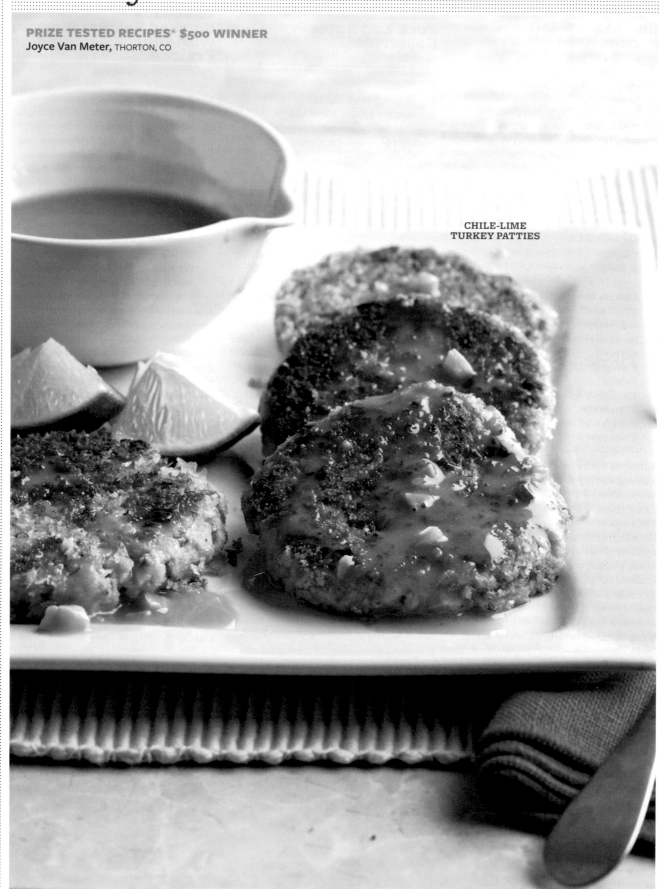

CHILE-LIME
TURKEY PATTIES

FAST LOW FAT
Chile-Lime Turkey Patties

PREP 20 min. COOK 10 min.

2   cups cut-up leftover cooked turkey
¼   cup fresh parsley
2   Tbsp. sliced celery
2   Tbsp. sliced green onion (1)
1   cup panko (Japanese-style bread crumbs)
¼   cup mayonnaise
1   egg, lightly beaten
1   Tbsp. lime juice
1   tsp. red chile paste
⅛   tsp. Worcestershire sauce
2   Tbsp. butter
1   recipe Lime Butter Sauce (below)
    Lime wedges

1. In a food processor, process turkey just until ground; transfer to a large bowl. Process parsley, celery, and onion until finely chopped; add to turkey in bowl. Add half the panko, the mayonnaise, egg, lime juice, chile paste, and Worcestershire sauce. Form eight 3-inch patties; coat with remaining panko.
2. In a 12-inch skillet heat 1 tablespoon of the butter over medium heat. Cook patties, half at a time, for 10 minutes, until browned and 165°F in centers, turning once halfway through. Serve with Lime Butter Sauce and lime wedges. Makes 8 servings.
Lime Butter Sauce In a small saucepan combine ⅓ cup white wine or chicken broth, 1 tablespoon lime juice, and 1 minced garlic clove. Bring to boiling; reduce heat. Simmer, uncovered, 5 minutes. Reduce heat to low. Whisk in 2 tablespoons whipping cream. Gradually whisk in ⅓ cup butter, cut up, until melted. Stir in 1 tablespoon Asian sweet chili sauce.
EACH SERVING *159 cal, 6 g fat, 36 mg chol, 566 mg sodium, 10 g carb, 2 g fiber, 16 g pro.*

KID-FRIENDLY
Asian Turkey à la King

PREP 30 min. BAKE 10 min.
OVEN 400°F

1   frozen puff pastry sheet (half a 17.3-oz. package), thawed
4   tsp. cornstarch
⅛   tsp. ground black pepper
¾   cup chicken broth
1   Tbsp. dry sherry or chicken broth
1   Tbsp. soy sauce
1   cup sliced carrots (2 medium)
1   cup chopped red sweet pepper (1 large)
¼   cup sliced green onions (2)
2   Tbsp. cooking oil
1   15-oz. can whole straw mushrooms, drained
3   cups chopped cooked turkey
1   8-oz. can sliced water chestnuts, drained
⅓   cup tub-style cream cheese spread with chive and onion
¼   cup chopped cashews

1. Preheat oven to 400°F. On a lightly floured surface, unfold puff pastry. Using a sharp knife, cut pastry in half lengthwise, then in thirds crosswise, making six rectangles. Cut each rectangle diagonally in half to make two triangles, for a total of 12 triangles. Arrange pastry triangles on a greased baking sheet. Bake for 10 to 15 minutes or until puffed and golden. Transfer to a wire rack and cool for 5 minutes.
2. Meanwhile, in a small bowl combine cornstarch and black pepper. Whisk in broth, sherry, and soy sauce; set aside. In a large skillet cook and stir carrots, sweet pepper, and green onions in hot oil over medium-high heat for 3 minutes. Add mushrooms. Cook and stir for 2 minutes. Stir cornstarch mixture; stir into vegetable mixture in skillet. Cook and stir until thickened and bubbly; cook and stir for 2 minutes more. Stir in turkey and water chestnuts; heat through.
3. For each serving, place a baked pastry triangle in each shallow bowl. Place about 1 tablespoon cream cheese on each pastry. Place another pastry triangle on the cream cheese. Spoon over turkey mixture then sprinkle with cashews. Makes 6 servings.
EACH SERVING *581 cal, 32 g fat, 78 mg chol, 804 mg sodium, 39 g carb, 5 g fiber, 33 g pro.*

FAST
Thai Turkey Soup

START TO FINISH 30 min.

    Nonstick cooking spray
1   medium onion, chopped
1   Tbsp. grated fresh ginger
3   cloves garlic, minced
2   14-oz. cans reduced-sodium chicken broth
1   14-oz. can unsweetened lite coconut milk
1   Tbsp. lime juice
2   tsp. Thai seasoning
2   medium carrots, thinly bias-sliced
½   a jalapeño, julienned or finely chopped (see note, page 11)
1½ cups shredded cooked turkey breast or chicken breast
1   cup fresh shiitake, straw, or button mushrooms, sliced
⅔   cup snow peas, trimmed and halved diagonally
1   Tbsp. chopped fresh basil

1. Lightly coat a 4-quart Dutch oven with nonstick cooking spray.
2. In the Dutch oven cook and stir onion, ginger, and garlic over medium heat for 2 to 3 minutes or until tender. Stir in broth, coconut milk, lime juice, and Thai seasoning. Bring to boiling; reduce heat. Add carrots and jalapeño; simmer, covered, for 5 minutes. Add turkey, mushrooms, snow peas, and basil. Cook for 3 minutes more or until heated through. Makes 5 servings.
EACH SERVING *159 cal, 6 g fat, 36 mg chol, 566 mg sodium, 10 g carb, 2 g fiber, 16 g pro.*

Pork Roasts

PRIZE TESTED RECIPES® **$500 WINNER**
Anne Galindo, FOSTORIA, OH

BLACKBERRY-
STUFFED PORK

LOW FAT | KID FRIENDLY

Blackberry-Stuffed Pork

PREP 35 min. COOK 1 hr. 15 min.
STAND 15 min. OVEN 325°F

1   recipe Blackberry Sauce
1   2-lb. boneless pork top loin roast
     (single loin)
½   cup chopped pecans, toasted

1. Preheat oven to 325°F. Prepare
Blackberry Sauce. Line a roasting pan with
foil; place rack in pan.
2. To butterfly roast, turn roast fat side
down. Make a lengthwise cut down
the center, cutting to within ½ inch of
opposite side. Place knife in the V. Cut
perpendicular to the first cut to within
½ inch of side. Repeat on opposite side.
Open flat. Sprinkle with ¼ tsp. each *salt*
and *pepper*. Spread with half the sauce;
sprinkle with half the nuts.
3. Starting from a short side, roll up meat
(some sauce may leak out). Place roast on
rack in pan. Roast, uncovered, 1¼ to
1½ hours or until thermometer inserted
into meat registers 145°F. Tent with foil;
let stand 15 minutes.
4. Reheat remaining Blackberry Sauce;
spoon over roast. Sprinkle with remaining
nuts. If desired, top with fresh blackberries
and snipped fresh rosemary. Makes
8 servings.
Blackberry Sauce Coat a medium saucepan with nonstick cooking spray; cook
½ cup chopped onion in pan over medium
heat for 5 minutes or just until tender. In
a bowl combine onion, ½ cup blackberry
spreadable fruit, ¼ cup green jalapeño
jelly, ½ teaspoon finely shredded lemon
peel, and ½ teaspoon reduced-sodium soy
sauce. Stir in 1 cup fresh blackberries.
EACH SERVING *310 cal, 14 g fat, 72 mg chol,
140 mg sodium, 20 g carb, 2 g fiber, 25 g pro.*

LOW FAT | KID FRIENDLY

Seeded Pork Roast

PREP 25 min. COOK 9 hr. (low) or
4 hr. 30 min. (high)

1   3- to 3½-lb. boneless pork
     shoulder roast
1   Tbsp. reduced-sodium
     soy sauce
2   tsp. anise seeds, crushed
2   tsp. fennel seeds, crushed
2   tsp. caraway seeds, crushed
2   tsp. dill seeds, crushed
2   tsp. celery seeds, crushed
½   cup lower-sodium beef broth
⅔   cup apple juice
1   Tbsp. cornstarch

1. Trim fat from meat. If necessary, cut
meat to fit in a 3½- or 4-quart slow cooker.
Brush soy sauce on meat. On a large piece
of foil or waxed paper combine anise seeds,
fennel seeds, caraway seeds, dill seeds, and
celery seeds. Roll roast in seeds to coat
evenly. Place meat in cooker. Pour broth
and ⅓ cup of the apple juice around meat.
2. Cover and cook on low-heat setting for
9 to 10 hours or high-heat setting for 4½ to
5 hours.
3. Transfer meat to a serving platter,
reserving cooking liquid. Cover meat to
keep warm.
4. For gravy, strain cooking liquid and skim
off fat. Transfer liquid to a small saucepan.
In a small bowl combine remaining ⅓ cup
apple juice and cornstarch; stir into liquid
in saucepan. Cook and stir over medium
heat until thickened and bubbly. Cook and
stir for 2 minutes more. Serve gravy with
meat. Makes 8 servings.
EACH SERVING *260 cal, 10 g fat, 110 mg
chol, 235 mg sodium, 5 g carb, 1 g fiber,
34 g pro.*

FAST | LOW FAT | KID FRIENDLY

Cranberry-and-Citrus-Glazed Pork Roast

PREP 15 min. ROAST 1 hr. 15 min.
STAND 15 min. OVEN 325°F

¼   tsp. salt
¼   tsp. black pepper
¼   tsp. ground sage
1   2½- to 3-lb. boneless pork
     top loin roast (single loin)
1   16-oz. can whole or jellied
     cranberry sauce
½   tsp. finely shredded
     orange peel
⅓   cup orange juice
¼   tsp. ground sage

1. Preheat oven to 325°F. For rub, in a
small bowl combine the salt, pepper, and
¼ teaspoon sage. Sprinkle rub evenly all
over pork roast; rub in mixture with your
fingers. Place meat on a rack in a shallow
roasting pan. Insert an oven-going meat
thermometer into center of roast. Roast,
uncovered, for 45 minutes.
2. Meanwhile, for sauce, in a medium
saucepan combine cranberry sauce, orange
peel, orange juice, and ¼ teaspoon sage.
Bring to boiling; reduce heat. Simmer,
uncovered, about 10 minutes or until
mixture has thickened slightly.
3. Spoon about ¼ cup of the sauce over
pork. Roast meat, uncovered, for 30 to
45 minutes more or until meat
thermometer registers 150°F. Remove
from oven. Cover meat loosely with foil; let
stand for 15 minutes before slicing. (The
temperature of the meat after standing
should be 160°F.) Serve remaining sauce
with meat. Makes 10 to 12 servings.
EACH SERVING *285 cal, 12 g fat, 66 mg chol,
120 mg sodium, 19 g carb, 1 g fiber, 23 g pro.*

Oh, Fudge

PRIZE TESTED RECIPES $500 WINNER

Sherry Day, PINCKNEY, MI

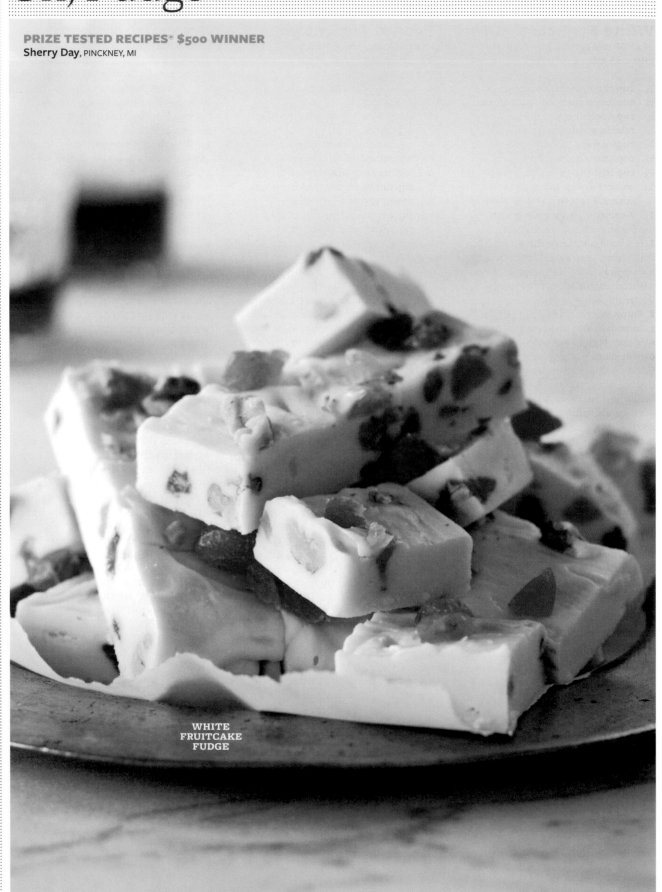

WHITE
FRUITCAKE
FUDGE

KID FRIENDLY
White Fruitcake Fudge
PREP 30 min. COOK 18 min.
CHILL 35 min.

¾ cup chopped walnuts, toasted
¾ cup finely chopped dried apricots
½ cup finely chopped golden
   raisins or raisins
2 cups sugar
¾ cup sour cream
½ cup butter
12 oz. white baking chocolate,
   coarsely chopped
1 7-oz. jar marshmallow creme

1. In a bowl combine walnuts, apricots, and raisins. Remove and set aside ¼ cup for topping. Line a 13×9×2-inch baking pan with foil; extend foil over edges of pan. Butter the foil.
2. Butter sides of a heavy 3-quart saucepan. In saucepan combine sugar, sour cream, and butter. Cook and stir over medium heat until mixture boils. Clip a candy thermometer to side of pan. Reduce heat to medium-low; continue boiling at a moderate, steady rate, stirring occasionally, until thermometer registers 236°F (18 to 20 minutes). Adjust heat as necessary to maintain a steady boil.
3. Remove saucepan from heat. Stir in chocolate and marshmallow creme. Continue stirring until chocolate is melted and mixture is combined. Stir in fruit and nut mixture. Immediately spread fudge evenly in prepared pan. Top with the reserved ¼ cup fruit and nut mixture. Chill fudge until firm. Use foil to lift fudge out of pan. Cut fudge into squares. Store in the refrigerator. Makes about 3 lb. (about 117 one-inch pieces).
EACH PIECE *53 cal, 2 g fat, 3 mg chol, 9 mg sodium, 8 g carb, 0 g fiber, 0 g pro.*

KID FRIENDLY
Peanut Butter Fudge
PREP 30 min. COOK 8 min.
CHILL 35 min.

4 cups sugar
1¼ cups whipping cream
⅓ cup light-color corn syrup
⅓ cup creamy peanut butter
¼ teaspoon salt
1 tablespoon vanilla
1 cup honey-roasted or dry roasted
   peanuts, chopped
   Honey-roasted or dry roasted
   peanuts, chopped (optional)

1. Line a 9×9×2-inch baking pan with foil, extending the foil over edges of pan. Butter foil; set pan aside.
2. Butter the sides of a heavy 3-quart saucepan. In the saucepan, combine sugar, cream, corn syrup, peanut butter, and salt. Cook and stir over medium-high heat until mixture is boiling. Clip a candy thermometer to the side of the pan. Reduce heat to medium-low; continue boiling at a moderate, steady rate, stirring occasionally, until thermometer registers 236°F, soft-ball stage (8 to 10 minutes). (Adjust heat as necessary to maintain a steady boil.)
3. Remove saucepan from heat. Add vanilla but do not stir. Cool, without stirring, to 110°F (35 to 40 minutes).
4. Remove thermometer from saucepan. Beat mixture vigorously with a clean wooden spoon just until candy starts to thicken. Add the 1 cup peanuts. Continue beating just until fudge starts to lose its gloss (7 to 8 minutes total).
5. Immediately spread fudge evenly in the prepared pan. If desired, sprinkle with additional peanuts and press them lightly into fudge. Score fudge into squares while warm. Let fudge cool to room temperature. When fudge is firm, use the edges of the foil to lift fudge from pan. Cut into squares. Makes 64 pieces.
EACH PIECE *85 cal, 3 g fat, 6 mg chol, 23 mg sodium, 14 g carb, 0 g fiber, 1 g pro.*

KID FRIENDLY
Rocky Route Fudge
PREP 30 min COOK 10 min CHILL 1 hr.

4 cups sugar
1¼ cups whipping cream
⅓ cup unsweetened cocoa powder
⅓ cup light-color corn syrup
¼ tsp. salt
1 Tbsp. vanilla
1 cup snipped tiny marshmallows
1 cup chopped pecans, toasted

1. Line an 8×8×2-inch baking pan with foil, extending the foil over edges of pan. Butter foil; set pan aside.
2. Butter the sides of a 3-quart heavy saucepan. In the saucepan combine sugar, cream, cocoa powder, corn syrup, and salt. Cook and stir over medium heat until mixture is boiling. Clip a candy thermometer to the side of the pan. Reduce heat to medium-low; continue boiling at a moderate, steady rate, stirring occasionally, until thermometer registers 236°F, soft-ball stage (about 10 minutes). (Adjust heat as necessary to maintain a steady boil.)
3. Remove saucepan from heat. Add vanilla but do not stir. Cool, without stirring, to 110°F (1 to 1¼ hours). Remove thermometer from saucepan. Beat mixture vigorously with a clean wooden spoon just until candy starts to thicken. Add marshmallows and pecans. Continue beating just until fudge starts to lose its gloss (6 to 8 minutes total).
4. Immediately spread fudge evenly in the prepared pan. Score fudge into squares while warm. Let fudge cool to room temperature. When fudge is firm, use the edges of the foil to lift from pan. Cut into squares. Makes 64 pieces
EACH PIECE *84 cal, 3 g fat, 6 mg chol, 13 mg sodium, 15 g carb, 0 g fiber, 0 g pro.*

A

B

M

N

Y

Z

Nutrition information. With each recipe, we give important nutrition

information you can easily apply to your own needs. You'll find the caloric count of each serving and the amount, in grams, of fat, saturated fat, cholesterol, sodium, carbohydrates, fiber, and protein to help you keep tabs on what you eat. These are noted in percentages of the Daily Values. The Daily Values are dietary standards determined by the Food and Drug Administration (FDA). To stay in line with the nutrition breakdown of each recipe, follow the suggested number of servings.

How we analyze. The Better Homes and Gardens® Test Kitchen computer

analyzes each recipe for the nutritional value of a single serving.
- The analysis does not include optional ingredients.
- We use the first serving size listed when a range is given. For example: If we say a recipe "Makes 4 to 6 servings," the nutrition information is based on 4 servings.
- When ingredient choices (such as butter or margarine) appear in a recipe, we use the first one mentioned for analysis. The ingredient order does not mean we prefer one ingredient over another.
- When milk and eggs are recipe ingredients, the analysis is calculated using 2 percent (reduced-fat) milk and large eggs.

What you need. The dietary guidelines below suggest nutrient levels that

moderately active adults should strive to eat each day. There is no real harm in going over or under these guidelines in any single day, but it is a good idea to aim for a balanced diet over time.

Calories: About 2,000
Total fat: Less than 65 grams
Saturated fat: Less than 20 grams
Cholesterol: Less than 300 milligrams
Carbohydrates: About 300 grams
Sodium: Less than 2,400 milligrams
Dietary fiber: 20 to 30 grams

Low Fat icon. Certain recipes throughout the book have an icon above the recipe

title that indicates the recipe is low fat. For a recipe to earn this icon, it must meet certain nutritional requirements. For a main dish one serving should have 12 grams of fat per serving or less, one serving of a side dish should have 5 grams of fat or less, an appetizer serving should have 2 grams of fat or less, and cookies and desserts should have 2 grams of fat or less per serving. Occasionally the fat level will slightly exceed one of the recommended numbers, but typically they remain below the listed amounts.

Metric Information

The charts on this page provide a guide for converting measurements from the U.S. customary system, which is used throughout this book, to the metric system.

Product Differences

Most of the ingredients called for in the recipes in this book are available in most countries. However, some are known by different names. Here are some common American ingredients and their possible counterparts:

- Sugar (white) is granulated, fine granulated, or castor sugar.
- Powdered sugar is icing sugar.
- All-purpose flour is enriched, bleached or unbleached white household flour. When self-rising flour is used in place of all-purpose flour in a recipe that calls for leavening, omit the leavening agent (baking soda or baking powder) and salt.
- Light-colorcorn syrup is golden syrup.
- Cornstarch is cornflour.
- Baking soda is bicarbonate of soda.
- Vanilla or vanilla extract is vanilla essence.
- Green, red, or yellow sweet peppers are capsicums or bell peppers.
- Golden raisins are sultanas.

Volume and Weight

The United States traditionally uses cup measures for liquid and solid ingredients. The chart below shows the approximate imperial and metric equivalents. If you are accustomed to weighing solid ingredients, the following approximate equivalents will be helpful.

- 1 cup butter, castor sugar, or rice = 8 ounces = ½ pound = 250 grams
- 1 cup flour = 4 ounces = ¼ pound = 125 grams
- 1 cup icing sugar = 5 ounces = 150 grams

Canadian and U.S. volume for a cup measure is 8 fluid ounces (237 ml), but the standard metric equivalent is 250 ml.

1 British imperial cup is 10 fluid ounces.

In Australia, 1 tablespoon equals 20 ml, and there are 4 teaspoons in the Australian tablespoon.

Spoon measures are used for smaller amounts of ingredients. Although the size of the tablespoon varies slightly in different countries, for practical purposes and for recipes in this book, a straight substitution is all that's necessary. Measurements made using cups or spoons always should be level unless stated otherwise.

Common Weight Range Replacements

Imperial / U.S.	Metric
½ ounce	15 g
1 ounce	25 g or 30 g
4 ounces (¼ pound)	115 g or 125 g
8 ounces (½ pound)	225 g or 250 g
16 ounces (1 pound)	450 g or 500 g
1¼ pounds	625 g
1½ pounds	750 g
2 pounds or 2¼ pounds	1,000 g or 1 Kg

Oven Temperature Equivalents

Fahrenheit Setting	Celsius Setting*	Gas Setting
300°F	150°C	Gas Mark 2 (very low)
325°F	160°C	Gas Mark 3 (low)
350°F	180°C	Gas Mark 4 (moderate)
375°F	190°C	Gas Mark 5 (moderate)
400°F	200°C	Gas Mark 6 (hot)
425°F	220°C	Gas Mark 7 (hot)
450°F	230°C	Gas Mark 8 (very hot)
475°F	240°C	Gas Mark 9 (very hot)
500°F	260°C	Gas Mark 10 (extremely hot)
Broil	Broil	Grill

*Electric and gas ovens may be calibrated using celsius. However, for an electric oven, increase celsius setting 10 to 20 degrees when cooking above 160°C. For convection or forced air ovens (gas or electric), lower the temperature setting 25°F/10°C when cooking at all heat levels.

Baking Pan Sizes

Imperial / U.S.	Metric
9×1½-inch round cake pan	22- or 23×4-cm (1.5 L)
9×1½-inch pie plate	22- or 23×4-cm (1 L)
8×8×2-inch square cake pan	20×5-cm (2 L)
9×9×2-inch square cake pan	22- or 23×4.5-cm (2.5 L)
11×7×1½-inch baking pan	28×17×4-cm (2 L)
2-quart rectangular baking pan	30×19×4.5-cm (3 L)
13×9×2-inch baking pan	34×22×4.5-cm (3.5 L)
15×10×1-inch jelly roll pan	40×25×2-cm
9×5×3-inch loaf pan	23×13×8-cm (2 L)
2-quart casserole	2 L

U.S. / Standard Metric Equivalents

⅛ teaspoon = 0.5 ml	
¼ teaspoon = 1 ml	
½ teaspoon = 2 ml	
1 teaspoon = 5 ml	
1 tablespoon = 15 ml	
2 tablespoons = 25 ml	
¼ cup = 2 fluid ounces = 50 ml	
⅓ cup = 3 fluid ounces = 75 ml	
½ cup = 4 fluid ounces = 125 ml	
⅔ cup = 5 fluid ounces = 150 ml	
¾ cup = 6 fluid ounces = 175 ml	
1 cup = 8 fluid ounces = 250 ml	
2 cups = 1 pint = 500 ml	
1 quart = 1 litre	